THE
BYZANTINE
EMPIRE

REVISED EDITION

THE
BYZANTINE
EMPIRE

REVISED EDITION

ROBERT BROWNING

THE CATHOLIC UNIVERSITY OF AMERICA PRESS
WASHINGTON, D.C.

Library of Congress Cataloging-in-Publication Data
Browning, Robert, 1914–
    The Byzantine Empire, revised edition / Robert
Browning.
        p.   cm.
    Includes bibliographical references (p.   ) and
    index.
    ISBN 0-8132-0754-1 (alk. paper)
    1. Byzantine Empire—Civilization.   I. Title.
DF531.B7   1992
949.5—dc20   91-25402

CONTENTS

PREFACE TO THE
REVISED EDITION

The first edition of this book, which appeared in 1981, very soon became out of print, and the publisher was reluctant to reprint it. As time went by, several teachers in North American universities and colleges told me that they found it a useful introduction to the Byzantine world to put into the hands of students, and urged me to try to make it once more available. I am most grateful to The Catholic University of America Press for offering to publish a second edition.

After ten years the temptation to rewrite a book is hard to resist. But after reflection and discussion with colleagues I decided that immediate revision was preferable to rewriting in the future. The present book is therefore substantially a reproduction of the 1981 edition. I have however corrected minor mistakes, removed some ambiguities and infelicities, and added some passages and modified others in the light of new knowledge or insight. I hope that the revised version will be found helpful by students and also be of interest to the general public.

I take this opportunity to thank David McGonagle for his encouragement and Susan Needham for her rigorous and sensitive copyediting.

ROBERT BROWNING
September 1991

PREFACE

It is no longer true that the Byzantine world is unknown to the English reader. Scholars like Norman Baynes, Steven Runciman, Joan Hussey, Dimitri Obolensky, and Cyril Mango have made the story of the Byzantine Empire accessible in broad outline and added insights of their own into Byzantine society and its place in the medieval world. George Ostrogorsky's *History of the Byzantine State* has been available in English translation for a quarter of a century. The new Volume IV of the *Cambridge Medieval History* surveys every aspect of the Byzantine world from the eighth century onwards. If I have ventured to follow these distinguished predecessors with yet another general book on Byzantium, it is because I believe that Byzantine society is often thought by the non-specialist to have been unhistorically rigid and unchanging, unresponsive alike to external pressures and to its own internal dynamic. In the present book I have tried to emphasize change and development, and the consequent tension between tradition and innovation. I am only too well aware how many aspects of Byzantine civilization I have neglected. But the book is already longer than either the publisher or the author intended. Thanks are due to the Australian National University, Canberra, on whose hospitable campus the early chapters were written; to Susan Archer, who in typing the manuscript drew my attention to many a slip; to Martha Caute, who took the book through the traumatic transition from intellectual exercise to industrial product with skill and tact; to Catherine Comfort, who obtained much of the illustrative material; and to my wife, who had to put up with even more absent-mindedness than usual.

R. B.

MAPS

INTRODUCTION

For Edward Gibbon, writing in 1776, the thousand years of Byzantine history could be dismissed as "the triumph of barbarism and Christianity." Voltaire declared it to be "a worthless collection of orations and miracles," and Montesquieu, in his survey of the grandeur and decadence of Rome, saw in the Byzantine Empire only "a tragic epilogue to the glory of Rome," "a tissue of rebellions, insurrections and treachery." These representatives of the Enlightenment make two implications: first, that Byzantine society had no development of its own, but remained, fossilized and unchanging, in a world of growth and development which culminated in the Renaissance and finally in the Age of Reason; and second, that the history of Europe and the Near East was independent of and uninfluenced by that of the Byzantine Empire, which played no significant part in shaping the world in which they themselves lived.

In the two centuries which have passed since Gibbon wrote *Decline and Fall* and particularly in the last hundred years, the study of Byzantine civilization has made great progress. Not only in the field of political history, but also in those of art, music, literature, technology, religion, philosophy, and many others, the role of Byzantium, sometimes dominant, always important, is better understood than ever before. The two propositions which underlay the attitude of the Age of Enlightenment would today be rejected by any serious historian. The Byzantine Empire was for many centuries the most powerful, the richest, and the most civilized state in Europe and the Near East. Its influence radiated in all directions, sometimes determining the course of events, and always influencing it. Centuries after its disappearance, its traces can still be discerned, as in a palimpsest. Even today the alert

traveller can observe the subtle changes in patterns of life and social
structures which mark the ancient frontiers of the Byzantine Empire.
From the political theory and practice of tsarist Russia to the theology
of the Anglican church, from the administrative organization of the
Islamic world to the dedications of churches in Scotland, the influence
of this wealthy and cultured society upon its neighbors can be traced.
Modern place names, too, sometimes perpetuate long-vanished features of the Byzantine world. The province of Romagna in Italy is so-
called because from the 560s to the middle of the eighth century it
was a province of the Byzantine Empire, known by its citizens as
Romania—the world of the Romans—and was sharply distinguished
from the barbarous world of the Lombard duchies.

The concept of the Byzantine Empire as a static and fossilized
society in an evolving world has been similarly overthrown by the
work of recent historians. It is true that it often presents an unvaried
façade—the ritual and ceremony of church and palace and the phrase-
ology of official communication show surprisingly little modification
through the centuries. But behind this façade we can now discern
continuous change and development. The Byzantines' view of their
own society and its place in the world, and the way in which they gave
expression to that vision in literature and art, passed through a series
of transformations. These in their turn reflected both changes within
Byzantine society in the relation of man to man, of man to the state,
and of man to the means of production and also shifts in the economic,
political, and cultural balance between the Byzantine world and the
related but different societies which surrounded it—western Europe,
the south Slav states, Russia, the nomad pastoralists of the Eurasian
steppe-lands, and the world of Islam.

Good books have been written in English in modern times on the
political history of the Byzantine world, and there are many surveys
of Byzantine civilization and culture. The former tend to neglect
those activities of a civilized society which are not directly political
or military, while the latter often pay insuffficient attention to evolu-
tion in Byzantine society. The aim of this book is to offer to the general

Constantine brought Xty to the Western world & the whole of the west - laws morals - is based on that. p.254
Justinian & the law   Introduction   xiii   West's own fault - they destroyed it

suger & st. Denis

reader a survey of Byzantine civilization, in the widest sense of the word, which takes account of the changing values of that society and of the Byzantines' developing perceptions both of their own society and of the larger world in which they lived. This book is therefore arranged by periods. A broad outline of the political history of the Byzantine world in each period is given, to provide a frame of reference for the discussion that follows.

First of all, however, a word about names is needed. The Byzantines did not call themselves Byzantines, but *Romaioi*—Romans. They were well aware of their role as heirs of the Roman Empire, which for many centuries had united under a single government the whole Mediterranean world and much that was outside it. They were also conscious that it was within the framework of the Roman Empire that Christianity had come into being, spread, and ultimately become the religion of the state and of virtually all its subjects. For the Byzantines "Roman" and "Christian" were often synonymous terms. So we find them calling themselves simply Christians or "the Christian people," although there were always many other Christian societies and Christian states outside the boundaries of the Byzantine Empire. The Greek word "Byzantine" is a rather literary term for an inhabitant of the city of Constantinople, the more usual word being *Konstantinou-polites*. French scholars of the seventeenth century were the first to use "Byzantine" with reference to the empire rather than to the city, and to speak of "Byzantine history." This has become normal usage in modern times, even in Greek. But "East Rome" and "East Roman," and their equivalents in other languages, are still used to denote the Byzantine Empire. What the Byzantines do not, for most of their long history, call themselves is Hellenes, though the dominant language and the dominant culture of the empire were always Greek. And Byzantine rulers and officials were always deeply offended when western potentates called them Greeks (*Graeci*) or described their emperor as "Emperor of the Greeks." This apparent paradox tells us something important about Byzantine society. A Frenchman or a German today regards the community to which he belongs as one defined primarily by a common language and all that goes with it. A Byzantine saw his society in a different light. The image he formed of his society changed along with historical circumstances, as will be seen. But it was never that of a nation—like France or England—nor even of a linguistic and ethnic group—like Italy or Germany before the mid-nineteenth century.

The boundaries of the Byzantine Empire, though they might remain for long periods with only very minor modifications, were subject from time to time to rapid and sometimes catastrophic upheavals. The maps make this point more forcefully than words. Leaving aside gradual expansions and contractions and mere frontier adjustments, sweeping and dynamic changes took place in the sixth century, when Justinian reconquered Italy, North Africa, and southern Spain from the Germanic kingdoms which had established themselves there; in the seventh century, when the first great expansion of Islam detached forever Syria and Palestine, Egypt and North Africa from allegiance to the Byzantine Empire; when Slavonic peoples, and later the Bulgarian state, occupied most of the northern Balkans, and when much of Italy was lost to the Lombards; in the ninth century, when Sicily and Crete were lost to the Arabs; in the tenth century, when Armenia, northern Mesopotamia and parts of northern Syria were reconquered from the Arabs, Crete was recovered, and large areas of southern Italy became once again Byzantine territory; in the eleventh century, when the Bulgarian state was destroyed and much of the northern Balkans restored to Byzantine rule, while at the same time the Seljuq Turks occupied much of Asia Minor; in the thirteenth century, at the beginning of which the armies of the Fourth Crusade captured Constantinople and divided most of the European territory of the empire between them, leaving a few tiny Byzantine successor states, one of which, based in western Asia Minor, succeeded in ousting the westerners from some of their European conquests, and ultimately recaptured Constantinople and restored a much weakened and diminished Byzantine Empire; and in the fourteenth century, when the Ottoman Turks drove the Byzantines out of Asia Minor, and established themselves in Thrace, while the Serbian Kingdom absorbed most of the

Early nineteenth-century engraving of Hagia Sophia, Constantinople. *Courtesy of Mansell Collection, London.*

rest of Byzantine territory in Europe, and the empire itself was reduced to Constantinople, Thessalonica, part of the Peloponnese, and a few islands in the Aegean.

Can we meaningfully speak of continuity in a state whose territories underwent such drastic changes? The answer must be that we can. The Byzantines themselves were never in any doubt—for them there were only restorations, never new beginnings. The continuity of political structure, of legitimacy, of religious and cultural unity was proof against the most violent territorial disruptions. Clearly the Byzantine state, and the civilization of which it was the bearer, were not territorial, as all post-Renaissance nation states have been. It needed some territory, naturally, but it could expand or contract to almost any extent without losing its political and cultural identity. One small territory, however, could not be lost for long without putting the continuing existence of the empire in doubt. That was Constantinople itself, the capital founded by Constantine in 330 to be a second Rome, and whose official name was always *Kōnstantinoupolis Nea Rōmē*—"the City of Constantine which is the New Rome." The successor states which survived the Latin conquest of 1204 did not regard themselves as fully embodying the heritage and traditions of the Byzantine Empire. Only when one of them reconquered the capital could it claim and be granted full legitimacy. When we look at the numerous usurpations of imperial power which took place, it is clear that no emperor ever succeeded in retaining even partial recognition for any length of time unless he had control of the capital, and that, conversely, once a rebel did establish himself there, opposition to him swiftly collapsed.

A further question arises on considering the gains and losses of territory by the Byzantine Empire over the centuries. Did the Byzantine world, the area in which Byzantine civilization developed, necessarily coincide in area with the territory of the empire? Clearly it did not in the last period of Byzantine history, when the empire had become a minuscule Balkan state while the Greek language and Greek culture, the Orthodox church, and a sense of Byzantine identity spread over a very much larger area which was subject to foreign powers. But this very discrepancy between the area of Byzantine power and that of Byzantine culture was perhaps a symptom of collapse, rather than a state of affairs capable of continuing. In particular, the fact that the ecclesiastical authority of the Orthodox church extended far more widely than the political authority of the Byzantine state at this late stage created many problems. It might therefore appear that state and civilization were essentially coterminous, and that only limited discrepancies could long be tolerated. But when the matter is examined more closely, it becomes clear that neither Byzantine political sovereignty nor Byzantine cultural domination had precise boundaries at all, but that both of them radiated into the surrounding world with different degrees of intensity. It is not always easy to define even the political frontiers of the empire. As soon as it is looked at in detail, anomalies are encountered—territories which acknowledged Byzantine sovereignty but lay outside the Byzantine administrative system, territories in which the Byzantines shared sovereignty with another power, territories which paid tribute to the Byzantine Empire but did not acknowledge its sovereignty, and finally a gamut of degrees of dependence ranging from thinly disguised and irreversible subjection to freely contracted alliance between equals. In this respect, too, the Byzantine Empire resembled neither modern nation states, with their all-or-nothing sovereignty, nor most medieval European states, in which notions of sovereignty and of personal dependence were not always easy to disentangle. In fact it formed the center of a zone of influence—political, religious, artistic, and cultural—which spread far beyond its boundaries. It thus often played a key role in determining the course of events in distant regions. A recent thought-provoking study, D. Obolensky's *The Byzantine Commonwealth*, developed the concept of a "Byzantine Commonwealth," which included all those communities whose links with the Byzantine Empire, whether formally recognized or not, were strong and lasting. The concept is a viable one, even if historians cannot always agree on how to define it. It is clear, for instance, that medieval Bulgaria or Georgia could exist in the form it did only thanks to the predominating power and prestige of the empire and its civilization. Many Italian city states, like Venice, Naples, and Amalfi, were originally constituent parts of the empire, strongly subject to Byzantine influence, and only gradually developed an independent political existence and pattern of life. Yet it would be very hard to say when, if ever, these communities ceased to belong to the "Byzantine Commonwealth." Kievan Russia in the eleventh to thirteenth centuries and the later Principality of Muscovy had never formed part of the Byzantine Empire in the political sense, yet their higher culture was almost wholly inspired by Byzantine models, their Church acknowledged its dependence on the Patriarch of Constantinople, and they always recognized themselves as standing in a special relationship to the empire. After Constantinople fell to the Ottoman Turks in 1453, the prince of Muscovy claimed to be the legitimate successor of the Byzantine Empire and declared that his principality was the Third Rome, in other words, the natural successor to the Byzantine and Roman empires.

This was no empty boast or arrogant self-aggrandizement, but reflected a real sense that Russia belonged essentially to a Byzantine "sphere of influence," though no Byzantine emperor had ever exercised even the most indirect sovereignty in that vast country.

This consideration brings us back to our original point, that the history of Europe and the Near East in the Middle Ages cannot be understood without taking into account the existence and influence of this usually powerful and always prestigious political and cultural community—the Byzantine Empire. Even in its period of greatest political weakness it possessed a quality of legitimacy which other states lacked—and sometimes envied—as well as a culture which offered direct access to the thought both of the Fathers of the Church and of the ancient Greeks. And its long survival was proof of its toughness and of the flexibility and viability of its political and cultural principles. Its unique and complex apparatus of administration, its sophisticated legal system, its wealth, its advanced technology, whether in the field of industry or in that of war, made the Byzantine Empire, at any rate until the disaster of the Fourth Crusade, what in modern times would be called a superpower.

It is easy to give a date for the end of the Byzantine Empire. On 29 May 1453 the Turkish army of Sultan Mehmet II took Constantinople by storm, and the Emperor Constantine XI was killed fighting in defense of his capital. On that day a political entity was destroyed, whose origin could be traced back without any break in continuity to the banks of the Tiber in the eighth century B.C. and to the historical reality reflected by the legends of Romulus and Remus and the foundation of Rome. There was still some Byzantine territory not under foreign occupation, particularly in the Peloponnese. But no new emperor was crowned, what remained of the original administrative apparatus ceased to function and even the most loyal subjects of the Byzantine Empire recognized that it no longer existed. The situation was unlike that pertaining after 1204, when several fragmented remnants of Byzantine power perpetuated the tradition of the empire, and one of them eventually established its claim to legitimacy. In 1453 the hope of a restoration was eschatological rather than political.

It has sometimes been argued that the Byzantine Empire really came to an end with the capture of Constantinople by the crusaders in 1204 and the partition of most of its territory. There is much to be said for this view. The restored Byzantine Empire of 1261–1453 was a pale shadow of its former self. Its economic role was greatly diminished in the new pan-Mediterranean market which was in process of formation in these years. Most of its power and wealth had been drained away and its territory was soon reduced to a handful of detached enclaves. But its citizens had a sense of continuity with the past. Their political ideology, though modified, was not transformed. The prestige of their culture was enhanced rather than diminished, perhaps in compensation for their loss of political power. And to the very last, the late Byzantine Empire was treated by its friends and foes alike as a special case. It was no ordinary state, nor was Constantinople an ordinary city. In this book, therefore, we shall follow the course of Byzantine civilization right up to the capture of the city by the Turks in 1453.

If we ask when Byzantine history begins, we face a different kind of problem. Byzantine society grew out of late Roman society. The late Roman Empire, distinct in its organization, its culture and its "feel" from the Roman Empire of Augustus, the Flavians, and the Antonines, resulted from the reaction of the ruling strata of Roman society to the half- century of anarchy and invasion that followed the death of the Emperor Severus Alexander in A.D. 235. Some historians have seen that half-century as the true beginning of the Byzantine period. Others have taken the inauguration by Constantine of his new capital city by the Bosphorus in 330 as marking the beginning of the new epoch. For others, again, the final separation of the eastern and western parts of the Empire in 395, or the dismissal of the last western Roman emperor in 476, is the crucial date. Finally, there are those historians who hold that it was only when the armies of nascent Islam conquered Syria, Palestine, Egypt, and North Africa that the Byzantine Empire attained its true form, and emerged, like a butterfly from a chrysalis, from the ruins of the old Roman Empire.

The truth is that, though historical periods are real, and are not

Christ Pantocrator in the main apse of the cathedral at Cefalù in Sicily, c. 1155. Although Sicily was under Norman domination from 1072, the mosaics at Cefalù are purely Byzantine in character, and were probably executed by Greek craftsmen who had been brought to Sicily to work for Norman patrons. *Courtesy of Colorphoto Hans Hinz, Basel.*

merely imposed by the historian upon a seamless continuum of events, they are not separated by clean-cut boundaries. They overlap, and features of the old and new worlds coexist for a time. So any particular date chosen to mark the beginning of a new age is largely arbitrary. One feature which distinguishes the Byzantine Empire from the world of the late Roman period is its Christianity. Not only was Christianity the religion of the state and that of the vast majority of its citizens, but Christian modes of thought, Christian ideals, and Christian imagery dominated the political, intellectual, and artistic life of the whole society and determined its peculiar quality. This state of affairs did not come into being all at once. There was a long transitional period during which Christianity became a permitted religion, then a favored religion, then the only tolerated religion. During this period the urban upper classes, who were the bearers of classical culture, gradually adopted Christianity. When they did so, they did not abandon all their previous intellectual baggage. Rather they adapted it to Christianity and Christianity to it. So the transitional period was marked by an extensive, though not total, fusion of Christianity and classical culture. Revealed religion gained intellectual respectability by being fitted into the framework of the Greek philosophical tradition. The fit was not perfect, and sometimes alternative attitudes to Christian dogma—an Aristotelian or a Platonic view— were adopted. At the same time much of classical literature and art, and the techniques and skills associated with them, were adapted to the needs of a Christian society by allegorical interpretation, or by being demoted to a kind of theoretical second rank as auxiliary or propaedeutic sciences.

The age in which this synthesis of classical and Christian culture took place, the age of Constantine and Julian and Theodosius, of the great fourth-century eastern Fathers Gregory of Nazianzus, Basil, Gregory of Nyssa, and John Chrysostom, of Ambrose, Jerome, and Augustine in the west, the age when the western, Latin-speaking half of the old Roman Empire largely passed under the domination of new Germanic kingdoms, the age when centralized power and its inevitable bureaucracy replaced the old balance between imperial administration and self-governing cities, has a peculiar character of its own. It cannot be adequately treated as a mere prologue to the thousand years of Byzantine history for two reasons. The first is its own complexity and importance and the wealth of information it has left us. The second is that it belongs in the last analysis to the ancient world and not to that of the Middle Ages. Constantine has more in common with Aurelian or Marcus Aurelius than he has with Justinian, let alone with any later Byzantine emperor. Gregory of Nazianzus and Augustine, though Christian bishops, are firmly rooted by their education, their values, their habits of thought and action, in the world of classical antiquity.

This book therefore takes up the story of Byzantine civilization after the definitive triumph of Christianity and the working out of the synthesis between classical and Christian traditions, and will not deal, except indirectly, with the age of the Church Fathers and the great Ecumenical Councils. If a date has to be chosen, it would be about A.D. 500. Not that many features of ancient society did not persist long after that date—indeed much of the peculiar quality of the first period of Byzantine history arises out of the contradictions between old and new. But the decisive changes had taken place, and were clearly irreversible. The butterfly had emerged from the chrysalis. Fragments of the chrysalis might still cling to its wings as they dried in the sun. But it could never creep back into it again.

THE
BYZANTINE
EMPIRE

REVISED EDITION

1

THE BIRTH OF A NEW EMPIRE 500–641

Head of the colossal statue of Heraclius in Barletta, southern Italy, early seventh century. *Courtesy of Hirmer Fotoarchiv, Munich.*

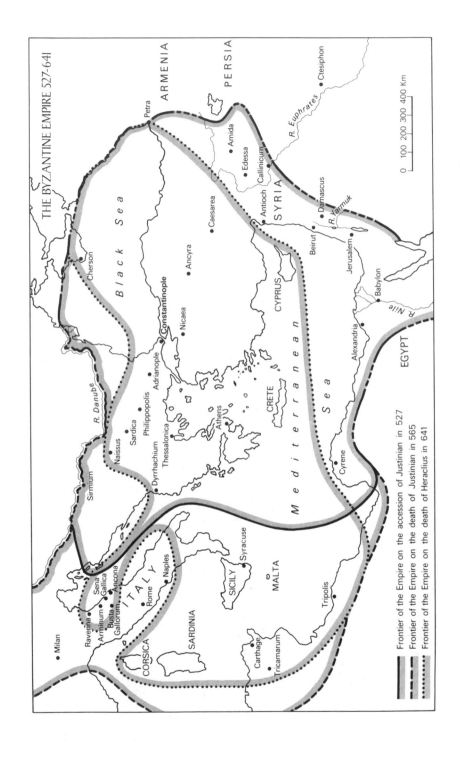

THE BYZANTINE EMPIRE 527–641

0   100 200 300 400 Km

ARMENIA

PERSIA

• Ctesiphon

R. Euphrates

Petra

• Amida

• Edessa

Callinicum

Antioch •

SYRIA

• Damascus

R. Yarmuk

Black Sea

• Caesarea

• Beirut

• Ancyra

• Jerusalem

CYPRUS

• Babylon

• Cherson

R. Nile

Constantinople •

• Nicaea

Adrianople

EGYPT

• Alexandria

Philippopolis

• Dyrrhachium

Thessalonica

Mediterranean Sea

Sardica

R. Danube

Athens •

CRETE

Naissus •

Sirmium •

• Cyrene

Syracuse •

SICILY

MALTA

• Naples

ITALY

Rome •

• Tripolis

Sena Gallica

Ancona •

Ravenna •

Arminum •

Busta Gallorum

Milan •

CORSICA

SARDINIA

• Carthage

Tricamarum •

━━━ Frontier of the Empire on the accession of Justinian in 527

╴ ╴ ╴ Frontier of the Empire on the death of Justinian in 565

• • • • • Frontier of the Empire on the death of Heraclius in 641

The first period to be looked at extends from 500 to the death of the Emperor Heraclius in 641. The political history of the age is marked by two great movements, one near the beginning, the other at the end. At the dawn of the sixth century A.D., the Emperor Anastasius reigned in Constantinople. There had been no Roman emperor in the west for a quarter of a century. Italy, with Sicily and part of the Dalmatian coast, formed the kingdom of the Ostrogoths, ruled by Theodoric from his capital at Ravenna. In the closing years of the fifth century he and his Gothic army had entered Italy and defeated another Germanic group with the blessing of the emperor in Constantinople, who was glad to see such dangerous guests leave his own territory. Farther west, the greater part of Gaul belonged to the kingdom of the Franks, a Germanic people from northwest Germany and Holland. They had displaced or destroyed earlier groups of Germanic invaders, the Visigoths and the Burgundians. The Visigoths moved into Spain and established their kingdom there, sharing the Iberian peninsula with their Germanic cousins, the Suevi. The former Roman Africa, together with Sardinia, Corsica, and the Balearic Islands, formed the kingdom of the Vandals. The Vandals were a Germanic people who had left their homeland by the Baltic under the twin pressures of overpopulation and lust for booty. Their long odyssey took them into northern Russia, down the river Dnieper to the Black Sea, across Europe to Gaul, and through Spain to the Straits of Gibraltar. For a time they settled in Spain, forming an alliance with another wandering group, the Iranian-speaking Alans. Then a rebellious Roman governor of Africa, Count Boniface, invited the Vandals under their king, Gaiseric, to join him in Africa and support him against the Roman government. In 429 the Vandals crossed from Spain. They numbered in all 80,000, of whom perhaps 15,000 would have been fighting men. Within a few years they had taken over Mauretania and Numidia, sweeping aside both Boniface and the Roman generals opposing him, and in 435 they signed an agreement with the Romans. A few years later they expelled the Roman forces from the old prov-

3

ince of Africa, and Gaiseric established himself in Carthage at the head of a Vandal kingdom. At the beginning of the sixth century his descendants were still firmly in control there.

These Germanic kingdoms which had established themselves upon the ruins of the western Roman Empire were curious states. In all of them the Germanic invaders were few in number compared with the Roman population, whom they did not expel. They could not afford to, since they lived off the rents paid by Roman tenants. They themselves remained a separate military caste, alone permitted to bear arms. Much of the Roman civil administration remained but served the new masters. The precise relations between Roman inhabitants and Germanic overlords varied from kingdom to kingdom. The Ostrogoths, Visigoths, and Vandals belonged, for historical reasons, to the Arian faith, which was rejected as heretical by the Christian Church of the empire in east and west alike. This fact alone imposed a barrier between the communities which strengthened that created by differences of language and lifestyle. The Franks, under King Clovis, were Catholics, and were probably more numerous than the other Germanic ruling groups. But they too were slow to fuse with their Roman subjects. And the openly parasitic nature of the Germanic states made it hard for the local population to entertain feelings of loyalty towards them. The Vandals were openly contemptuous of their subjects, and from time to time persecuted the Catholic Church, though the Vandal court affected a taste for Roman culture and provided patronage for a circle of minor Latin poets. The Ostrogoths, under the far-seeing and brilliant King Theodoric, sought to win the support of the population of Italy, so far as this could be done without weakening the reality of Ostrogothic power. Theodoric probably looked forward to the ultimate blending of Roman and Ostrogoth, but that was for the distant future.

Meanwhile the eastern half of the Empire had continued to prosper and to enjoy freedom from invasion. The Danube frontier was less secure than it had been in the heyday of the empire, and the Danubian provinces were from time to time attacked and pillaged. But the lands round the eastern Mediterranean, with their populous cities, enjoyed peace and tranquillity. To the east of them, it is true, lay the Persian Empire of the Sasanid kings. Incidents occurred frequently enough along the long frontier that stretched from the Caucasus to the Arabian desert. From time to time there was full-scale war between the two powers. But neither was able, under the conditions of ancient warfare, to strike a mortal blow at the other. So once the demands of prestige were satisfied, and some booty taken, a peace treaty was usually signed.

The government in Constantinople was confident that it could handle hostilities with Persia and trouble on the Danube. They were traditional problems that had faced the Roman Empire for five centuries. The loss of Italy and the western provinces was another matter. This was something without precedent, something damaging to the unity of an empire which had for centuries embraced the whole Mediterranean world. And if that empire, as its rulers and many of its citizens now believed, was not merely a product of history but was part of a providential plan to bring salvation to all mankind, then it was impossible that its territory should be permanently diminished. The old Roman pride and the new Christian sense of mission conspired to urge upon the rulers in Constantinople a policy of reconquest. An attempt had indeed been made in 468 to regain Africa from the Vandals, but had failed miserably. In the meantime pressure groups of western exiles in Constantinople and of dissidents in Italy and Africa continued to reinforce the claims of imperial tradition and Christian piety.

In 527 the Emperor Justinian succeeded to the throne in Constantinople. He had been the effective ruler during the nine-year reign of his elderly uncle Justin I, a peasant from the neighborhood of Naissus who had made his way to power through long service in the army. Justinian was clever and ambitious, and had boundless confidence in his own ability. He saw himself both as the elect of God and as the restorer of Roman power and prestige, at home and abroad. His great codification of Roman law, which dominated legal theory and practice in Europe until the nineteenth century, was of course the work of a team of lawyers, headed by the brilliant Tribonian, but without

Mosaic over the south door of Hagia Sophia, Constantinople, showing Justinian offering his church, and Constantine the city he founded, to the Virgin. The mosaic probably dates from the late tenth century. *Courtesy of Sonia Halliday.*

Justinian's enthusiastic and unfailing support it would never have been carried out. His rebuilding of the great church of the Holy Wisdom (Hagia Sophia), destroyed by fire during a riot in 532, was the work of two talented architects, Anthemius and Isidore. It was Justinian, though, who provided the driving force and the immense material resources needed. Early in his reign he determined to restore the unity of the Roman Empire by regaining the lost western provinces. Clever diplomacy sowed discord both within and between the Germanic kingdoms. A single campaign, conceived and led by the young general Belisarius, destroyed the Vandal Kingdom and brought Africa back under Roman rule in 534. A year or two later Belisarius was operating against the Ostrogoths in Italy, where things were not to prove so easy. Ravenna, the Gothic capital, was captured in 540. But soon a new Gothic leader, Totila, who knew how to appeal to the poor and oppressed of Italy, turned the tables on the Romans and drove them from Italy again. All the resources of the Empire in men and money were brought to bear, and slowly, city by city, Italy was reconquered. But it was not until the late 550s that the last Gothic garrisons north of the Po surrendered. In those years Italy had been devastated, its city walls destroyed, its population uprooted, its rich and cultured senatorial class extirpated.

That was not the full price to be paid for restoration in the west, which was completed by the conquest of southern Spain in the early 550s. The immense military effort in the west had exhausted the treasury, and preoccupation in that direction had led to dangerous neglect of the long-standing problems in the east. Justinian wanted peace with Persia and was willing to pay for it so that he might have a free hand in the west. And though he constructed a network of fortified posts in the northern Balkans, he never provided the military manpower called for in that region by increasing pressure both from Slav tribesmen spreading out from their homeland in Poland and from pastoral nomads from the steppes, driven westwards by changes in the balance of power beyond the Great Wall of China. And the empire's ability to face these new military problems had been weakened by a devastating epidemic of bubonic plague in 542, followed by secondary outbreaks at intervals afterwards. So the great achievement of his reign, the reconquest of Italy, Africa, and part of Spain, left a heritage of trouble to his successors. For all its display of power and for all the lustre of art and intellect which it fostered, his reign was not, as he had hoped, the beginning of a new era of glory, but rather a last, doomed attempt to shore up a structure whose collapse was inevitable.

Within a few years of Justinian's death in 565, much of Italy had been lost to the Germanic Lombards who swept in from the plains of Hungary. Southern Spain was soon regained by the Visigoths. And even in Africa, Roman authority was never effectively established over the Berber tribes and principalities. Only in the old Roman province of Africa itself—modern Tunisia—and in a few coastal cities elsewhere was an effective administration maintained. Justinian's immediate successors, Justin II (565–78), Tiberius (578–82), and Maurice (582–602), could do little about the deteriorating situation in the west because they were fully occupied in the east. Along the thousand-mile eastern frontier the initiative now lay with the Persians, and they made good use of it. On the Danube frontier the increasing penetration and settlement by Slavonic tribes was complicated by pressure from a new group of nomads with a strong state structure, the Avars. Sometimes the Avars acted as powerful but self-willed allies of the Romans against the Slavs, and sometimes they coordinated and supported the Slav attacks. A long series of desperate campaigns led to the devastation of much of the northern Balkans and the destruction for ever of many of the inland cities. In time the Avars became involved in hostilities with the Franks to the west, and their pressure on the Balkans diminished. This enabled the Emperor Maurice, who had already succeeded in restoring Roman initiative on the Persian frontier, gradually to drive Slavs and Avars back across the Danube. But it was too late to restore the situation. Nepotism, severe taxation, and finally an attempt to reduce the soldiers' pay lost Maurice what support he had. A military revolt put a junior officer named Phocas on the throne. Phocas's combination of irresponsible populism and brutal repression enabled him neither to win and retain the affection of his subjects (though Pope Gregory the Great [590–604] treated him with respect) nor to cope with the military threat on the frontiers. The greater part of the northern Balkans was reoccupied by Slavs and Avars, and such of the hard pressed Roman population as still survived either migrated to the south, to Thessalonica and Constantinople, or took to the hills. In the east the Persians were again pressing hard.

Phocas's ineffectual reign of terror was ended in 610 when Heraclius, the son of the governor of Africa, sailed into the Bosphorus with his fleet and overthrew the usurper. Heraclius, an able soldier and wholly devoted to his duty as ruler, found himself from the beginning facing a war on two fronts. On the north the Slavs and Avars ranged almost unopposed over the northern Balkans, often establishing their rustic hamlets under the ruined walls of abandoned Roman cities. On occasion their armies besieged Thessalonica and Constantinople itself. The danger in the east was even more menacing. The Persian thrust carried their armies beyond the usual frontier zones of Armenia and Mesopotamia. In 613 they took Antioch, and in the following year, Jerusalem. All of Syria and Palestine was in Persian hands, Egypt was occupied by them, and their inroads into Asia Minor became ever more penetrating. Heraclius was forced to sign a humiliating peace treaty with the khan of the Avars in order to have his hands free in the east. In 622 he set out at the head of his army into Asia Minor. His object was to strike at the center of Persian power, not to fight pitched battles with the Persian field army. By exercising great strategic and tactical skill, he forced his way into Armenia, from which he made a series of drives to the south. While Heraclius was in Armenia, in 626 Constantinople had to face a siege by the combined armies of the Persians and Avars, who had renounced their peace treaty. It was a critical situation. The very existence of the empire was at stake. But Roman sea power decided the issue, and the besieger had to withdraw. At last Heraclius could launch his counterattack. Building up a system of alliances with the peoples of the Caucasus and with the powerful kingdom of the Khazars to the north, he began his steady advance southwards into Mesopotamia. By December 627 Heraclius faced the main Persian army before Nineveh, and shattered it. Within a few months he had occupied the Persian royal residence of Ctesiphon, the king of Persia had been deposed and murdered, and his successor had signed a peace treaty with Heraclius. All Roman territory was returned, and Heraclius was proclaimed guardian and protector of the new king's infant son.

When Heraclius returned to the capital, to be greeted by the acclamation of his subjects and the benediction of patriarch and clergy, it seemed to everyone that the position of the empire was now secure. Radical administrative reorganization, which will be described later, provided an army based on local manpower, and no longer dependent, as was that of Justinian, on foreign tributaries and mercenaries. The

Revelation brought to Mohammed by the Archangel Gabriel, from a manuscript of the
Universal History **of Rashid al-Din (1247–1318).** *Courtesy of Edinburgh University Library.*

power and prestige of Heraclius appeared unchallengeable. With Roman help and encouragement the Slav and Bulgar subjects of the Avars rose in revolt against them. The weakened Avar kingdom was no longer in a position to threaten Constantinople. To men of the time it must have appeared that the Roman Empire and east Roman society had survived a desperate crisis and could now resume their old way of life.

In the very year in which Heraclius set out from Constantinople to destroy the Persian empire, Mohammed and his followers migrated from Mecca to the safety of Medina, where the Prophet soon won many new adherents and, more from necessity than from design, began to lay the foundations of a Moslem Arab state. The success of the new movement was in large part due to the weakness displayed by the two great empires, which for so long had confined the Arabs to carrying out as auxiliaries the policies of others. Both Rome and Persia had conquered and been conquered in turn, and now it was time for the Arabs to make their own history. Within a few years of the death of Mohammed in 632, Moslem armies had broken out of the Arabian peninsula, invaded Roman and Persian territory, and begun the career of conquest that in the course of a century was to take them to the banks of the Loire in the west and the Indus in the east. In 635 Damascus surrendered to the Arabs. In 636, by the river Yarmuk, a left-bank tributary of the Jordan, the Arabs inflicted a crushing defeat on the Roman army; this marked the end of Roman power in Syria. Jerusalem held out longer against Arab besiegers under the leadership of Patriarch Sophronios, a former teacher of rhetoric, but in 638 hunger forced him to surrender the Holy City to Caliph 'Umar. In 640 the Armenian stronghold of Dvin fell, and the conquest of Egypt was begun, to be completed in a few years. All of the southern, largely Syriac- and Coptic-speaking provinces of the empire were lost, never to be recovered, and Arab raiding parties were already penetrating Asia Minor. Heraclius's life's work lay in ruins before his eyes. The balance of his mind was disturbed by this succession of disasters, all the more terrible because they were unforeseen. For the last few years of his reign, until his death in 641, his government made no serious attempt at a counterattack.

Shorn of its western and southern possessions, reduced in size, but ethnically more homogeneous, the empire, which from now on will be termed "Byzantine" rather than "Roman," had to adapt itself to very different conditions of life.

CIVILIZATION IN TRANSITION

Justinian and Heraclius were both obstinately devoted to the restoration and aggrandizement of the Roman Empire. Yet they did not see this patriotic enterprise in the same light; nor did their contemporaries. In his legal enactments Justinian occasionally made a bow, as it were, to divine providence, as for instance in the decree giving validity to the *Digest*, the systematic compilation of excerpts from the

works of the classical Roman jurists. But in that same decree he went
on to speak at length and in traditional Roman terms of the imposition
of eternal peace on the Persians, the destruction of the Vandals, and
the restoration of Africa to Roman rule. In the decree introducing his
Institutes, or epitome of Roman law for students, God appeared only
in a brief subordinate clause. Instead the emperor spoke of armed
force and law as the two bastions of Roman society, of barbarian peoples brought under the Roman yoke, of new provinces added to the
Roman Empire. And at the head of each of these decrees Justinian
himself appeared with the traditional resounding titulature of a Roman emperor—*Imperator Caesar Flavius Justinianus, Alamannicus,
Gothicus, Francicus, Germanicus, Anticus, Alanicus, Vandalicus, Afri-
canus, Pius Felix Inclitus, Victor ac Triumphator, semper Augustus*.
When his general Belisarius returned to Constantinople after his
great African victory, Justinian organized for him a kind of revival of
the ancient Roman triumph. It was a remarkable piece of antiquarian-
ism, for no triumph had ever been held in the new capital of Constantinople in the two centuries of its existence, and more than five and
one-half centuries had elapsed since the last time a private citizen
celebrated a triumph in Rome. The victorious Belisarius did not, of
course, dedicate the spoils of his victory to Jupiter Capitolinus. This
was a Christian society, and there were no pagan temples in Constantinople. Yet there were virtually no Christian elements in the elaborate
symbolism of Belisarius's triumph. It was left to the defeated king of
the Vandals, Gelimer, to murmur a quotation from Ecclesiastes—
"Vanity of vanities, all is vanity"—as he grovelled before Justinian in
the Hippodrome.

    How different were things in the time of Heraclius! George of
Pisidia, the court poet who wrote panegyric accounts of the emperor's
campaigns against the Persians, had very little to say about the Roman
duty to spare the submissive and to vanquish the proud; indeed he
made very little use of traditional Roman imagery of war and conquest. Instead Heraclius was depicted as the chosen vessel of God,
divinely inspired in all his actions, and his campaigns were seen as a
holy war in defense of Christianity against the infidel. He drew up

The Emperor Justinian, surrounded by court officials, ecclesiastics, and guards, brings an offering to the Church; sixth-century mosaic from the church of St. Vitale, Ravenna. *Courtesy of Alinari Art Resource, New York.*

his line of battle *theiōs* ("divinely"). And after his final decisive victory the whole army raised its hands and hearts to the God of creation. It was not only in "official" poetry that this fervently Christian tone was adopted. When Heraclius left Constantinople on his long march into enemy territory, his departure was preceded by a religious service in Hagia Sophia, in which the emperor prayed for victory over the enemies of God. As he marched down to the harbor at the head of his army he held in his hands an icon of Christ which was reputed not to be the work of human hands. When he returned victorious to the capital after his long and hard-fought war, his triumphal procession probably outdid that of Belisarius in magnificence. But it is noteworthy that it went, not to the Hippodrome, the center of secular celebrations, but to the church of Hagia Sophia. At the door of the Great Church the victorious emperor was greeted by the Patriarch Sergios, and then emperor and patriarch together prostrated themselves in thanksgiving before an icon of the Virgin. Only after his religious celebration did Heraclius, mounted on a white horse and escorted by captured Persian elephants, make his entry into the Hippodrome and present himself to his subjects.

Both Justinian and Heraclius, like most of their contemporaries, saw the empire as a unique political entity, the heir of the Roman Empire of pagan times, with its pretensions to universality. They also saw it as a unique theological entity, a part of God's grand design for the salvation of mankind. But in the ninety years that elapsed between Justinian's wars of conquest and those of Heraclius, the emphasis changed. Men looked less to the historical Roman past and more to the eschatological Roman future when they sought to define and understand the place of their own community in the world. One can detect intermediate stages in this process of change. In contemporary accounts of Justinian's wars, the symbol of authority, the sight of which rallies and inspires the soldiery, was the standard. In Maurice's wars this role was often played by icons, which were sometimes brought to the army by leading bishops. The public life of the emperor took on a liturgical quality. More and more of his time was taken up by processions to churches in and around the capital on fixed days.

In a sense, then, the religious side of public life was emphasized more as time went on. But we must beware of false analogies. It was not a matter of the influence of the Church increasing as that of the state decreased. "Church and state" was not a Byzantine concept. The clergy did not form a distinct and self-conscious social group. Nor did its members hold high state office. With a few notable exceptions—notable for the Byzantines as well as for us—there were no clerical statesmen in the late Roman and Byzantine world. The clergy were not even the bearers of high culture. Rather the reverse, as will be seen. Literacy and literary education were commoner among laymen

The interior of Hagia Sophia, Constantinople, built by Justinian between 533 and 537. The Arabic medallions date from the Ottoman period when the building was used as a mosque. *Courtesy of Weidenfeld & Nicolson Archives, London.*

than among clerics. And the Church did not control great wealth at this time. If late Roman society became more religious in its outlook between the sixth and the seventh centuries, it certainly did not become more clerical. The "liturgification" of much public state business increased the prestige and authority of the emperor and his principal officers of state. Speeches and written documents were accessible only to those who heard them or who had the education to read them. The regularly recurring ritual appearances and acts of the emperor were open to all in the capital to see, and could be described in the provinces. They established a far more direct bond between the ruler and his subjects than was possible by more overtly political means.

However, if religion could be a powerful cement binding together the members of a political community, it could also be a solvent, separating them into distinct, self-conscious groups. If the prosperity of the state depends on the favor of God, and the favor of God depends on correct belief—and few in the sixth century would have questioned either of these propositions—then it follows that those who do not entertain correct belief cannot be true members of the body politic. So long as heretics were discriminated against as individuals or as members of unimportant conventicles, no great harm came to the community as a whole. But if they set up a parallel Church, with its own hierarchy and its own network of communication, then serious and permanent alienation of a significant body of citizens could be expected. This is exactly what happened in the sixth and seventh centuries. The Church had long been divided on the issue of the relationship between Christ's divine and human natures. The details of the argument are complex and need not concern us here. Justinian in his later years, and his immediate successor Justin II, supported by the Church hierarchy of the capital, took punitive measures against the Monophysites, those who believed that Christ's human nature was wholly absorbed by his divine nature. The Monophysite clergy were forced underground, and set up their own Church organization. From being a loosely structured faction within the Church, the Monophysites became a counterchurch. For reasons that are not completely clear, they found their strongest support in Syria, Mesopotamia, and

Egypt, regions where the mass of the people did not speak Greek. A whole body of homilies, hymns, pastoral letters, polemical treatises, and the like in Syriac and Coptic grew up, the tone of which was hostile to the established Church and, by implication, to the state. Thus religious sectarianism reinforced ethnic and cultural distinction, creating a sense of alienation from the political society of the empire. In the reign of Heraclius it was precisely those regions which were overrun and occupied by the Persians and then recaptured by the Romans. Their inhabitants bore the brunt of the devastation and privation of war, and felt that they had not had the protection which was their right as citizens of the empire. Thus when the Arab invasions began at the end of Heraclius's reign, the Arabs found little enthusiasm for Roman rule in the areas they attacked. If not positively welcoming the invaders, many of the inhabitants displayed sullen neutrality. This was a major factor in the ease with which the Moslems took over some of the richest and most populous provinces of the Roman Empire.

If different and sometimes conflicting tendencies can be seen in attitudes towards the Roman state, the same is true of attitudes towards the universe. The mutual adaptation of Christian theology and Greek philosophical thought had already in a large measure been completed. Fourth-century Fathers like Gregory of Nyssa had begun to provide a Neoplatonist interpretation of Christian doctrine. The unknown fifth-century author of the works attributed spuriously to Dionysius the Areopagite, an Athenian who is mentioned in the Acts of the Apostles, completed the work begun by Gregory and constructed an elaborate system of downward-reaching emanations from the One, who was God, to the created world, balanced by corresponding stages of ascent towards the One. In the first half of the sixth century, Leontios of Byzantium, a monk in Palestine, provided a more Aristotelian interpretation of Christology as his attempt to render intellectually acceptable the dogmas of the Church.

But philosophy was not wholly absorbed by theology, nor was all of theology translated into philosophical terms. In Athens the venerable Academy, founded by Plato himself nearly a thousand years earlier,

was still in existence and numbered among its teachers men who, if
not in the first rank of philosophers, were steeped in ancient philosophical tradition. The greatest of the Neoplatonist Academicians,
Proklos, had died in 485. But Simplikios was busy compiling his erudite and judicious commentaries on Aristotle, in which he preserved
much of the thought of older philosophers. Damaskios was applying
a strange mixture of genuine philosophical analysis and superstitious
demonology to the elucidation of Plato. Yet the school of Athens was
out of touch with the times. Much of the effort of its scholars was
devoted to finicky logic-chopping. And above all, it was a center of
paganism in a world that had become Christian. Like other university
cities in later times, Athens had become a home of lost causes. In 529,
as part of a general policy of discrimination against heretics, pagans
and other intellectual dissidents, Justinian confiscated the rich endowments of the Academy and ordered its members to cease teaching.
Some of these distinguished and eccentric scholars for a time migrated to Persia, hoping to set up a school of philosophy there, but
soon returned. Recent studies have suggested that the closure of the
school of Athens was a temporary rather than a permanent measure,
and that the teaching of philosophy went on in the ancient city,
though with reduced endowments, till the end of the sixth century or
later.

Athens was in any case no longer of much importance. The greatest
intellectual center of the late Roman world was Alexandria, where
the Museum, founded by Ptolemy I in 280 BC, still flourished as a
research institution and a community of scholars. The philosophers
of Alexandria had adopted, or at least reconciled themselves to, Christianity, and avoided the exhibitionist paganism of their Athenian colleagues. The greatest of them—though he may not have held an official chair—John Philoponos, took issue with Proklos of Athens on
the question of whether the universe had always existed or had been
created in time. It is an important philosophical problem, which survives today in some of the arguments of cosmologists on the origin of
the universe. Philoponos, like Proklos, treated it with the seriousness
it deserved. At the same time his work, which he wrote about 529,

was perhaps meant to defend the Alexandrian school from the fate which befell the Academy of Athens. In his numerous other works he not only tried to reconcile dogma and dialectic but developed in a creative way many of Aristotle's ideas on physics. Much of his wide-ranging work has been lost, because as a Monophysite he was an object of suspicion to orthodox Christian copyists and teachers. But what survives shows him to be a philosopher of near first rank, and an attractive man of the utmost intellectual integrity. He died some time in the reign of Justinian, but the Alexandrian school of philosophy survived him. David and Elias, who published studies on Aristotle, were probably younger contemporaries of John Philoponos. Stephen of Alexandria, who was summoned by Heraclius to Constantinople in 612 to teach philosophy there, was a versatile scholar who commented not only on Aristotle but also on the medical writings of Hippocrates and Galen. His establishment under imperial patronage as head of the newly restored "university" of Constantinople indicates the prestige still enjoyed by a philosophical tradition which went back to Plato and Aristotle, so long as its adherents refrained from attacking entrenched Christian positions. The teaching of Stephen is probably reflected in the theological writing of his contemporary, Maximos the Confessor (580–662), who made sophisticated use of the concepts and methods of ancient philosophy in his treatment of dogmatic questions. A contemporary at Alexandria of John Philoponos was Cosmas Indicopleustes (the Voyager to India). Cosmas was a retired sea captain who had travelled widely in pursuit of eastern trade. Whether he had himself ever actually visited Taprobane (Sri Lanka) is a matter of uncertainty, but he knew those who had. He devoted his years of retirement to expounding, with many fascinating digressions and reminiscences, his view of the universe. Far from being spherical, as the Greek philosophers had generally held, it was, he declared, rectangular in plan, with a kind of conical summit, above which was situated Paradise. In fact its shape resembled that of Noah's ark, which was modelled on it. The heavenly bodies, he believed, were manipulated by angels. Cosmas rejected the whole philosophical tradition, against which he launched a number of polemical asides. He based himself firmly on the Old Testament, as interpreted allegorically by the Church Fathers. In spite of the almost maniacal detail with which he worked out the implications of Old Testament passages torn from their historical context, Cosmas was not an isolated figure from the lunatic fringe. Many manuscripts of his work survive, and a cycle of illustrations to it was created very early, perhaps by the author himself.

So we can trace in the sixth century three different approaches to the central problems of philosophy. The Athenian school maintained in a somewhat scholastic fashion the position of the later pagan Neoplatonists. The Alexandrian school conceded the central points of Christian doctrine and proceeded to analyze their implications by the use of Aristotelian logic and to build a system of philosophy which would not come into open confrontation with Christianity. Cosmas the Voyager to India (who may have been a Nestorian, and hence a heretic in the eyes of the official church) and those who thought like him tried to reject the whole Hellenic philosophical tradition and to make a fresh start on the basis of interpreting Holy Writ. In doing so they inevitably let in certain elements of traditional philosophy again by the back door. All three tendencies coexist throughout much of the Byzantine period, influencing and influenced by one another.

In medicine too one can see a conflict between the new and the old. There was a good deal of medical writing, most of it compilatory in character and based on the vast medical encyclopedia of Oreibasios, personal physician to the Emperor Julian in the fourth century. Alexander of Tralles, brother of Anthemios, the architect of the church of Hagia Sophia, wrote a voluminous handbook on therapeutics and minor works on parasitic worms and on the eyes. Alexander is clear-headed, careful, and familiar with the great works of Greek medicine and their cool and objective approach. But he is not above including superstitions and old wives' tales in his work. His contemporary Aetios of Amida was court doctor, probably to Justinian. His lengthy textbook of medicine is largely a compilation from earlier writers. Yet he reflects the ideas and practices of his own time by occasionally prescribing prayer or the use of incense from a church. Gessius of

Illustration of a leguminous plant from the Vienna manuscript of the Herbal of Dioscorides, written in Constantinople in 512 for Juliana Anicia, daughter, grand-daughter, and great-grand-daughter of western Roman emperors. *Courtesy of Osterreichische Nationalbibliothek.*

Petra, a teacher of medicine around 500, already conflates scientific and hieratic medicine in his work. Paul of Aegina (seventh century), in his handbook of practical medicine, tries in the same way to reconcile the traditional medical thought of the Greek world with the growing tendency to attribute illness to the work of evil spirits. We get an interesting glimpse of how medicine worked in practice in the *Life of St. Theodore of Sykeon*, a holy man living in a small town in Northwest Asia Minor in the closing decades of the sixth century. The world of Theodore and his companions was demon ridden. Every kind of untoward event, including illness, was attributed to demons, who were often identified with extreme precision. Much of Theodore's work consisted of driving out demons, often by methods familiar to psychotherapists today. But he did not regard himself as a rival to the local doctors. On the contrary they often sent one another patients who, they felt, could not be treated by their particular methods. The old and the new, the scientific and the superstitious, the pagan and the Christian, persisted side by side in the daily medical practice of this little provincial town.

When we turn to the sphere of literature, we find the same coexistence of old and new, sometimes in confrontation, sometimes supplementing one another. Many of the classical Greek literary genres had died out centuries before, when the social and political conditions which favored them were superseded. Men no longer wrote tragedies, or comedies, or lyric poetry in the original sense of the expression— poetry to be sung. Political oratory had vanished with the disappearance of sovereign assemblies to harangue, and forensic oratory with the disappearance of jury courts. But speeches continued to be made—everything from wedding speeches to funeral orations, from pyrotechnic displays of rhetorical skill to serious comment on public affairs. Chance has preserved a number of public speeches delivered in the Palestinian city of Gaza in the late fifth and early sixth centuries, which reveal the continuing importance of oratory both in reflecting and molding public opinion and in providing intellectual entertainment. And let us not forget the rhetoric of the pulpit, which often betrays the influence of classical tradition. Indeed rhetoric had taken over much of literature. The immense *Dionysiaca* of Nonnos of Panopolis, written about the middle of the fifth century, though in form an epic, has no real story to tell; it is an inflated, digressive, descriptive panegyric of the god in the language and style of traditional epic poetry. The boundaries between prose and verse were no longer clear. The same matter could often be cast in either mould. Dioscorus, a minor versifier living in the little town of Aphrodito in the Nile valley in the middle of the sixth century, composed occasional poems in Homeric or tragic language and meter to celebrate the arrival of a portrait of Justin II, the visits of minor officials, the promotion of fellow citizens in the civil service, or the weddings of local notables. Christian literature addressed to laymen was equally dominated by rhetoric—technical writing addressed to fellow theologians was another matter. All this literature was essentially learned. It was couched in a language originally intended as an imitation of that of the writers of Athens in the classical age, but which had by now developed rules of its own, which had to be learned by long study. It was packed with quotations from and allusions to the literature and mythology of the distant classical past—or, in the case of Christian literature, to the Bible. It avoided precise reference to those features of the contemporary world which had no classical—or biblical—counterpart, and cultivated a curious air of detachment from the society to which both writers and readers belonged. It was to some extent a status symbol, the possession of a class of leisured, cultivated men who had spent their youth in the study of grammar and rhetoric.

Side by side with this classicizing literature we find another type of literature, which did not share its values or methods, and which was often more overtly contemporary in tone. Two examples will illustrate the point. History in the classical manner, with speeches, grand descriptive passages, serious study of the causes and effects of events, was written by men who clearly saw themselves as the heirs of Herodotus, Thucydides, and Polybius. The greatest of these was Procopius, of Caesarea in Palestine, whose account of the wars of Justinian ranks among the masterpieces of Greek historiography. Austere, serious, and erudite, he writes in classicizing language, avoids the technical terms of contemporary life, strikes a high moral tone, and shuns the trivial and anecdotal. In the organization of his narrative, in his use of fictitious speeches, in his elevated language, in his grave and censorious literary persona, he deliberately links himself with the long tradition of Greek historiography. A little later, in the early years of Justin II, Procopius found an heir in Agathias, who, though clearly of lighter weight than his predecessor and not above recounting an amusing anecdote, adopts the same imitative language and style, the same generally serious tone, and the same learned digressions. Agathias in his turn was followed by Menander the Protector, of whose work only excerpts survive, but they show that Menander pursued the same aims as Agathias. In the reign of Heraclius, Theophylact Simocatta wrote a history of the reign of the Emperor Maurice (582–602). He too was a historian of serious purpose, interested in establishing the truth, and in command of all the devices of classical historiography. Only his florid style, crammed with poetic words and images, and his interest in the lives and miracles of holy men and women, marked the beginning of a break in a long tradition.

Side by side with these historians who follow—albeit at a respectful distance—in the footsteps of Thucydides, a new type of history made its appearance. This was the chronicle, which surveyed the history of the world from the creation or some other arbitrary early date to the time of the writer. The chroniclers were not interested in establishing causal links or in exploring the relations between the character of a statesman and his acts. They had little feeling for the much-prized art of rhetoric, and did not insert fictitious speeches into their narrative. Their language was not consistently atticizing, but rather macaronic, with many elements of vocabulary, morphology, and syntax belonging to the spoken language of the time and carefully avoided by classicizing writers. Their view of history, so far as they could be said to have one, was naively theological—misfortune was considered a punishment for sin—and their characters were black and white, either good or evil. They were uncritical and undiscriminating in the choice of events which they narrated, and included much that was trivial or sensational. The chronicles have often been termed monkish, the implication being that they were written by and for members of monastic communities. There is no reason to think this generally true. What is true is that they were written to entertain as much as to edify, and that they were addressed to a readership which was fully literate but whose taste was uninfluenced by the high culture of the classically educated. They were manifestations of a popular culture, firmly Christian in tone, ignorant of or confused concerning classical tradition, eager for information but uncritical in handling it. They provided an answer to the naïve questions of the man in the street about the past of the society in which he lived.

Two chronicles have survived from this period. The Chronicle of John Malalas was written in Antioch early in the reign of Justinian, and contains much information—and misinformation—about events in that city. Lively, undiscriminating, often muddled, firmly orthodox in theology, a jumble of battles, high politics, ecclesiastical intrigue, earthquakes, tittle-tattle, and sensationalism, it offers a fascinating glimpse of the intellectual world of the ordinary man under Justinian. The second, the Paschal or Easter Chronicle, so called because of the attention it devoted to the date of Easter, was written by an unknown author in the reign of Heraclius. More "ecclesiastical" in tone than the Chronicle of Malalas, it may well have been written by a cleric. It shows the same simple, annalistic presentation of events, the same black-and-white characterization, the same inability to discriminate between the significant and the trivial, the same theological view of historical causes. But it is less lively and entertaining than the work of Malalas, who had a certain almost journalistic talent. Both these works marked a clear break with a millenial historical tradition, and the beginning of a new kind of historiography, addressed to readers whose intellectual demands were of a different kind from those of the readers of Procopius and Agathias.

Poetry in the classical tradition also continued to be written, although the range of genres was limited, and much of the poetry of the time was really declamation in verse. The special poetic language, going back to Homer, and the quantitative verse, which depended on distinctions between long and short syllables no longer made in pronunciation, made this traditional poetry a form of literary expression practicable only by the learned. And only the learned could fully appreciate its tissue of allusion and imitation. Historical epics were composed by Christodoros of Koptos early in the sixth century. There still survive poems on the Capture of Troy by Tryphiodoros, and on the Rape of Helen by Colluthus. Musaeus's poem on Hero and Leander probably belongs to the early sixth century. This traditional narrative poetry in the Homeric manner seems to have been losing some of its appeal to readers. At any rate in the reign of Anastasius, one Marianos devoted his modest poetic talent to recasting in simpler iambic verse the works of Theocritus, Callimachus, Apollonius Rhodius, Aratus, and Nicander. Soon the iambic trimeter replaced the dactylic hexameter as the appropriate meter for lengthy narrative poems. This was more than a technical metrical change. With the abandonment of the hexameter went that of the Homeric poetic language, with its special vocabulary, its strange inflexional forms, and its traditional formulae. A number of historical and mythological poems were written in iambic meter in the sixth century, but they no longer survive. What does survive is the extensive corpus of poetry composed in the reign of Heraclius by George of Pisidia. This includes a long poem on the Creation, and a series of panegyrical accounts of Heraclius's campaigns against the Persians. George's overt and often passionate expression of Christian belief marked a radical break with classical poetic tradition. With it went much, but not all, of the allusive reference to earlier poetry so characteristic of the imitators of Homer and Callimachus. Its place was partly taken by biblical allusions. In spite of his declamatory tone of voice, George of Pisidia was a vigorous poet, capable of carrying on a narrative with grandeur, master of a great store of imagery. But his poetry was very different from classical narrative poetry and more like a series of very long messenger's speeches from Greek tragedy.

Side by side with narrative poetry in the classical manner and in the new manner represented by George of Pisidia, there was a lively production of short occasional poems in classical form. The historian Agathias belonged to a coterie of such poets in the third quarter of the sixth century. Some of their poems dealt with contemporary events and personalities, while others were literary exercises, variations on themes by Alexandrian and later epigrammatists. Agathias made a collection of his poems and those of his friends; it survives in part in a later anthology. And we have two longer descriptive poems by a member of the circle, Paul the Silentiary, written on the occasion of the reopening in 562 of the church of Hagia Sophia after the dome had collapsed. These were recited in the presence of the by then octogenarian Justinian. It is clear that there was still interest in and patronage for classicizing poetry in the ruling circles of Roman society.

Alongside these developments in poetry, another of a quite different character was taking place. From its earliest days the Christian Church had made use of sung poetry in its liturgy, following the model set by contemporary Judaism. To the biblical psalms and canticles there were added in due course short poems of praise or supplication, in classical quantitative meters. As the feeling for syllabic length was lost, similar short poems appeared in simple meters based on recurring stress accent. These usually had the same rhythmical pattern repeated line after line. In the Syriac-speaking regions of the empire, the Semitic tradition of religious poetry in short lines of stress rhythm, as old as the Song of Deborah in the Old Testament, underwent further developments, including that of a short, sermon-like address to the congregation in verse. Out of such unpromising beginnings there suddenly arose in the sixth century a new and elaborate kind of Greek liturgical poetry and music—the new genre was known as the *Kontakion*. It was essentially a sermon, recounting some event in Old Testament or New Testament history or in the life of a saint and drawing brief lessons from it. In form it consisted of a series of stanzas in a complex accentual meter—no longer monotonous repetition of similar lines—each sung to the same melody, and all ending in the same repeated line or refrain. The range of metrical and musical patterns was inexhaustible, and their complexity of structure rivalled that of classical Greek lyric. The music of these early liturgical hymns is lost, but its rhythm can be reconstructed from the meter of the poems. The subject matter of this new lyric poetry was essentially narrative, and the narrative was presented largely through dramatic dialogue between the characters.

The *Kontakion* is associated with Romanos, who may have invented the genre and who certainly developed and perfected it. He was a native of Emesa (Homs) in Syria, possibly of Jewish origin, who came to Constantinople in the reign of Anastasius and became a deacon in the church of Hagia Sophia. According to his biographer, he saw in a dream one Christmas Eve the Virgin Mary, who gave him a roll of papyrus and bade him eat it. When he awoke the next morning he went straight to the pulpit of the great church and sang a

Christmas *Kontakion* which still has a place in the liturgy of the Orthodox Church. He was apparently still composing poems, and the music to which they were sung, as late as 555.

The poetry of Romanos was written in what can best be described as an enhanced form of the language of formal prose, the linguistic register in which sermons, laws, and other official pronouncements were couched. He was a master of lively and psychologically plausible dialogue. His work is full of rich imagery, taken largely from the world of nature, agriculture, and craft, and owing little or nothing to earlier literary models. Biblical echoes were naturally frequent, but allusions to classical literature were absent, apart from stylized expressions of rejection of the classical tradition. He dismissed as worthless Aratos "the accursed" (*triskataratos*), Demosthenes "the feeble" (*asthenes*) and so on.

This new lyric poetry, in a new meter and a new style, and with a new subject matter, was functional in the sense that the poetry of Pindar or the tragedies of Aeschylus were functional—it formed part of a ceremony or ritual. It was also inseparable from its musical accompaniment, like the poetry of Pindar or the choral odes of tragedy. In both these respects it was quite unlike contemporary classicizing poetry. It was also readily comprehensible to the relatively uneducated, though no doubt its full appreciation called for more than average familiarity with the Bible and the Church Fathers. It represented a quite unexpected renewal of a poetic tradition which in many ways had become fossilized and handed over to mandarins. It was to have a long future, though it was rarely to produce a poet of the stature of Romanos.

The material surroundings of life in late antiquity changed only slowly. The monumental city of the high Roman Empire, with its colonnades, temples, and open *agora* surrounded by public buildings, had already entered a process of transformation with the closure of the temples at the end of the fourth or beginning of the fifth century, and the building of large churches, around which a new city center tended to grow up. Broad, colonnaded streets began to be replaced by narrow, sometimes winding, alleys, lined by two- or three-story houses with overhanging upper floors and balconies. But by the age of Justinian, the classical city had not yet become the medieval city. Justinian carried out a great deal of public building, partly from military necessity and partly as a display and assertion of imperial grandeur. The historian Procopius devoted a special work to a description, province by province, of the buildings constructed under his direction. Few of his countless fortresses remain standing. The most striking survival is the impregnable castle at Dara near the Euphrates, a testimony to the power of the empire and to the ingenuity of the architect Anthemius. It was never taken by assault, but a resourceful enemy could simply walk around it. The foundations of the great fortresses on the Danube at Belgrade and Vidin, upon which successive conquerors have built through the centuries, were the work of Justinian. Many of his defense works still stand in Tunisia, though usually with later Arab or Turkish additions, as at Kelebia.

Of his other secular buildings which survive, the most notable are the huge underground cisterns in Constantinople, the roofs of which are supported upon hundreds of columns. Solidity, dignity, and technical excellence marked all these constructions. But it was above all by the churches which he ordered to be built that Justinian impressed the men of his time. Since the Christian communities emerged from their semi-underground existence in the reign of Constantine, the churches they constructed had taken one of two forms. The basilica followed a pattern established for public buildings in Hellenistic times and much used in the Roman Empire. It was a rectangular building, usually with a central nave and two or four side aisles. The nave was separated from the aisles by a row of columns on which rested walls, usually with windows, and the pitched roof of the central nave. The aisles were covered by lean-to roofs beneath the level of the windows. There was usually a curved apse at the east end, and there might be an enclosed portico or entrance hall at the west end, communicating with the main body of the church by doors. Such a building was easy to construct, economical of space, and reassuring in its rectilinearity. It enabled a large number of people to see and hear what was going on around the altar at the east end, which might be raised on a platform reached by a few steps. The flat architrave resting on the capitals of the columns was soon generally replaced by a row of arches, which gave a greater lightness to the building, emphasizing its perpendicular rather than its horizontal aspect.

The other type of church was a round or polygonal building roofed by a dome, which might rest either directly upon the outer walls or upon interior pillars or piers. This type of construction, which was often used for tombs, was generally fairly small. But the example of the Pantheon at Rome reminds us that Roman architects were well able to build large, circular, domed buildings. The earliest Christian churches of this form were probably martyria, built over the supposed tombs of those who had died for the faith. By the fourth and fifth centuries, larger round churches were either being built or being converted from earlier secular use. Examples are the mausoleum of Constantia and the church of St. Stephen in Rome, and the church of St. George in Thessalonica, probably originally built as a mausoleum for the Emperor Galerius. The round building with its lofty, domed roof was less suitable for mass communication than the rectangular basilica. But it provided a "total" environment, disorienting those within and cutting them off from the outside world. It could also be seen as a symbol of the universe, with the earth below and heaven above.

Attempts were made to combine the best features of both types of church. In parts of Asia Minor and Syria, basilical churches were provided with vaulted roofs, and the rows of columns were replaced by large arches. But the technical difficulties of superimposing a dome upon a rectangular building were great. Justinian and the architects whom he employed seem to have devoted much thought and experiment to this problem. The church of San Vitale in Ravenna, begun in the days of the Ostrogoths, though probably with funds and designs from Constantinople, and completed by Justinian after the capture of the Gothic capital, is essentially an octagonal building surmounted by a dome resting on four piers, and with a small, vaulted apse attached. The great church of St. John the Evangelist at Ephesus, now in ruins, was a church of basilical pattern, with a transverse aisle or transept, roofed by several small domes. Early in his reign Justinian

The interior of Ss. Sergius and Bacchus in Constantinople, built in 525, in which Justinian's architects attempted to solve the problem of superimposing a dome on a rectangular building. *Courtesy of Josephine Powell, Rome.*

rebuilt the small church of SS. Sergius and Bacchus in Constantinople—his dedicatory inscription running round the base of the dome can still be read. The architect has here succeeded in imposing a dome upon a distorted rectangular building by the use of pendentives—spherical triangles filling the space between the corners of the rectangle and the base of the dome. But it was in the great church of Hagia Sophia that the problem of combining the firm regularity of the aisled basilica and the disoriented space of the round building was solved in a way which has excited the amazed admiration of visitors and architects alike for fourteen centuries.

In the church, which was begun in 533 and completed in 537, a rectangular brick exterior wall encloses a nave and two aisles, separated by marble columns supporting a gallery on each side. In the line of the columns stand four vast piers supporting via pendentives a huge dome over the center of the aisle. Two half-domes, supported partly by the same piers, partly by smaller piers set slightly inwards, cover the east and west ends of the aisles. At the east end is a single apse, at the west end a wide narthex, or porch, divided into an inner and an outer section by a wall pierced by several doors. In front of the narthex there was originally a large colonnaded forecourt. The bare technical description gives little idea of the impression this superb building made, and still makes, on the visitor. First of all, the enclosed space is enormous—77 meters long, 71.7 wide, and 31.5 high. Second, the huge dome rests on a short drum with windows all around: thus the inner space is filled with light, the source and direction of which are not immediately recognizable. At night it was lit by a system of chandeliers suspended from chains. By modern standards it must have been rather dim, but to the sixth-century observer, used to illumination by olive-oil lamps, it seemed ablaze with light. Third, the interior walls and floor were all lined with highly polished polychrome marble, and the dome and other parts contained mosaics of reflective colored glass. The original decoration has almost entirely vanished, and the mosaics the visitor sees today are all of later date. The effect of all these factors, and of the plan of the church with its columns and piers, is that, as one moves about, fresh vistas constantly open up; the sense of horizontal direction is soon lost. The only fixed point becomes that over which hangs the center of the huge dome. The visitor is as if lost in a vast underwater cavern, brightly illuminated from a hidden source and lined with glittering gemstones. The technical perfection of the church of Hagia Sophia is demonstrated by the fact that it still stands, virtually undamaged, after more than a hundred recorded earthquakes and who knows how many which escaped the notice of historians. It was Justinian's showpiece. He is said to have looked around in amazement when he first entered the completed building, and murmured, "Solomon, I have surpassed thee." No other church was ever built on the same pattern and the same scale. But the artistic and technical breakthroughs of the age of Justinian paved the way towards the classical type of Byzantine church, the cross in a square surmounted by a dome or domes set upon drums, a type of building wholly without precedent in the classical world.

The original mosaic decorations of Hagia Sophia appear to have been nonfigurative. That in the great dome represented a cross. There was, however, plenty of representational art in the period, in the form of mosaic, fresco, portable painting (usually encaustic), relief carving in ivory, steatite, and other materials, and repoussé or engraved silver. Freestanding stone sculpture was not prominent in the art of the period, though a huge equestrian statue of Justinian was erected in the main square of Constantinople across which the Great Church and the Great Palace faced one another. From the surviving examples of the representational art of the age we can discern a number of styles, each embodying a different view of man and his place in the universe. The realistic, illusionistic art of the classical period, which sought to represent objects as they actually appeared modelled in three-dimensional space, was fully alive. The floor mosaics of the Great Palace, probably of the mid-sixth century, the fresco of the Maccabees and their mother in St. Maria Antiqua in Rome (620–40), the silver dish of 613–29 depicting Meleager and Atalanta, now in the Hermitage in Leningrad, the silver dish depicting a herdsman and goats, and found

Two silver dishes showing the excellence of Byzantine metalwork in the early seventh century. Left: Herdsman and goats on a plate found at Klimova in Russia. Right: David fighting Goliath, one of a series of plates decorated with scenes of David's life found at Kyrenia in Cyprus. *Courtesy of The Hermitage, Leningrad. Courtesy of The Metropolitan Museum of Art (Gift of J. Pierpont Morgan, 1917).*

at Klimova near Perm in the Soviet Union, and some of the superb David plates from Cyprus are all examples of the continuity in style and motif of this classicizing, realistic art.

Side by side with this we find an art in which the constraints of three-dimensional space are forgotten. Human figures are flat and frontal, their feet walk on no real ground, they are unrelated to one another and communicate only with the beholder through their large and striking eyes. And what they communicate is emotions and states of mind, rather than outward and physical features. This "abstract" art has two roots. One is an age-long tradition of the Syrian and Palestinian world, the spawning ground of religions and religious art. The other is the Neoplatonist view that the artist must not merely copy physical objects, including human beings, but must strive to provide insight into the higher reality, the form, of which they are only derivatives or reflections. These two factors, one provincial and non-Hellenic, the other profoundly Greek, conspired to produce an art that sought to depict the inner man rather than his outer shell, the holiness which made a saint rather than the accidental features of his physical body. Realistic art used true perspective. This abstract art often uses reverse perspective, in which the background figures are larger than those in the foreground. The artist—and those who contemplated his work—was concerned with relations of essential importance, not with Euclidean space. Examples of this abstract, idealist art are the mosaics of the church of St. Demetrius in Thessalonica made before the disastrous fire in the early seventh century; the mosaic over the triumphal arch in the church of St. Lorenzo Fuori le Mura in Rome (dated 578–90); the apse mosaics of St. Agnese in Rome (c. 630) and of Kiti, near Larnaca, in Cyprus; and the sixth-century icon of the Virgin and Child flanked by saints from the monastery of St. Catherine on Mount Sinai.

Art of both styles could be found side by side in the same building, even in the same picture. The conflict was not one between different schools of artists; it was one within the human consciousness. There were other tendencies, too, often of provincial origin. Many works of art show curiously squat, flattened figures, the drapery of whose clothing has become purely decorative rather than representing three-dimensional reality. Good examples are the seventh-century relief of Christ enthroned, accompanied by an apostle, from the monastery of St. John of Studios in Constantinople, or the sixth-century reliquary lid with gospel scenes in the Vatican Museum. Others are associated with Egypt, such as the frescos from Bawit and from Saqqarah in the Coptic Museum in Cairo, and several of the tombstones with human figures in an attitude of prayer in the same museum. The mosaic from Jerusalem now in the Archaeological Museum in Istanbul, showing Orpheus/Christ among the animals (which include a Pan and a Centaur) is noteworthy not only for its carefree fusion of Christian and pagan motifs, but also for the childlike naïveté of its style. This naïveté is also to be found in some ivories of the period, like the diptych of St. Lupicinus in the Bibliothèque Nationale in Paris or the diptych with Virgin and Child in the Matenadaran in Erevan.

Floor mosaic showing Christ as Orpheus among the animals from Jerusalem, now in the Archaeological Museum in Istanbul. *Courtesy of Istanbul Archaeological Museum.*

Much work remains to be done in discerning and distinguishing the different styles prevalent in art of the sixth and early seventh centuries. What is clear, however, is the break in the artistic uniformity so long imposed upon the Mediterranean world by the cultural leveling of the Roman Empire. Ways of looking at and representing things long confined to a kind of underground life in remoter provinces and at a low social level now become acceptable in the great centers. In particular, since the loss of the western, Latin half of the empire, oriental influences of all kinds confront, mingle with, and modify the naturalistic tradition of classical art. Above all, the emotional art of the Fertile Crescent meets and finds an echo in the Christian Neoplatonist idealism of much of the élite of society. And out of this there begins to emerge a new, abstract religious art which turns aside from representing things as they happen to be and concentrates upon what they essentially are, or ought to be, an art which leads men to a transcendent world. This movement is not unconnected with the growing liturgification of life and the emphasis on the Christian as opposed to the Roman aspect of the Christian Roman Empire.

In all that concerns civilization and culture, the Roman Empire of the period from Justinian to Heraclius was polycentric. Rome, Carthage, Alexandria, Jerusalem, Antioch—to name only the principal cities—were lively centers of intellectual and artistic development side by side with Constantinople. Regular movement of men and ideas took place among all these centers, in which the traditional cultures of many peoples played a part. This cultural diversity and regionalism—which extended, as has been pointed out, to religion—contrasted sharply with the political unity and centralization of the empire. Power resided at Constantinople, and there alone. However the outward aspect of that state power underwent a change during this period. Though Greek was the mother tongue of most of the inhabitants of Constantinople and the lingua franca of all of them, the imperial government clung tenaciously to Latin as the language of the state and the mark of its Roman origin. The high officers of state transacted their business in Latin, the army was commanded in Latin, laws were promulgated in Latin. No emperor was more passionately attached to the traditions of Roman universalism than Justinian, the codifier and restorer of Roman law. Yet he was the first emperor to issue the majority of his laws in Greek, the language of the greater part of his subjects. His successors followed his example, and the Latin façade of court and government grew thinner. Finally, about the time of his victory over the Persians, Heraclius dropped the resounding traditional Latin imperial titles, and called himself in official acts and proclamations simply *basileus* or king. This remained both the official title and the everyday designation of Byzantine emperors until the end of the empire. Latin continued in use in coin inscriptions in Byzantium for a century or two more—as it did in Britain until recently. And a few Latin phrases were fossilized in imperial ceremonial, as Norman-French is fossilized in British royal and judicial ceremonial. But from the end of the reign of Heraclius, the Roman Empire had become Greek in language at all levels—and this only two generations after Corippus, the last Latin poet to write in the classical, Virgilian tradition, had come to Constantinople to seek patronage and fame.

Lastly, it is worth mentioning a perhaps trivial symbol of the change in outlook and lifestyle in the period from Justinian to Heraclius. Since the stormy third century the Roman governing classes were clean-shaven—only philosophers were bearded. The emperor Julian was laughed at for his beard. Soon the mantle of the philosopher passed to monks and bishops, and they too might be bearded. But all the figures in Justinian's entourage in the Ravenna mosaic are clean-shaven. Justinian's three successors, Justin II, Tiberius and Maurice, are depicted on their coins as clean-shaven. Suddenly with Heraclius we are in a world of bearded men, and none more so than the emperor himself. Whether this change in personal appearance is the outward sign of an inward change in mentality is for others to decide. It is worth noting that it coincides with the completion of a radical change in clothing styles which extended over several generations. Classical garments were draped round the body rather than tailored; and those worn by men were generally without decoration. In late antiquity tailored garments, including even oriental trousers, become more and more frequent. And the cloth from which they were made often had colored stripes, woven designs, or appliqué decoration varying from simple embroidery to costly and elaborate arrangements of jewels. These bearded, tailored men in their polychrome clothes certainly looked very different from their plain, clean-shaven grandfathers and great-grandfathers.

2

THE STRUGGLE TO
SURVIVE 641–867

The walls of Constantinople, built by Theodosius II in the fifth century, protected
the city from invaders for more than a thousand years, and are still standing. *Courtesy
of Weidenfeld & Nicolson Archives, London.*

The loss of Syria, Palestine, Egypt, and soon the whole of North Africa in the middle of the seventh century was a shattering blow to the Byzantine Empire. These regions were the most densely populated in the empire and in every respect the most advanced economically and technologically. They included some of its largest and most important cities—Alexandria, a center of christianized Hellenic culture and the entrepôt through which the agricultural surplus of Egypt was exported to feed the vast population of Constantinople; Antioch, another ancient center of art and letters with a centuries-old Christian tradition, and the terminal point of overland trade routes to Persia and ultimately to India and China; Jerusalem, the holiest of cities to all Christians, orthodox and heretic alike; Gaza, the seat of a lively school of philosophy and literature, and the débouché of caravan routes to the Yemen and to the Persian Gulf; Edessa, a fortress and trading center, and the home of Syriac culture; and many others.

The economic loss was considerable, though we must beware of thinking of it in modern terms. There was no empire-wide market, let alone a world market, except for a handful of luxury consumer goods; most trade was local, and very often between a city and its own agrarian hinterland. But the loss of corn from Egypt was a serious matter. Free distribution of bread to the citizens of Constantinople was suspended, and there were problems in feeding the army. These sudden shortages in such politically sensitive areas caused great instability. The capital had now to be fed from its own hinterland in Thrace, like any other city. A new impulse was given to agriculture in Thrace and Bithynia, and no doubt land values rose, fortunes were made, and a new influential group of landowners came to the fore. Another aspect of the economic consequences of the Moslem conquests was the loss of revenue to the state from taxation of the rich southern provinces. Suddenly there was no money available for paying mercenary soldiers, for the construction of prestigious public buildings, for the conspicuous spending so important in a deferential soci-

Scenes of rural life from a tenth-century manuscript. On the left, peasants are pick-ing olives; on the right, a cheese-maker, bees, and a beehive. *Courtesy of Biblioteca Marci-ana, Venice.*

ety. All men did not of course become equal. But they became more equal than they had been for many centuries.

The military implications of the new situation were even more alarming. The Moslem conquerors, who were few in number com-pared with those whom they ruled and from whose produce they lived, halted for a while at the natural frontier of the Taurus Moun-tains and the highlands of Armenia. The mountain ranges and the plateau of Asia Minor which lay beyond them were a new and diffi-cult terrain for warriors who had learned their craft in the torrid desert lands of Arabia. They presented special problems for an army whose rapid mobility depended on the camel—problems never satis-factorily solved. In any case the new-born Moslem state was fully occupied at first in organizing its vast territories which it had won not only from the Byzantines but from the Persians too. Indeed the Persian Empire, weakened and ridden by dissidence since its defeat by Heraclius, was completely destroyed by the Arabs. The absorption of its immense lands and their proud and alien population was per-haps the greatest task which faced the new caliphate.

Yet there was no lasting peace for the Byzantines. In 647 an Arab force under Mu'āwiya, the Moslem governor of Syria, penetrated deep into the interior of Asia Minor, and sacked Caesarea in Cappadocia. In 649 a new threat appeared. The Arabs had a fleet constructed and manned by Egyptian and Syrian sailors, with which they landed in Cyprus and captured and destroyed Constantia, the capital. On the appearance in Cypriot waters of the Byzantine navy, the invaders discreetly withdrew. But the Byzantines could no longer count on control of the sea, which had been theirs without effort for so long. A few years later, in 654, the Arab fleet attacked again, and this time seized and occupied Cyprus, Rhodes, and Cos. Their ultimate goal was only too clear—it was Constantinople itself. In the next year the Byzantine fleet was crushingly defeated by the Arabs off the southern coast of Asia Minor. The rulers of the empire and its citizens could have no illusions—they faced a long and desperate struggle for their very existence. The Persian Kingdom had vanished. Was the Byzantine Empire to follow it?

Events in Europe made the situation of the empire even more perilous. The long campaigns of the Emperor Maurice at the end of the sixth century had largely restored Byzantine authority in the northern Balkans. The cities of the interior were woefully diminished in population. Some were abandoned, and many others had reverted to an agrarian lifestyle. And the Slav settlers, who had been pouring in for a generation, remained, occupying the place of those peasants who had fled or been killed during the years of invasion. But the frontier seemed firmly reestablished and the Avars were disposed to recognize it. A new beginning might be made by absorbing the Slav settlers and reestablishing the Roman way of life in this extensive region. The deposition and death of Maurice in 602 as a result of a mutiny by the soldiers, whose pay had been reduced and who were ordered to overwinter north of the Danube, put an end to this balance of power and to the hopes arising from it. His successor, Phocas, made no serious attempt to defend the Danube frontier, and Heraclius was, throughout his reign, too desperately involved first with the Persians and later with the Moslem Arabs to spare troops and resources for the Balkans. The result was that the Slavs and the Avars were able once again to range as they pleased south of the Danube. The Black Sea coastal cities remained firmly in Byzantine hands, as did Thessalonica on the Mediterranean. The immediate hinterland of Constantinople was protected by a ring of powerful fortresses in Thrace—Develtos, Adrianople, and Philippopolis were the chief among them—and Sardica (Sofia) was held as a strongly garrisoned outpost on the great road from central Europe to the Bosphorus. The rest of the Balkans passed largely out of Byzantine control. Not only the north, but the whole of the Greek peninsula as far as the southernmost tip of the Peloponnese, lay open to settlement by Slavs. Only a few coastal cities, such as Athens, Patras, and Corinth, remained permanently in Byzantine hands.

In the middle of the nineteenth century, Johann Jakob Fallmerayer propounded the view that the whole of Greece was settled by Slavs at this time and that the original population either fled or was exterminated, from which it allegedly followed that the modern Greeks are not the descendants of the ancient Greeks at all. Fallmerayer's theory aroused the keenest passions among both Greek and Slavonic scholars, whose arguments often generated more heat than light. Today we can look at the matter more coolly. The frequency of Slavonic place-names in many parts of Greece shows the extent and density of the Slav settlements, though we must not assume that a Slavonic place-name always implies a permanent settlement by Slavs. Recent discoveries by archeologists of remains of village settlements near Argos and elsewhere similar to those of the Slavs in the northern Balkans have brought added evidence of the Slav presence. Some Greek peasants withdrew to inaccessible mountainous territory in the eastern Peloponnese. Others probably took refuge in less attractive regions of Greece, or adopted a wandering, pastoral way of life. Still others, perhaps the majority, lived on side by side with the new settlers, but out of the reach of the tax collector from Constantinople. The Slav tribal nobility began to feel the attraction of Greek ways. A long period of coexistence began, which ended in the absorption of the Slavs of the southern Balkans by the preexisting population, and their adoption of Christianity and of the Greek language and civilization. And as Isocrates had observed a thousand years earlier, it is culture, not blood, that makes a man a Hellene.

The military threat to the empire in Europe was very different from that in Asia. Here it faced no expansive, aggressive state with an ideology of conquest, but rather the relentless pressure of a peasant population on the move in search of land to cultivate. Only occasionally was this pressure given an overall organization and direction, as by the Avars, and later by the Bulgars. The provinces occupied by the Slavs were not among the richest or the most populous of the empire. Even as suppliers of military manpower they had long passed their zenith. What made the invasions of the Slavs menacing was the nearness of their conquests to Constantinople itself. Since the days of Justinian the threat of an enemy army appearing before the walls of the capital had been ever present. Those walls, built under Theodosius II, were virtually impregnable. And so long as they retained command of the sea, the Byzantines could hope to withstand a siege, however long. But the political consequences of failing to keep the enemy away from the capital could be disastrous for an emperor. And since the loss of Egypt the plains of Thrace had become the granary of Constantinople. Repeated invasion and devastation of Thrace threatened the food supply of the city in the long run, and undermined the position of a class of landowners and officials who played a role of growing importance in Byzantine society.

The Byzantine world's response to this catastrophic change in its situation was complex. First we must look at the political, military, and administrative reaction of the imperial government. Since the days of Diocletian and Constantine, at the turn of the third and fourth centuries, rigid separation of civil and military authority had been the rule. Civilian governors of provinces had no authority over troops stationed in their area. Army commanders had none over the civilian population. This was the theory, and on the whole the practice, of the empire. It was a system designed to keep generals from dabbling in politics and staging military coups, and it worked. But it was cumbersome, it depended on the cooperation of the governing bodies of cities, which had to undertake much of the execution of government policy, and it made coordination of military and civil policy slow and difficult.

Now that no region of the empire was safe from attack, something different was needed. Already in the later sixth century, civilian and military authority had been combined in the same hands in two regions cut off from the rest of the empire—Italy, or such of it as was left under Byzantine sovereignty after the Lombard invasion, and Africa. In each of these provinces an exarch both commanded the troops and carried on the civil government, acting as a kind of delegate of the emperor. Heraclius may have instituted a similar system in parts of Asia Minor and Syria during his long war against the Persians. Territories still under Byzantine control were formed into military districts under the command of a *strategos*, who was responsible for all aspects of government, civil and military. The first *strategoi* would be the commanders of the military units stationed in, or which had fallen back into, the territory in question. The old civilian administration did not entirely disappear at first. Indeed some features of it survived vestigially for centuries. But the civilian provincial governor became the subordinate of the *strategos* instead of his equal. These new military districts were called *themes*, a word whose primary connotation is that of a division of troops.

Gradually the practice developed of giving the soldiers in each *theme* inalienable grants of land and freedom from most taxation. In return they had to provide a man, a horse, and arms when called upon. These citizen-soldiers largely replaced the mercenaries of late antiquity, who had become a luxury which the empire could no longer afford. The owner of the lot of land would serve if he was of military age, and if not a son or other relative would serve for him. On his death his eldest son would inherit the land and the obligations which went with it. Any other sons would find holdings in the land which had fallen out of cultivation during the invasions, and thus swell the number of free peasants paying taxes. Enemy prisoners were often settled in such military holdings, which both satisfied their desire for

land and made them the defenders of the empire instead of its enemies. However, it is clear that the system of paying soldiers by granting them land was not universally applied. The *theme* system was not
merely an administrative innovation. It rested upon, and in its turn
fostered, a change in the social structure of the countryside, a change
that had begun before the administrative reforms. Peasant-soldiers
and tax-paying farmers replaced latifundist landlords and serfs, for
many of the great estates were broken up as their owners fled or were
killed during the invasions. In addition to the *theme* armies, composed
largely of peasant-soldiers, a central mobile army, based on Constantinople and composed of fulltime soldiers, remained in being.

The earliest *themes* may have been set up by Heraclius in Syria,
each with its port, its inland city, and its stretch of open frontier. By
the later seventh century the new organization had been extended to
Thrace, and by the end of the century to central Greece. As time went
on most of the empire was organized in *themes*, each furnishing its
own army division, whose commander was in charge of the government of the *theme*.

At the same time the system of taxation instituted by Diocletian
was abandoned. Under this system the unit on which direct taxation
was levied was an area of land and the man who cultivated it. The
value of such a unit was calculated by complex rules. Land which was
uncultivated generally escaped taxation, as did men who were neither
landlords nor tenants, in particular the inhabitants of cities and the
landless rural poor. The new system was based upon separate land
taxes and poll taxes. The land tax was payable even if the land was
left uncultivated, in which event the duty of payment fell upon the
neighbors, who also had the right to take over and cultivate the vacant
land. The complicated Roman law of ownership was replaced by the
simple doctrine that he who paid the land tax was the owner. The
poll tax was payable by all classes of citizens, urban or rural, whatever
might be their relation to the land. By the eighth century it appears
to have been superseded or supplemented by a tax on households, the
kapnikon or hearth tax, which was easier to collect.

The immediate result of these changes was to make early Byzantine society more socially homogeneous and cohesive than that of late antiquity. There were still slaves—largely domestic servants—and there were still very rich men. But the wealth and power of the great landowners had been broken by the years of invasion and devastation. The *coloni*, serfs tied to the great estates in perpetuity, had been largely replaced by peasant-soldiers and free peasants owing allegiance only to the state. A new class of officials in the central government, usually owning estates of moderate size in the neighborhood of the capital, had attained some prominence and exercised its influence through its membership of the Senate. Great regions whose inhabitants largely felt themselves to be divided by language, culture, and religion from the orthodox Greek majority had been severed from the empire. Byzantine society was thus able to present a more unified face to the terrible and long-lasting challenge from the east and the north. But it had its own internal dynamic of development, and during this period a new, power-hungry group began to appear, as the *strategoi* of the *themes* and their senior officials began accumulating landed property in their provinces and turning into a class of feudal magnates in embryo. From the end of the eighth century we begin to find, at first occasionally and then more and more frequently, provincial land-owning families with family names which are passed on from generation to generation, a sign of a developing aristocracy.

When Heraclius died on 11 February 641 he was succeeded by his eldest son, who died within a few months, and then by his grandson, Constans II. At first Constans could only attempt rather unsuccessfully to resist continuing Arab pressure on land and sea. However, strife among the Arab leaders after the assassination of Caliph ʿUmar in Medina in 656 gave the Byzantines breathing space. Expeditions were mounted against the *Sclaviniae*, the areas of Slav settlement in the Balkans which had passed out of Byzantine control. Constans seems to have hoped to mobilize the resources of the Byzantine west to redress the situation in the east. At any rate he removed his court to Italy in 663. But he had no success against the Lombards and had to face a revolt in Africa. In 668 he was murdered in his bath in

Syracuse, and succeeded by his son Constantine IV, who at once returned to Constantinople.

Constantine had to face the full weight of Arab assault, as the caliphate regained the initiative. In 670 the Arabs seized the Cyzicus peninsula in the Sea of Marmara as a base for their attack on Constantinople. In 674 they began a siege of the city by land and sea. At the same time the Avars were making threatening gestures and inciting their Slav subjects to press forward local attacks on Byzantine strongholds. The fall of the city would mean the collapse and disappearance of the empire as a political entity. But the resilience of the new peasant-soldiers and sailors and the technological superiority of Byzantine civilization over that of their adversaries enabled the city to hold out. An architect and mathematician named Kallinikos, himself a refugee from Syria, invented a method of propelling through tubes an inflammable compound which caught fire spontaneously as it touched its target, an enemy ship. This was the famous "Greek fire," the secret weapon of the Byzantines, the nature of which is still a matter of discussion among specialists. In 678 the Arabs raised the siege of Constantinople after suffering crippling losses, and concluded a thirty-year peace with the Byzantines. At once the Avars ceased their attacks and acknowledged a largely theoretical Byzantine sovereignty.

Within a few years, however, new invaders from the steppe zone appeared. The Bulgars had for a long time been moving between the Volga and the plain of Hungary, and had been in contact with the Roman Empire as invaders or mercenaries since the days of Justinian. In 681 a group of Bulgars from north of the Danube delta crossed over to the Roman side and subjected some of the Slav tribes settled there. Perhaps they were originally invited by the Byzantines. Constantine IV tried to expel them, but his campaign ended in failure. He had to sign a formal treaty with the Bulgar leader Asparuch recognizing the existence of the Bulgar Kingdom. In itself the matter was of little importance. The region had long been outside effective Byzantine control in any case. But it was the first time since the Arab conquests that the Byzantine government had formally ceded the territory of the empire to a foreign power. And it was a development which augured badly, as the Bulgar Kingdom improved its position and extended its territory. Constantine IV did not live to face these problems—in 685 he died and was succeeded by his son, Justinian II.

Justinian was able to profit by the deep divisions within the Moslem community to impose a new peace treaty on the Arabs which aimed at setting up a belt of demilitarized territory between the two powers, extending from the Caucasus to Cyprus. On the mainland the project soon fell through, as both sides sought advantages for themselves. In Cyprus, however, a curious condominium was established which lasted, in spite of interruptions and frontier incidents, for nearly three centuries. Taxes from Cyprus were divided between the two powers, neither of which maintained forces on the island, and the inhabitants were left to run their own internal affairs. Justinian also made a show of force against the Slavs in the Balkans, many of whom he transferred to Asia Minor, where he settled them on abandoned land as peasant-soldiers. By this and other population transfers he tried to build up the empire's power of resistance. A disastrous defeat in 691, however, led to the whole of Armenia falling to the Arabs. As a result of this defeat, and of the unpopularity aroused by his forced transfers of population, Justinian was overthrown in 695 by a revolt in Constantinople, was mutilated—his nose was cut off—and banished to a remote fortress in the Crimea. For a few years coup and counter-coup succeeded one another, as powerless and undistinguished emperors rose and fell. Externally things went from bad to worse. In 697 the Arabs captured Carthage, and the empire had to abandon the whole of Roman Africa except the distant outpost of Septem (Ceuta), which held out till 711. Meanwhile Justinian escaped from prison and fled first to the Khazars, north of the Caucasus, and later to the Bulgars. It was with the support of a Bulgar army that he reentered Constantinople in 705, and in return he agreed to pay tribute to the Bulgars and conferred high dignities upon their ruler, Tervel. Most of his energies were now devoted to a reign of terror against those who had earlier deposed and mutilated him, and little care was given to external danger. In 709 the Arabs captured Tyana, and pursued their devastating raids in Asia Minor. In 711 a revolt in the Crimea supported by the Khazars proclaimed a rival emperor, Philippicus, who at once sailed to Constantinople. Justinian had lost all support in the capital, and was deposed and killed.

Philippicus did not long outlast him. Arab attacks continued, and Tervel once more brought his Bulgar army to the walls of Constantinople. Civil war broke out between units of the army supporting different candidates, a war which was ended when Leo, the *strategos* of Anatolikon, defeated his rival in March 717 and ended twenty years of more and more violent changes of rulers. Meanwhile the Moslem caliphate had prepared another all-out attack on Constantinople. In August 717 an Arab army appeared on the Asiatic coast of the Bosphorus, and an Arab fleet sailed up the Sea of Marmara. But once again Greek fire and the walls of Constantinople—as well as an unusually severe winter—frustrated Moslem designs. After a year the siege was lifted and the enemy withdrew. This success strengthened the position of the new emperor, who turned out to be one of the most energetic and far-seeing men ever to exercise the imperial office.

The first need of the empire was to keep the Arabs and Bulgars at a distance. As early as 726 the Arabs recommenced their annual invasions of Asia Minor, and the Bulgars were constantly seeking opportunities to extend their territory. Leo led a long series of campaigns against both enemies, culminating in his decisive victory over the Arabs at Akroinion, near Amorium.

Military strength was not, however, in itself enough to guarantee security. The empire needed a powerful ally, and found one in the Khazars, a Turkic people who had established a potent state north of the Caucasus and the Caspian Sea and who had for a time given shelter to the fugitive Justinian II. They were able to threaten both Bulgars and Arabs. In 733 the alliance was cemented by the marriage of Leo's son and co-emperor to the daughter of the khan of the Khazars. The Khazar alliance stood Byzantium in good stead till the end of the century.

In 726 Leo promulgated a new code of law, the *Ecloga* or Selection. This brief and simple code did not replace the legislation of Justinian, which was still studied, in Greek translation, by students of law in the capital. What it did was to provide subordinate judges in the provinces with a handbook covering the cases they would most frequently encounter; it embodied the modifications of Justinian's law resulting from subsequent legislation, from ecclesiastical influence, and from the traditional customary law of the Asiatic provinces. In this way Leo strengthened the effectiveness of central control throughout the empire, for it must not be forgotten that the introduction of the *theme* system did not lead to the militarization of Byzantine society. Government was firmly retained in the hands of the emperor and his hierarchy of civilian officials in the capital. There was no question of military dictatorship or martial law.

It was clear to Leo, as to all his subjects, that things had not gone well for the empire. Twice within a generation it had been brought to the brink of destruction. It was still forced to adopt a defensive strategy. The quality of life had diminished. Ancient cities were now heaps of ruins in which miserable squatters eked out a squalid existence. None could fail to note with pain and anxiety what a change had taken place since the great days of Justinian, or even of Heraclius. If the Byzantines were the chosen people, destined in the fullness of time to lead the rest of the world to salvation, their present sorry state must be the result, if not of positive sin, at least of backsliding. The community as a whole must be doing something displeasing to God. It was the duty of a monarch consecrated by God to put an end to error and to lead his subjects back to the course which was their destiny. Leo and his advisers must have pondered such questions greatly. It could scarcely be argued that such moral deviations as perjury, fornication, and adultery were any more widespread than in previous ages. The trouble must therefore lie in theological error, so Leo increased the pressure for religious conformity. Jews found themselves threatened with forced baptism, although their religion had always been regarded as legitimate by Roman civil law. But what if there was something wrong with the very orthodoxy to which the heterodox were being forced to conform? One feature of the religious practice of Leo's own day which was something of an innovation was the reverence paid to holy images both in liturgical worship and in private devotion. Beginning perhaps in the sixth century, the cult of icons had now permeated the religious life of the Byzantines. But was it not a kind of idolatry, a foolish attempt to circumscribe the uncircumscribable, to represent with wood and paint that which had no form or color and could be apprehended only by intellect and faith? Leo and his counsellors came to feel with ever-growing certainty that this was the error for which God was turning his face from them. It was Leo's duty to combat such deviation from true doctrine. Thus began the great movement of Iconoclasm, which was to dominate Byzantine history for the next century. Scholars have long discussed its nature. Was it a movement of social and economic protest or one of popular piety? Was it a protest by the peasant-soldiers of the provinces against the bureaucrats of the capital? Had it any links with Islam, which also forbade the representation of the human figure? No movement which carries so many people with it for so long is plausibly explained by a single cause. Men supported Iconoclasm for different reasons. Some of the more important considerations will be discussed in the following chapter, but in the meantime we shall continue with an outline of the main events.

In 726 the emperor gave clear official support to the Iconoclast theology of many bishops from Asia Minor by himself preaching a series of sermons in the Hagia Sophia denouncing the worship of icons as idolatry. Shortly afterwards a detachment of palace guards removed the huge picture of Christ which stood above the bronze gate of the Great Palace in the Augusteion Square, facing the Hagia Sophia. This act was greeted with demonstrations of opposition, and the officer commanding the guards' detachment was lynched by a hostile crowd. When the news reached such regions of Greece as were under effective Byzantine control a revolt broke out which had to be suppressed by the army. Shocked by these developments—or believing them to be only what was to be expected from a people led astray by false doctrine—Leo held back for a time. In 730, however, he convened a formal meeting of high officers of state and clergy and issued an edict ordering the immediate destruction of all holy images. This order was not universally obeyed. Laymen who continued to venerate icons might find their prospects of an official career diminished, but were in general not actively persecuted. Clergy who persisted in venerating icons risked dismissal, imprisonment, public humiliation, and even mutilation. Many began to flee to regions where they would be safe from the long arm of emperor and patriarch—regions such as Cherson in the Crimea, neutral Cyprus, the Dalmatian cities or the Byzantine provinces of south Italy, where many of the cities enjoyed effective independence. A breach ensued with the pope, who was wary of imperial intervention in matters of doctrine. The papacy looked more and more to the Lombards as a military counterweight to the emperor in Constantinople.

In 741 Leo III died, and was succeeded by his eldest son and co-emperor Constantine V, an even more radical Iconoclast than his father. The succession was not unchallenged. A *theme* governor, Artavasdes, rose in revolt and succeeded in gaining possession of Constantinople. Confused fighting broke out between the various *theme* armies. In 743 Constantine defeated the usurper and returned in triumph to the capital. The war had not been fought solely on the issue of image worship—it was in part a traditional attempt by an army commander to seize power at the center. But the conflicting armies tended to take up firm positions for or against Iconoclasm, the issue which most divided the people.

Constantine knew that only victory against the common enemy could unite his divided army. After long and careful preparation he took the offensive in 746, invading Syria and recapturing Germaniceia (Marash). It was the first time for a century that the Byzantines had operated successfully in Moslem territory, and the impact of the victory was immense. To the doubters it was evidence that the young emperor's theology was acceptable to God. To the soldiers it was a signal that at last they had a brilliant and imaginative commander. In the next year the Byzantine fleet defeated the Arab fleet off Asia Minor and ensured that, for a time at least, the Aegean would remain under Byzantine control.

These successes convinced Constantine and his advisers, if they needed any convincing, that their theological views were correct and that the Byzantine Empire once again enjoyed that divine favor which was its right. The time had come to put an end once and for all to the veneration of images and to remove from positions of authority in the Church those who practiced such idolatry. The emperor summoned a Church council which met in 754 and declared the veneration of images to be contrary to the doctrines of the Church, and those who persisted in it to be subject to anathema. Though Constantine and his supporters deemed it to be an ecumenical council, it was not recognized by the pope nor by the Orthodox church after the rejection of Iconoclasm. The council gave rise to a period of conflict, in which not only clergymen but also laymen were persecuted for the mere possession of holy images. But the cult of icons was not eradicated. On the contrary, a dangerous split was created in Byzantine society, which did not always follow geographical, ethnic, or class lines.

Constantine's military efforts thus far had been mainly directed against the Moslems. Now he turned to the empire's other enemy, the Bulgars, and began building extensive fortifications along the frontier in the Balkans. The Bulgars at once reacted by invading Byzantine territory, and a long period of hostilities began. At first Constantine counterattacked and fought a series of campaigns on Bulgar soil. But by 762 a new Bulgar ruler, Teletz, was able to return to the offensive. Constantine responded with an attack in force, and in 763 inflicted a crushing defeat on the main Bulgar army at Anchialos, near the modern town of Burgas. So decisive did he feel this victory to be that he celebrated it by returning to Constantinople in ceremonial procession, the equivalent of the ancient Roman triumph. But Bulgar society had great human resources and notable powers of recovery. In 770 they regained the initiative under another new ruler, Telerig, and began once again to make devastating raids into Byzantine territory. Once again, in 773, Constantine was able to defeat them decisively.

During the long reign of Constantine V the military effort of the empire was concentrated on the Moslem and Bulgar frontiers, and no resources could be spared for Italy. In 751 Ravenna fell to the Lombards, and with it the extensive Byzantine possessions in northern

Italy. This was the end of the exarchate of Italy. The popes now felt that they could not count on Byzantine support, and they turned increasingly to the major Christian power in the west, the Frankish kingdom. In 754 Pope Stephen II met the Frankish King Pippin at Ponthiou, and an understanding was reached that the Franks would protect Rome and the papal territories against Lombard attack. Meanwhile the cities of south Italy that were theoretically under Byzantine suzerainty, such as Naples, Gaeta, and Amalfi, looked more and more to their own resources for defense, set up their own militia, and enjoyed virtual autonomy. So too in the north, where the communities on the islands of the Venetian lagoons, no longer protected by the exarchate, began their long, slow development into the Serenissima Repubblica. The break between Byzantium and the popes soon led to the removal of Sicily, southern Italy, and the western and central Balkans from the religious jurisdiction of the pope to that of the Patriarch of Constantinople. Byzantine sovereignty over Sardinia and the Balearic Islands could no longer be exercised. These islands had to make their own arrangements for defense against the Arabs, and thus became effectively independent. The division between the western and eastern Mediterranean worlds was now clear, and Byzantine interest was henceforth confined to the latter.

In 775 Constantine V died while on a campaign in Bulgaria and was succeeded by his son and long-time co-emperor, Leo IV. Leo, who did not have his father's decisive character, and who was perhaps more aware than his father of the danger of division in Byzantine society, eased the pressure on image worshippers without of course challenging the decisions of the Church council of 754. He did not live long enough to develop an independent policy of his own. In 780 he died, leaving a ten-year-old son and successor, Constantine VI. In the meantime the regency was held by Leo's widow, Irene, the daughter of a rich Athenian family. The position of a woman in a man's world is often a difficult one, and nowhere was it more difficult than in the Byzantine Empire. No sooner had Irene taken up the reins of power than she was faced by a rebellion led by her late husband's brother Nicephorus, supported by many units of the army. Knowing that if she hesitated she and her son were doomed, Irene ruthlessly suppressed the rebellion, the leaders of which she had put to death or blinded.

The Arabs, ever on the alert for signs of Byzantine weakness, renewed their attacks, and in 781 penetrated deep into Asia Minor. Byzantine countermeasures soon restored the situation. But Irene was conscious of the danger of internal feuding, and she herself came from a region of the empire in which support for the cult of icons seems to have been strong. Probably her own religious convictions favored icons. At any rate she decided to try to defuse the situation by removing the ban on the veneration of icons. This could be done only by an ecumenical council of the Church. In the meantime, when a vacancy occurred in the patriarchate in 784, she appointed a high officer in the civil service, Tarasios, whom she knew to be opposed to the Iconoclasts. Tarasios carried on preparations for a council, which had probably been begun by his predecessor Paul, a Cypriot by origin. In 787 the council met in Nicaea and restored the cult of icons.

As often occurs in such situations, there was a cleavage among the victors. One faction, whose strength lay particularly in the monasteries, was anxious to exact vengeance for persecution of its members, and to oust all supporters of Iconoclasm from positions in ecclesiastical and public life. The other, headed by Patriarch Tarasios and supported by Irene, wanted to heal the breach and to reunite Byzantine society. The division gave the Iconoclasts their chance. By 790 the young Emperor Constantine VI was already of age, but his mother still showed no sign of handing over power. Chafing at his subordinate position, the young emperor made overtures to leading Iconoclasts in the high command of the army. Faced with conspiracy and imminent rebellion, Irene proclaimed herself no longer regent for her son, but his senior co-ruler. This action triggered the rebellion which she feared, and a military revolt forced her to withdraw to a convent and to yield power to her son. But the wiser heads among the civilian and army leaders realized that nothing would be achieved by one section of Byzantine society subduing another. Already the Bulgars had resumed the offensive and had to be bought off by the payment of tribute. Negotiations were begun between the parties. In 792 Irene was reconciled with her son and once again became co-emperor with him and effective ruler of the empire. A year later a further military revolt, this time in support of Nicephorus, was put down decisively and with great cruelty.

The young Constantine VI turned out weak and irresponsible—perhaps he was never given a chance to be anything else. In 793 he divorced his wife and, with the grudging approval of the ecclesiastical authorities, married his mistress. This rash move lost him most of what popular support he still enjoyed, and sharpened the conflict between the moderate and radical wings of the Church. By 797 Constantine had become an embarrassment to his mother's government. Irene, after we know not what hesitation, had her son arrested, deposed, and blinded. Henceforth she governed the empire as sole ruler. On her coins she called herself *basileus* (emperor) and never *basilissa* (empress as wife of an emperor). Her conduct towards her son and the military inactivity of her reign provided grounds for attack by the Iconoclast opposition, which was still influential. To counter this Irene took the populist course of reducing taxes. It was not long before the bullion reserves of the government—in the absence of a credit system, its only means of meeting necessary expenditure—were reduced to a dangerously low level.

In the meantime events were moving fast in the west. Charlemagne had reorganized, revitalized, and extended the Frankish kingdom, which was no longer the ramshackle dominion of his Merovingian predecessors but a powerful centralized state, whose court saw itself as a reincarnation of that of Augustus. The popes looked more than ever to the Franks for protection and support. Since the deposition of Constantine VI they regarded the throne of Constantinople as vacant, refusing to recognize the abomination of a woman emperor. When Charlemagne visited Rome at the end of 800 he was treated by Pope Hadrian I not as one territorial ruler among others, but as the only wholly legitimate monarch in Europe. On Christmas Day, when Charlemagne attended mass in St. Peter's basilica, the pope crowned him and consecrated him as emperor. Though Charlemagne did not instigate this move, it was not unwelcome to him. In the eyes of his subjects and of the western Church he was set by God above all other rulers, including the pseudo-emperor Irene. For Irene it was a new threat. Obscure negotiations took place between the two rulers, delayed by the painful slowness of communications. It is probable that in 802 Charlemagne actually proposed marriage to Irene as a solution to the problem of two emperors. What Irene's reply would have been we cannot know, for when the message arrived she had been overthrown by a palace revolution and exiled to an island. She had held power for twenty-two years in the face of immeasurable difficulties.

The successor chosen by the conspirators was one Nicephorus, the chief finance officer of the empire and, like Irene, an icon worshipper. He set to work to undo the damage caused by Irene's financial policy, cancelling her tax remissions and reorganizing the whole structure of taxation. He also strengthened the armed forces, which Irene had neglected, and began to reestablish effective Byzantine power in continental Greece.

Careful husbandry and good internal security measures were not, however, enough to deter the empire's external enemies, who had recovered from the blows inflicted on them by Constantine V. In the east the caliphate was once again united and strong. In 806 Hārūn al-Rashīd seized the key fortress of Tyana and pressed on deep into Asia Minor. Nicephorus was obliged to sign a humiliating peace treaty and to pay tribute to the Moslems. In the north, now that Charlemagne had destroyed the Avar Kingdom, the Bulgars were free to concentrate their forces against Byzantium. In 809 they took Sardica, which for nearly two centuries had been a Byzantine strong point in Slav territory. Nicephorus made a counterattack in force two years later, intending to teach the Bulgars a lesson. He captured and destroyed their capital, Pliska, in northeastern Bulgaria, but during the return march his army, laden with booty, was ambushed in a defile in the Balkan range. In the ensuing battle the Byzantines suffered a devastating defeat; Nicephorus himself was killed and his son Staurakios seriously wounded. The Bulgar ruler Krum, following an ancient custom of his people, had a drinking cup made from the skull of the Byzantine emperor.

After a brief reign by Staurakios, whose wounds proved mortal, army and senate proclaimed a high civilian official, Michael Rhangabes, emperor in October 811. Desperately eager to gain allies against the Bulgars, Michael sent envoys to Aachen to announce his recognition of Charlemagne as his co-emperor. But the Franks could not be persuaded to open hostilities against the Bulgars. Krum began mopping up one by one the Byzantine cities on the west coast of the Black Sea, which earlier Bulgarian rulers had left untouched. When Michael led out his army against them, it was crushingly defeated. Michael no longer retained any credibility as emperor, and was deposed by the senate, who nominated as his successor a man of military experience, Leo, commander of one of the Asia Minor *themes*.

The task before Leo was formidable. As he assumed office, the Bulgarian army and its terrible commander, Krum, were encamped before the walls of Constantinople. They withdrew in autumn 813, but returned again the following spring. There was nothing the demoralized Byzantines could do to stop them. An attempted meeting between Leo and Krum went wrong when a Byzantine officer, either on his own initiative or acting on secret orders, attempted to assassinate the Bulgarian ruler. The capital faced a long siege by a resolute enemy, well served by Byzantine engineers and technicians—either prisoners or deserters. It was a moment of crisis no less grave than those of 674–78 or 717–18. Suddenly, on 13 April 814, King Krum died. Leaderless and demoralized, the Bulgars withdrew to their own territory. Constantinople, and with it the empire, were safe again. The new Bulgar ruler, Omurtag, was not interested in costly and dangerous attacks on Constantinople. He concentrated on internal consolidation of his rule and on the extension of Bulgar power to the northwest, into the vacuum created by the destruction of the Avar Kingdom. He was therefore ready to sign a thirty years' peace with the Byzantines.

Leo V was a man of Iconoclast sympathies. He depended on the

King Krum feasting after his victory over the Byzantines; on the right, his cupbearer brings in a goblet carved out of the skull of the Emperor Nicephorus. Illustration from a fourteenth-century manuscript of the Slavonic version of the Chronicle of Manasses. *Courtesy of Biblioteca Apostolica Vaticana. MS. Vat. Slav. 2, fol. 145ᵛ.*

support of the largely Iconoclast soldiers of Asia Minor, and he may well have seen in the unexpected deliverance of Constantinople a token of divine approval. In 815 he called a synod of the Church, which once again came out against the veneration of images. The new Iconoclasm, however, was a pale shadow of that of the previous century. The uncompromising theology of the council of 754 was watered down. And though there was persecution, it lacked the ferocity and extent of that of Constantine V's time.

In 820 Leo was murdered in Hagia Sophia by a passionate partisan of icons. His successor, Michael II the Amorian, though personally an Iconoclast, adopted a reserved position, not wishing to alienate either party. He had good reason to seek all the support he could find. A high military officer, apparently a hellenized Slav of humble origin, Thomas the Slav, was heading an armed revolt in Asia Minor; the rebellion not only enjoyed strong support among the peasantry but was also encouraged by the Moslem caliphate. This movement appears to have had some kind of rudimentary program of social change, and was distinct in nature and extent from earlier revolts in which a division of the army tried to place its commander on the throne. It was a measure of the distress of the common people, faced by repeated invasion and devastation, and of the lack of sympathy between provinces and capital which often manifested itself in the course of Byzantine history.

By the end of 821 Thomas's forces, which had been joined by many elements of the *theme* armies, were encamped before the walls of Constantinople. So long as the fleet kept the sea routes open, and so long as there was no treachery, the capital was safe. But Michael II could not himself muster a good enough army to defeat Thomas, and the siege dragged on. Meanwhile Michael was in negotiation with the Bulgars. The details of the agreement between them are not known, but in 823 a Bulgarian army attacked Thomas's forces from the rear and dispersed them. Thomas himself was captured and put to death, as were many of his subordinates. Most of his followers returned disillusioned to their provincial homes, and it was some years before the Byzantine army became once again an effective fighting force.

During these years Moslem pressure was kept up, but from a new quarter. About 827 a Moslem group which had come from Spain via Egypt landed in Crete and soon gained control of the whole island. Another Moslem force from North Africa established itself in Sicily and began to attack and capture the cities one by one. In 831 Palermo fell. After that the Moslem impetus slowed down for a time. But Sicily enjoyed peace no more, and within a century it was entirely under Moslem rule.

Before Palermo fell, Michael II had died, in 829, and been succeeded by his son Theophilus. The new ruler profited by the accumulation of money in the hands of the state since the reforms of Nicephorus. Extensive building was carried out in the capital and elsewhere, sometimes modeled on the Moslem architecture of Baghdad. The walls of Constantinople were repaired and strengthened; Theophilus's inscriptions can still be read on many of the towers along the seawalls. Theophilus had not only money but also an army which had recovered from the havoc caused by Thomas the Slav. He pressed forward in a series of local advances on the eastern frontier. The Byzantine Black Sea possessions were reorganized and strengthened. There was a feeling abroad that things were changing, and that the empire was no longer always on the defensive. Yet there were shocks. In 838 an Arab raid in force occupied Ancyra and captured Amorium, the city from which the imperial family originated. The tables were not yet turned.

Theophilus was formally an Iconoclast, but in practice cared little for the quarrels of theologians, and the confrontation between Iconoclasts and icon-worshippers, from being one which divided the whole of Byzantine society, was now rapidly becoming a matter of concern for theologians alone. In 837 John the Grammarian was appointed patriarch. What we know of him we owe to his enemies, and he remains an enigmatic character. Enlightened and interested in the intellectual tradition of the past, he was also a passionate Iconoclast. The persecution of icon worshippers, which had been virtually abandoned, was taken up again, though this time its victims were almost exclusively clergymen. In 842 Theophilus died, and was succeeded by his infant son Michael III, under the regency of his mother, the Empress Theodora. Theodora was not another Irene. She always depended on the guidance and support of kinsmen or high officers of state, but she was a sincere believer in the veneration of icons. Supported by a council of state including her brothers Bardas and Petronas, and Theoktistos, a senior minister, Theodora had John the Grammarian deposed and exiled, and in 843 she summoned a synod which proclaimed the restoration of the veneration of icons. This marked the end of Iconoclasm as a social force, though doubts about the validity of holy images continued to be felt by many theologians. It did not end the ill feeling between the moderates and the zealots among the victorious icon worshippers. Though the Church had not become a mere department of state, it never gained the kind of autonomy which the zealots aspired to. Their resentment continued to smoulder and from time to time broke out into open hostility to the moderate leadership of the Church.

Careful financial policy and imaginative strategy enabled the Byzantines to resume the offensive against the caliphate. A Byzantine fleet captured and burned Damietta in Egypt. Crete was briefly recaptured. But there were also some chastening defeats. The balance of military power did not lie wholly in favor of the Byzantines. This was partly the result of the unexpectedly tough resistance put up by some Slav communities in Greece, but mostly the result of the campaign of suppression against the Paulicians. This dualist, quasi-Manichaean sect, which believed that the world had been created not by God but by the Devil, enjoyed considerable support in the eastern provinces. It had been favored by the Iconoclast emperors of the eighth century, and so had grown in numbers and confidence. Unlike many heretical groups, the Paulicians did not lie low and adopt the protective camouflage of orthodoxy. They stood up and fought with arms in their hands. The hostile attitude of the Byzantine government towards them since the death of Nicephorus I had driven many of them to make common cause with the Arabs. Many Paulicians actually migrated to Arab territory, especially near Melitene (Malatya), and fought with the Moslems against the Byzantines. Thus a theological difference became first a problem of internal security, then one of foreign policy and strategy. Theodora's government proceeded against the Paulicians with remarkable ferocity and cruelty.

In 856 the young Emperor Michael III, resentful of his mother's tutelage and of the concentration of power in the hands of Theoktistos, conspired with other members of his family. In a palace coup Theoktistos was murdered and Theodora shut up in a convent. Michael was a weak and indecisive man, though not the monster of iniquity that his enemies claimed. The real power during his reign was his uncle, Bardas, a far-seeing and resolute man with a deep understanding of the complex classical and Christian heritage of Byzantium. The war against the Arabs was carried on with many local successes but little change in the strategic situation until 863, when the Byzantines won an overwhelming victory in northern Asia Minor and destroyed a major Arab army. If there is one event which marked the decisive shift in the balance of power between Byzantines and Arabs, this was it.

The logistic problems of fighting the Arabs in Sicily were immense, and there the Byzantines continually fell back, till at the end of Michael III's reign they held only a few towns in the east of the island. A new enemy appeared in the shape of the Rhos, eastern Slavs led by slavized Scandinavians, the eastern equivalent of the Vikings of the west. In 860 they made their first terrifying attack on Constantinople, sweeping down the Bosphorus from the Black Sea in their long ships. Unable to storm the walls of the city, the marauders pillaged and burned the surrounding countryside before returning to their homeland on the middle Dnieper. Their raid alerted the Byzantine government to a new danger from the north. It was this which made it vital for the Bulgar Kingdom to be won as an ally for Byzantium. The Bulgar King Boris was at this time in negotiation with the western Emperor Louis and the pope, and was involved in war on his western frontier. In 864 Michael marched into Bulgaria at the head of his army, fresh from its victory over the Arabs. The Bulgar ruler had no

A symbolic portrayal of the conversion of Bulgaria to Christianity in 865, from the
Chronicle of Manasses. On the left, the Emperor Michael III and the Empress hold
out their arms to receive their godson, Boris, who is being baptized by the Patriarch.
Courtesy of Biblioteca Apostolica Vaticana. MS. Vat. Slav. 2, fol. 263ʳ.

choice. He accepted Michael's terms, which included the baptism of
himself and his subjects and their ecclesiastical subordination to the
patriarch of Constantinople. Without a blow being struck, a powerful
potential enemy had been turned into an ally and Bulgaria brought
once and for all within the Byzantine sphere of influence. Or so it
appeared at the time.

   This brilliant stroke of policy owed much to Patriarch Photios,
whose appointment in 858 was a victory for the moderate party in the
Church. The discomfited zealots, as was their custom, appealed for
support to the pope, who declared Photios's appointment invalid,
since his predecessor Ignatios had been uncanonically deposed. So
began a schism between the eastern and western Churches, which

was patched up from time to time but never healed. This is why it was important, if Bulgaria was to be a reliable ally for the Byzantines, that its conversion should be organized and sponsored from Constantinople rather than from Rome.

Photios and Bardas took the lead in providing institutional forms for a new cultural upsurge in the middle of the ninth century, which embraced the study of ancient literature and science, a classicizing movement in the visual arts, and much besides. It was as if Byzantine intellectual life had reawakened after a sleep of three centuries. Bardas founded a center of higher education in which all branches of secular learning then known were cultivated, and he summoned the most learned men of the age to teach in it. All these events led to great tension in Byzantine society, and made many enemies for Michael III. The end came, however, not from a discontented faction among his subjects, but from a sordid palace coup. Basil the Macedonian, a peasant's son, who began his career as a groom at court, made himself serviceable to Michael, and the irresolute emperor came to depend on his tough-minded and ambitious favorite. Basil aimed high, had striking tenacity of purpose and no scruples. First he removed the emperor's uncle Bardas in 865. Then in 867 he had Michael murdered in the palace as he slept off a drunken debauch. On the next day he was installed in power as Basil I, the founder of the Macedonian dynasty, which ruled the empire for nearly two centuries, during which Byzantium reached the zenith of its power.

THE NEW ORDER

After the great Arab conquests of the mid-seventh century, the Byzantine Empire was not merely reduced in size—it was poorer, its very existence was threatened, and its structure was radically changed. As society adapted itself, willingly or unwillingly, to the changed world in which it lived, many of the ideals and values of the age of Justinian or even that of Heraclius had to be abandoned and replaced by others more in accord with the needs of the age. But as always in a society with a long and tenacious tradition, the changes were neither sudden nor complete. Often old features survived long after they had ceased to perform any function. Sometimes they were adapted to fulfil a function quite different from that which they had originally served. Old and new coexisted, interpenetrated, and influenced one another, contributing to that appearance of immutability which often strikes those looking at the Byzantine world for the first time.

The territories that had been lost—Syria, Mesopotamia, Palestine, Egypt, and soon all of North Africa—had been the most populous and economically developed of the late Roman Empire. The loss of the tax revenue alone left the state impoverished and forced it to follow a policy of financial retrenchment. The loss of the agricultural surplus produced by the toiling farmers of Egypt meant, among other things, the end of free distribution of basic foodstuffs to the population of Constantinople. It also no doubt brought about a series of changes in agricultural and land prices throughout the empire, which must have caused formerly marginal land to be brought into use. This is one—but only one—of the factors underlying the wholesale transfer of population undertaken towards the end of the seventh century, in particular by Justinian II. New land was opened up for cultivation. But to bring land into agricultural use, not only manpower, but also a large investment of capital, is needed, even under the relatively simple agricultural regimes of the Middle Ages. And capital was always in short supply. Thus there arose a constant conflict between needs and possibilities of development, which was further complicated by the frequent military operations in Asia Minor and the Balkans, and the overriding requirements of defense.

One ultimate result of these changing pressures was that Byzantine society could support fewer nonproductive members. In practice this meant a fall in the proportion of the urban population. Not that all city dwellers were unproductive parasites. Many were artisans, shopkeepers, and the like providing essential services for the agricultural population. But side by side with these was a vast superstructure of landowners and those who served them—lawyers, doctors, teachers of rhetoric, purveyors of luxuries, hangers-on, domestic servants. Economic necessity trimmed this class down to a shadow of its former proportions.

Many landowners lost their estates in the original Arab conquest. Others saw theirs absorbed or made unviable in the course of the long struggles against Slav, Avar, and Bulgar invaders in Europe, or the continuing Arab invasions of Asia Minor, culminating in the two great sieges of Constantinople of 674–78 and 717–18. Cities, large and small, were invested again and again by hostile armies and not infrequently captured and sacked. Some vanished altogether, abandoned by their inhabitants. Others gradually lost the complex division of labor and the structures of self-government which were the mark of a city, and became merely large agricultural villages. Some became military fortresses, under the command of an army officer. Others abandoned their vulnerable situation in a fertile plain or by a main road, and were rebuilt on a nearby hilltop or some other defensible position, usually with a much smaller area included within their walls. Such migrations are more likely to have been undertaken at the behest of the military authorities than by a spontaneous decision of the dwindling citizen body.

For some thirty years there has been controversy among historians on the fate of Byzantine cities during the seventh and eighth centuries. Some argue that city life on the ancient pattern vanished altogether, and that virtually all cities were destroyed and abandoned, or were converted into military strong points, or reverted to village status, and that therefore the cities which make their appearance in the Byzantine world in the later Middle Ages are new creations and have no direct continuity with the cities of late antiquity, even when they occupy the same area and grow up within the ancient walls. Other historians maintain that while in some regions of the empire cities did disappear, in others a genuine urban life, with some kind of self-government and with highly developed division of labor between specialist craftsmen and merchants, was maintained throughout the so-called Dark Ages. The question is a difficult one. If a definitive answer is possible, it is likely to be provided by the archeologist rather than by the student of narrative histories, bishops' lists or the decisions of church councils, valuable though the evidence of these is. But the archeologists will have to be able and willing to excavate whole settlements systematically, and not to concentrate, as many have done in the past, on churches and fortifications.

It appears likely, on the evidence at present available, that the collapse of city life was widespread but far from total. In many places cities appear to have survived and even thrived by providing services to regions, most of whose inhabitants practiced subsistence agriculture. And the superimposition of a military garrison does not necessarily mark the end of those features which distinguish a small city from a large village. It may even be the cause of the city's further development.

Nevertheless it is clear that cutting down the nonproductive element in Byzantine society did lead to a drastic reduction in the number and size of cities, and in the quality of life of their citizens. A striking example is that of baths. In late antiquity every city, however small and unimportant, had its public baths, the maintenance of which was often one of the main duties of the city council. The baths were often lavish in scale and luxurious in their appointments, and provided a center for the social life of the community comparable to that offered by the theater. The baths seem to have gradually gone out of use in the seventh or eighth century in those cities which survived in their original location, and those which were rebuilt or moved to a new location usually had none at all. Where baths survived they were small and inconvenient and no longer performed their old social function. However there is archeological evidence for the construction of a new public bath in Sparta in the late tenth century. Michael Choniates, metropolitan of Athens in the late twelfth century, describes with disgust the poky and uncomfortable bath house of the city. Monastic rules often speak of washing twice a month, or even three times a year, as normal practice. The unwashed world of the Middle Ages had begun.

In one city, however, the baths remained open—Constantinople. More and more the capital, from being the principal city of the empire, became its only true city. The gulf that separated Constantinople from the provincial cities of the empire after the Arab conquests was qualitatively different from that between Constantinople and such great cities as Antioch and Alexandria in the earlier period. There was now only one center of political power, of culture, of art, and of theology. Gradually local artistic traditions gave way before metropolitan uniformity, without ever disappearing completely. Where they survived they became socially degraded, often to the status of "peasant" or "folk" art. The oriental patriarchates of Alexandria, Antioch, and Jerusalem were now in Moslem territory, and in any case the majority of the Christians in the regions which they ruled were Monophysites, no longer in communion with the Orthodox Church. So their voice in matters of theology counted for little. From the old pentarchy of five independent patriarchates there survived in effect only two, Constantinople and Rome.

The second city of the empire was now Thessalonica, which had a long and brilliant future before it. In the seventh and eighth centuries, however, it was often a beleaguered fortress, under regular attack by Slavs and Avars. The territory of Macedonia and Thrace, which separated Thessalonica from the capital, was for much of the period lost to Byzantine control. Justinian II's march from Constantinople to Thessalonica was a hard-fought military operation. Thessalonica as yet counted for little as a center of political power or of culture. The new, trimmed-down Byzantine Empire of the early Middle Ages was monocentric, while that of late antiquity had been polycentric.

Economic factors were not the only ones which made the Byzantine Empire of the later seventh and eighth centuries oriented more towards the countryside and less towards the cities than had been the empire of late antiquity. The pressing needs of defense also had to be met. The empire could no longer afford to pay mercenary soldiers from the barbarian world. City dwellers were on the whole useless to the army, so it was on the peasants of the countryside that the unrelenting burden of defense fell. Although the institution of peasant-soldiers, whose maintenance was guaranteed by the grant of a farm free of most taxes, and the new administrative organization of the empire in military districts may well have had different origins, they fitted together admirably in an effective system of defense, providing every province with a reserve of trained and equipped men who could be mobilized at very short notice against an Arab—or later, in Europe, a Slav or Bulgar—invasion. The same provincial army could, if the fortunes of war changed, form part of a counterattacking force engaged in reprisals against the enemy. In such a case the provincial, or *theme*, army would usually be supplemented by units of the central army, a fulltime professional force normally stationed in camps near the capital, and commanded by a general—the Domestic of the Schools—whose duty had in origin been to command the palace guard. This central army drew its volunteer recruits from the same source as the *theme* armies, the peasantry. Many a younger son, who could not count on inheriting his father's farm or military holding, would sign on as a soldier in one of the *tagmata*, the divisions of the central army.

The Balkan provinces of the empire were by the mid-seventh century largely submerged beneath a wave of Slavonic invaders. Not that the Greek population was extirpated entirely, as some early nineteenth-century historians believed; harassed and reduced in numbers, it survived in many regions, often enough living in close contact with the new settlers. But the machinery of government and control had broken down, and the inhabitants of the Balkan provinces, whether Greek or Slav, were not available for recruitment. Those of the remoter west, in Byzantine Italy and Sicily, were barely able to provide for their own local defense. And even if they had been available, the logistic problems of using them on the eastern front would have been insurmountable for the impoverished Byzantine state. It was upon the peasants of Asia Minor that the survival of the empire depended. They and they alone provided the manpower which defeated two long sieges of the capital, fought the Arabs in the highlands of Armenia, the arid plateau of Cappadocia, and the gorges of the Taurus Mountains, as well as the Avars and Bulgars in the passes of the Balkan range and the plains of Thrace.

If once their will to fight wavered, all would be lost. The alienated detachment of the people of Syria and Egypt in the face of Moslem expansion provided an ever-present lesson to the minds of Byzantine rulers in the centuries immediately following. So the views and interests of the peasantry had to be considered, and a new, national solidarity had to be created. The people of the countryside, who had been largely excluded from the public life of the empire of late antiquity, as indeed they had been since Hellenistic times, were now brought into Byzantine society. Their importance was recognized. The law was modified in their favor. Their religious views were listened to. Organized in their military units, they sometimes succeeded in placing their candidate upon the imperial throne.

To these peasants of Asia Minor the millennary traditions of Roman imperialism meant little. The restoration of Roman power in the west was not even an attractive dream. The world they were willing to fight for was that in which they lived—Greek, but with little interest in classical tradition; Christian, devoutly so, but often enough sectarian. Suspicious of, and even hostile to, the great city on the Bosphorus and its elegant and refined inhabitants, who span subtle arguments in words they could scarcely understand, they yet knew that if that city fell, their own Greek and Christian world would fall with it. Patriotism and religious fervor fused into a sense of unity and solidarity which inspired these men, living lives of deprivation and danger, to fight bravely and often desperately for the empire for generation after generation. But they had to feel that it was theirs, and that the spoils of victory over the infidel in this world and in the next would belong to them. As they set off for battle they sang hymns in which they compared themselves to the ancient Israelites fighting the Amalekites or the hosts of Midian. They learned these hymns from special officers—the *cantatores*—attached to each unit, who also had the task of haranguing them on the motives which must inspire their struggle. A military handbook—compiled towards the end of the ninth century, but, as is the way with textbooks, containing much earlier material—set out with admirable clarity the leading themes of this propaganda, the ideas which turned individualist peasants into tough soldiers who, in Cromwell's words, "knew what they fought for and loved what they knew."

> The cantatores should use such arguments as these to arouse the support of the army. They should remind the soldiers of the rewards for faith in God and those granted by the generosity of the emperor, and of their former successes. And they should say that the struggle is for the sake of God, and his love, and the entire nation. Furthermore they should add that the soldiers will be fighting for their brothers in the faith, when this is the case, and for their wives and their children and their native land, and that the memory of those who distinguish themselves in war for the liberation of their brothers will be everlasting, and that this great struggle is one against the enemies of God, and that we have God on our side, who has authority over the fortunes of war, while the enemy fight against him since they do not believe in him.[1]

The new political and social importance of the peasantry of Asia Minor is the major factor accounting for the origin and success of the Iconoclast movement. These men, whether as soldiers or as peasants, bore the brunt of Moslem pressure. Their simple but passionate piety led them to seek a direct theological explanation for their dire situation. Their conduct must in some way be displeasing to God. They knew that God had forbidden the Israelites, whom they saw as foreshadowing themselves, to make any graven image. They were in close contact with communities practising aniconic cults—in the first place the Moslems themselves, who, though enemies, were familiar enough to the Asia Minor frontiersmen. There was plenty of coming and going between the empire and the caliphate, and many conversions took place in both directions. Moslem and Christian were like fish swimming in the same water. The curious combination of hostility and easy-going familiarity which linked the two communities is reflected in the later epic poem on Digenis Akritas, which probably draws on traditions going back to the ninth or even the eighth century.

Another religious community whose influence ran deep among the peasants of Asia Minor was that of the Paulicians. Although in the later ninth century the Paulicians developed a clearly dualistic doctrine, asserting that the world was created not by God but by the

Devil, they appear to have been originally adherents of a quasi-Nestorian adoptionist point of view, that Jesus was a man, upon whom, on account of his justice and virtue, God later conferred a share in his own divinity. Other scholars have seen in early Paulician theology traces of aphthartodocetism, the doctrine that Christ's body, being divine, was in reality incorruptible, and that hence the crucifixion was an illusion. Be that as it may, the Paulicians were bitterly opposed to the adoration of holy images, which to their eyes was idolatry. And they knew and studied their Bible. A story relates that one of the great leaders of the Paulicians, Sergios, was converted from Orthodoxy by a woman who asked him why he did not read the Gospels. Sergios replied that it was forbidden to laymen. The Paulician woman went on to insist that all must read the Bible, and that the Orthodox clergy dealt with the Scriptures like shopkeepers, doling it out to the faithful in small quantities. There is in fact no trace in the canons of the Orthodox church of any such prohibition. But in general, Orthodox laymen were familiar only with those portions of the Bible used in the liturgy. The Paulicians, and other heretical groups, studied it closely and interpreted it literally—not for them the subtleties of allegorical interpretation elaborated by generations of learned theologians. Leo III was himself a native of one of the frontier zones and had for many years commanded armies on the eastern front. He was the spokesman of his soldiers, as well as a sincere critic of icon worship. The Iconoclast movement derived its power from the peasant armies of Asia Minor with their simple, fundamentalist faith. When in the ninth century the Arab threat faded, and the empire no longer depended on the soldiers for its very existence, Iconoclasm lost its powerful drive and became a question for theologians to argue about.

Stated thus baldly, this is an oversimplification. Any movement so powerful and so lasting draws its strength from a multitude of sources, and one of them was certainly widespread opposition to monasticism. This did not arise, as has sometimes been suggested, because monasteries were by one means or another taking over peasant land holdings. There is no evidence that monastic property was extensive at this period. A more likely reason is distrust of the monk as one who with-

Iconoclasts daubing an image of Christ with whitewash, from the twelfth-century
Barberini Psalter. More frequently, however, images were torn down or destroyed,
so that little remains of representational religious art from the pre-Iconoclast period
except in areas outside of Byzantine control at the time, such as Cyprus and Italy.
Courtesy of Biblioteca Apostolica Vaticana. MS. Barb. gr. 372, fol. 43ʳ.

draws from the society in which he lives and contributes nothing to
it. At a time when strong social solidarity was essential, those who
rejected the bonds of this solidarity were likely to be seen as potential
enemies. On the other hand, it was traditionally from the monk rather
than from the priest that the Byzantines sought spiritual guidance. So
the Iconoclast movement could never become wholly anti-monastic.
Nevertheless it is noteworthy that within the Church, resistance to
Iconoclasm was virtually confined to monks, and that they provided
almost all the victims of persecution by the Iconoclasts. There is little
record of resistance by, or persecution of, the secular clergy. Another
suggested source of support for Iconoclasm is a changed attitude to
holiness, the quality which marked something, or someone, as having
more direct access to the transcendent, spiritual world than is permitted to the ordinary man. This is an interesting suggestion but difficult

to verify, and it seems perhaps to be another way of describing the rugged, passionate, fundamentalist faith discussed above.

The tone of Iconoclasm, as well as its power and impetus, varied with place and time. Persecution was always uneven and depended on the zeal of local officials, and no doubt also on the pressure exerted upon them by the local population. The second wave of Iconoclasm, in the early ninth century, was probably a reaction to the humiliations and disasters which marked the reigns of Irene, Nicephorus, and Michael I—a kind of nostalgic yearning for the great days of Leo III and Constantine V, when the empire was at least victorious in defense.

The early Iconoclasts appear to have maintained friendly relations with the Paulicians on the eastern frontier, and perhaps to have seen in them men who shared their own biblical and fundamentalist attitude to religion and their own distrust of the intellectualism of Constantinople. It was only after the restoration of icon worship by the Council of 787 that the Paulicians adopted a thoroughgoing dualist philosophy, were actively persecuted by the imperial authorities, and set up their own independent state on the upper Euphrates, which often acted as a de facto ally of the Moslem caliphate.

The Byzantine Empire in the late seventh and eighth centuries was a military state in several senses of the expression. The old structure of civil administration of the provinces was gradually replaced by the *theme* system, in which military commanders exercised civil power in their areas. A larger proportion of the population was actively engaged in the army and the fleet than at any period before or after. And military commanders aspired to and sometimes seized imperial power in a way reminiscent of the great crisis of the Roman Empire in the third century A.D. Leo III was the most successful of a series of generals who marched their troops to Constantinople. But none of them set up anything resembling a modern military dictatorship or proclaimed martial law—a concept which would have been incomprehensible to a Byzantine. They realized, as did every citizen of the empire, that Constantinople was not just a strong point to be captured, but a unique city of almost mystical significance, and that he who possessed it, provided he did not do so by mere brute force, enjoyed a legitimacy of divine origin. So the successful leader of a military coup always sought and obtained the formal approbation of senate and people, and in several instances of disputed succession the senate took the initiative and presented its candidate to the people for approval. Once installed upon the throne, many emperors of the period called meetings of the people of the capital to explain to them their policies and beliefs. Legitimate authority required at least occasional manifestations of consent from those whom it ruled.

The senate, which was often involved in the choice of an emperor and in other matters of high policy, especially in the turbulent decades of the late seventh and early eighth century, was a very different body from the Roman senate of the west and even from the Constantinopolitan senate of the age of Justinian. No longer did its members belong to the old class of provincial landowners and city magnates who had often enjoyed a near monopoly of high office in the capital. The power of that class had been drastically reduced by the Arab and Slav invasions and the long years of warfare which followed. The new senatorial aristocracy was a class of officials and bureaucrats. They owed their position in society to the offices they held, rather than the reverse.

Byzantine society of the late seventh and eighth centuries had room for considerable social mobility. Several emperors were of humble origin, such as Leo V and Michael II, and probably also Leo III. Patriarch Nicetas (766–80) was of Slav origin, as was Thomas the Slav, the army commander who headed a dangerous rebellion in the early years of the ninth century. Lives of saints and historical chronicles passed quickly over their subject's family and wealth, and concentrated in particular on the titles and offices he held. These were of course not hereditary. One of the paths of upward mobility was provided by a successful career in the civil service of the capital. This was not a new feature in the society of the time. John of Cappadocia had risen from obscure beginnings in this way in the reign of Justinian, and others were to do so later. But because provincial landed families lost their grip on high civil office, such careers evidently became more open to talent.

Another channel of upward mobility was provided by a career in the army. An army commander could build up a power base independent of the capital, as did Leo III and Thomas the Slav. He could use his local power to acquire landed property in the province which he governed, though this was in theory against the law. It is out of this stratum of successful military men that a new landowning provincial aristocracy began to emerge in the later ninth century. But so long as Asia Minor and Thrace remained theaters of war, the possibility of building up great estates there was limited, and this new aristocracy remained in an embryonic state. It was the successful wars of the later ninth century that enabled it to take off.

A peasant could begin to move upwards in the social scale by buying up the land of his less fortunate colleagues, or by bringing new land into cultivation provided he could acquire the necessary initial capital by good husbandry or good luck. *The Life of St. Philaret,* a landowner in Cappadocia in the eighth century, recounts that he owned 600 oxen, 100 bullocks, 800 horses, 1,000 sheep, and 48 farms. The saint's precise position in society is a little mysterious, but he appears to have had no connection either with the palace bureaucracy or with the army. Many circumstantial details in his story suggest a very successful peasant rather than an aristocratic landowner of ancient stock. Philaret also provides an example of downward social mobility, as he lost all his wealth through foreign invasions and ended up with only a horse and a pair of bullocks. Another possible route of upward social mobility is suggested by the career of the widow Danielis, a wealthy landowner of the western Peloponnese who helped the future Emperor Basil I. She appears to have had not only land but a very large number of persons of semi-servile status under her control. As the region in which she lived was one in which the Slavonic population had only recently been reduced to subjection to the empire, it seems likely that her numerous dependents were conquered Slavs living in a state of limited freedom, like those whom a chronicle describes as subject to the church of Patras, in the same region of the Peloponnese. It may be that internal reconquest of areas long out of effective Byzantine control gave an opportunity to able citizens to increase their wealth dramatically.

A world in which city life was dying out in many regions, in which invasion and devastation sometimes reached the walls of the capital itself, in which few families retained wealth and influence through several generations, and in which the balance of power was tipped in favor of the army, was not one favorable to the survival of inherited classical culture. Rhetoric, philosophy, and belles-lettres were both the product and the status symbol of an urban aristocracy, confident of its position and sure of its future. Artists needed patrons, who usually belonged to the same class. The reduction in the revenues of the state put an end to the lavish imperial patronage of an earlier age. And the opposition of the Iconoclasts to the representation of the personages of Scripture or hagiographical tradition imposed new limitations upon the work of artists. There is no doubt that the period under discussion was one of drastic cultural recession. Little literature remains, and what does remain is reduced in scope and quality in comparison with that of the preceding age. Few works of art survive; those that do are often of depressingly low quality. Few major buildings that were not strictly utilitarian in character appear to have been constructed until the reign of Theophilus in the second quarter of the ninth century. The whole period is often dismissed as a "Dark Age." Yet it is worth looking a little more closely at the evidence to see which were the areas of continuity, which those of loss, and which those of innovation.

First of all, the three-tier educational system—elementary education, secondary education under the *grammaticus*, and higher education under the *rhetor*—seems to have largely broken down outside Constantinople itself. Elementary schools—or rather elementary teachers, since the school as a continuing, structured organization scarcely existed at this level—were to be found in many cities and occasionally even in villages. Literacy must have been widespread in comparison with western Europe, and it was not confined to clergymen, or indeed to men. Girls not infrequently attended school. It is interesting that pupils often passed from the study of letters and syllables to that of the Psalms, for which a simple grammatical commentary was composed. It was now possible to learn to read and write literary Greek without making contact with classical Greek literature. Here and there *grammatici* and teachers of rhetoric were to be found, providing some training in classical literature; or an elementary school teacher might take his pupils beyond merely learning to read and write. But as a rule it was only in the capital that a full secondary and higher education, indispensable for a career in the higher ranks of the bureaucracy, was available. Paradoxically, the old three-tier pattern of education may have survived more tenaciously in the cities of Syria and Palestine than on Byzantine territory. In those regions, rapidly and permanently conquered by the Moslems, city life was less disturbed and threatened than in Asia Minor.

There were neither the people to write, nor those to read, the kind of literature which called for a full classical education. No more historians followed in the footsteps of Procopius and Agathias. Or at any rate none survived, for we must bear in mind that works of an overtly Iconoclast tone would not be copied by later generations. What did continue to be written were chronicles like that of Malalas and the Paschal Chronicle, in which the events of each year were set down baldly and undiscriminatingly, with little or no attempt to establish causal connections or to explore motive and character, and certainly no eye for the great movements of history. Several of these survive, and are the main source of knowledge of the events of the period. The most noteworthy is the *Chronographia* of Theophanes the Confessor, which records year by year events from 284 to 813. Their language is often popular in tone—without being a faithful reflection of the spoken language—and their style simple, with little use of the techniques of rhetoric and no veneer of allusion and reference to older literature, other than occasional biblical phrases. Many lives of saints were produced. Though some of these rise in their opening paragraphs to a certain height of literary pretension, they are generally couched in simple, straightforward language, without obscure and recherché words or recondite classical allusions. We hear often enough of speeches being made—usually by generals to their soldiers or by emperors to the people massed in the Hippodrome—but none survives. The circumstances in which they were made would call for forcefulness and clarity rather than for the more subtle features of classical rhetoric.

Poetry in classical styles and meters virtually disappeared. But the knowledge of how to read it—and even how to write it—was maintained among some sections of the official class in the capital. Tarasios, the imperial secretary and future patriarch, who must have been born about 750, taught the meters of classical poetry to the deacon Ignatios. It would be impossible to teach meter without actually reading some of the poems. And Ignatios, in the curious dialogue in verse between Adam, Eve, and the serpent which he later wrote, shows more than superficial acquaintance with Greek tragedy. There must have been others like him.

Plenty of religious poetry was produced for liturgical use. Some of it was written in classical iambic meter, notably the canons of John of Damascus and his brother Cosmas of Maiuma, both of whom lived and worked in Moslem territory. But the great bulk of the liturgical poetry of the period was in the accentual meter used by Romanos in the age of Justinian. The *Kontakion* continued to be written, though it now drew its subjects from the lives of saints rather than from the Bible. But the principal form of religious poem was now the canon, a much longer, more diffuse composition, often panegyrical rather than narrative in structure. There seems to have been a change in the relative importance of words and music. The canon called for a greater variety of melodies than the *Kontakion*. Though some of the countless surviving canons are well-structured and moving poems, the majority strike the modern reader as verbose, repetitive, and confused in imagery. But we must bear in mind that they were sung, not read, and that the music has perished. Among the principal writers of canons were Andrew of Crete, born in Jerusalem about 660 and Joseph the Hymnographer (816–86) a native of Sicily who emigrated to Constantinople as the Arabs gradually occupied his native island.

The Iconoclast controversy gave rise to much polemical theological writing. That of the Iconoclasts survives only in citations by their adversaries. Most of this literature is compilatory in character and lacks originality, but originality was the last thing the opposing factions aimed at, since each claimed to represent the true tradition of the Church. Though the theology of the so-called Dark Age cannot bear comparison with that of the great fourth-century Fathers or even with that of Maximus the Confessor (580–662), who survived into the beginning of the period under discussion, it was not the work of ignoramuses. These men were acquainted with the rich theological literature of the eastern Church and were able to use it selectively for their own practical and polemical purposes. John of Damascus (active c. 750), son of a Syrian Greek who held high office under the Umayyad caliphs and a pupil of a monk from Sicily, was a systematizer and polemicist on the grand scale as well as a writer of religious poetry. His work is largely compilatory—indeed he claims to have said nothing of his own. But there is much originality in the way he arranges his arguments. He, of course, worked in the safety of the Moslem caliphate, beyond the reach of the long arm of the Iconoclast emperors. Patriarch Nicephorus I (806–11) was the leading theologian of the second period of Iconoclasm, and a vigorous and ingenious theologian. He wrote in a style which bore witness to some training in classical rhetoric. He was also the author of a short chronicle covering the period 602–769. The monk Theodore of Studios (759–826) was born of a family of Constantinopolitan officials, and was the leader of monastic opposition in the second period of Iconoclasm. A gifted writer, and no stranger to classical literature, he wrote in a variety of genres, including liturgical poetry, ascetic manuals for monks, polemical treatises, etc. His most interesting works for the present-day reader are his letters—he maintained a wide-ranging correspondence with men of influence within and without the empire, and his letters are never mere displays of style—and the epigrams or short poems which he wrote as guidance for the monks performing various functions in the monastery of which he was abbot. On more than one occasion monastic libraries in the nearby provinces were ransacked for patristic texts by the ecclesiastical authorities in the capital. This testifies to a shortage of books—they were always luxury products in the Middle Ages—and also to an awareness of the existence of a rich and important literature.

Lawyers never ceased to practice, and there were teachers of law in Constantinople, apparently officially appointed, towards the end of the seventh century, and a professor of law under Leo V in the middle of the eighth. But no speculative or theoretical treatises on jurisprudence survive, nor is there any indication that any such works existed. A short practical handbook of law for provincial judges, the *Ecloga*, issued by Leo III in 726, does survive, as well as an interesting and apparently unofficial account of the law as applied in peasant communities, the *Farmer's Law*. Both of these enjoyed wide influence in succeeding centuries. They are not systematic expositions of the law of the empire, which continued to be based on the *Corpus* of Justinian—now read in Greek translation with notes and explanations in that language—as modified by the legislation of subsequent emperors, of which little has survived. They are selections of those sections of the law most important in practice in country districts, and do not on the whole deal with the more complex situations which might arise in the society of the metropolis. Leo III, in the preface to the *Ecloga*, declared that he had gathered together the laws of earlier emperors which were hard to understand, especially for those living "outside this God-protected imperial city of ours" and modified them in the direction of greater humanity. He urged those who administered the law not to despise the poor nor to allow the mighty to do wrong unpunished. They were to restore equality and to take away from the rich what the poor were in need of. They would be paid an adequate salary and were thereafter to avoid corruption, which would be stamped out ruthlessly. Only if justice was done, concluded the emperor, would we be able to face our enemies.

The "humanity" of the *Ecloga* is not evident at first sight, since it provides for the various punishments by mutilation which came into use in this period. These brutal penalties very often replaced the death penalty, and aimed at marking a man as permanently incapacitated to perform certain functions, while still permitting him to live as a member of society. The earliest examples are the mutilation of Heraclonas and Martina after the death of Heraclius, the purpose of which was to exclude them from power. In 681 Constantine IV cut off the noses of his two brothers and co-emperors with the same aim in view. And nearly a century later Irene blinded or otherwise mutilated her late consort's four brothers to prevent them conspiring against her own sole rule; later she blinded her own son. Whether these penalties were ever widely applied outside the highest circles of power is unknown. The saints' lives of the period scarcely mention them. But it would be naive to suppose, for instance, that it was not common for a habitual thief to have his hand cut off.

The "humanity" of the Iconoclasts' legislation is rather to be sought in its attitude towards family law, which recognized the nuclear family as the basic social and economic unit of society. This was reflected in the provisions for intestate succession, in the greater rights of inheritance given to women, and in the insistence on the consent of the wife as well as the husband to certain transactions involving the children of the marriage. The *Ecloga* probably also provided simpler, less costly and more rapid settlement of many of the disputes arising in a predominantly agrarian society.

Medicine too was not wholly neglected. A few works survive from this period, notably the handbook of medicine by Paul of Aegina in the early seventh century, the commentaries on Hippocrates and Galen of Stephen of Alexandria a little later, the brief manual of Leo the Iatrosophist in the early ninth century; and perhaps the curious work on human physiology and anatomy by the monk Meletios is also of this date. Like all later Greek medical writings, these are essentially compilations, drawing via the fourth-century medical encyclopaedist Oreibasios—the Emperor Julian's physician and friend—on Galen and his great predecessors. But they do occasionally contain a new and personal observation. Sometimes they depart from the scientific and pragmatic tradition of Greek medicine by suggesting supernatural treatment such as prayer or the use of saints' relics. What they indicate, however, is that the medical profession had not lost contact with its Greek roots, although its interests now tended to be severely practical.

So too in the mathematical and physical sciences the emphasis was on practical applications. During the first Arab siege of Constantinople in 674–78 an engineer called Kallinikos invented Greek fire, the much feared secret weapon of the Byzantines, which ignited spontaneously and set fire to all that it touched. The composition of Greek fire was a closely guarded secret in Byzantine times, and modern chemists propound very different theories. Some believe it to have been largely crude petroleum plus a spontaneously inflammable additive; others suggest a mixture of saltpeter and other substances. We shall probably never know the answer. According to one tradition, the secret of Greek fire was revealed to Constantine I by an angel. What is clear, however, is that the development of this "secret weapon" required the practical solution of a number of problems, not only in chemistry but also in engineering, for the means of delivery were as important as the substance itself. Greek fire played a part in the defeat of the two Moslem sieges of the capital, and for centuries gave the Byzantines a powerful advantage, particularly in naval warfare.

Contact was not altogether lost, however, with the distinguished tradition of Greek theoretical science. In the second quarter of the ninth century, Leo the Mathematician, a future teacher of "philosophy" in Constantinople and archbishop of Thessalonica, found an old monk on the island of Andros who was able to teach him higher mathematics—and who must have possessed or had access to manuscripts of such classical mathematicians as Euclid, Archimedes, Diophantus, and Pappus. Leo seems to have reintroduced the study of higher mathematics in the capital, and became a legend in his lifetime. The caliph is said to have tried to persuade him to come to Baghdad. He is credited with the invention of a number of useful devices, including a visual telegraph system for rapid communication between Constantinople and the eastern frontier which recent research has shown to be not entirely impracticable.

It is not easy to assess the situation in the visual arts and architecture. Many monuments have perished through the ravages of time. Many others were destroyed by Iconoclasts or icon worshippers for doctrinal reasons. It is clear, however, that the shrinkage of the urban upper classes and the economic retrenchment forced upon the state must have resulted in a marked diminution of patronage, and there-

Seventh-century mosaic from the church of St. Demetrius in Thessalonica, showing the saint between Bishop John, who restored the building around 634, and a layman, who probably contributed the money for the restoration. *Courtesy of Colorphoto Hans Hinz, Basel.*

fore of artistic production. A few large churches were constructed
or reconstructed by Iconoclast emperors. The church of St. Irene at
Constantinople was rebuilt on its Justinianic foundations after a severe earthquake in 740. A large mosaic cross in the apse is all that
survives of the original decoration. Towards the end of the eighth
century the metropolitan church of Hagia Sophia in Thessalonica
was built, no doubt as a symbol of Byzantine power in a city often
threatened by Slavs and Bulgars. It is a massive, domed, three-aisled
basilica in which some decorative, nonfigurative mosaics still survive.
Other, smaller, churches were certainly built by the Iconoclasts, but
none can be identified with certainty today. The period of restored
icon worship under Irene saw the building of a number of small
churches in various parts of the empire. The extensive use made in
them of columns and other material from ancient buildings suggests a
certain poverty of resources. It may be that the cross-in-square church
(rectangular in ground plan and cruciform in roof plan) surmounted
by a dome set on a drum supported by internal pillars, which became
the regular pattern for churches from the late ninth century, was
worked out by architects of the Iconoclast period.

   Many religious pictures were effaced or chipped off the walls of
churches and other buildings by the Iconoclasts, and replaced by nonfigurative motifs, often involving a cross. Some examples of this Iconoclast redecoration survive, for instance, in some of the rooms over
the southwest ramp of Hagia Sophia in Constantinople; these rooms
probably formed part of the patriarch's quarters. The ban on figurative decoration applied only to religious pictures. Whether the palaces,
and indeed some of the churches, of the Iconoclast period were decorated in the rich, naturalistic, nonfigurative decoration which was executed, probably by Greek artists, in the Great Mosque of Damascus
in the early eighth century, is at present an open question. The new
palace built by Theophilus in Constantinople is said to have been
modelled on that of the caliphs in Baghdad, and to have been richly
decorated in mosaic. These mosaics would have included both nonfigurative motifs and figurative representations with no religious reference, such as hunting scenes. We can only speculate on their style—

if more illuminated manuscripts or portable icons survived from the period we would be better placed. As it is, only one illuminated manuscript can be dated with certainty to the Iconoclast period, and the few icons of the period are now, and may always have been, in the monastery of St. Catherine on Mount Sinai, which was in Moslem territory. However, there is some evidence of three main types of artistic expression being continuously practiced throughout the period— the non-figurative or decorative; the abstract or stylized representation of the human figure, as exemplified by the early seventh-century mosaics in the church of St. Demetrius in Thessalonica; and the classical or illusionist art inherited by Byzantium from the Hellenistic world. The traditions were there to be taken up and developed in the following period of economic, political, and cultural expansion. But during the period under discussion their practitioners must have been few in number and perhaps mediocre in skill.

The culture of the seventh and eighth centuries was marked throughout by a kind of levelling, in which "élitist" and elaborately sophisticated modes of expression were abandoned. It was the practically oriented culture of a people fighting for survival, with little time or taste for refinement and elegance. But the tradition of a more complex and elaborate literature, art, and science was maintained, often with difficulty, by a small class of cultured men in official circles in the capital, who must often have felt that they were swimming against the tide, and who were occasionally actually subject to persecution. They built up a resentment of and a contempt for the egalitarian culture of their age which were among the mainsprings of the cultural revival of the succeeding period.

3

THE GOLDEN AGE OF
BYZANTIUM 867–1081

The Harbaville Triptych, now in the Louvre, Paris. An ivory carving of the late
tenth century, it shows Christ flanked by John the Baptist and the Virgin Mary, who
intercede for mankind; in the lower and side panels are saints. The ivory is a slightly
lush example of high-quality metropolitan art. *Courtesy of The Louvre, Paris (Hirmer Foto-*
archiv).

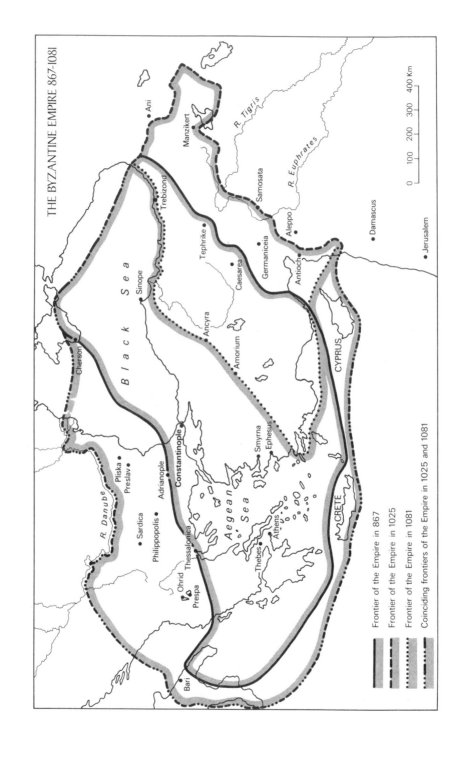

THE BYZANTINE EMPIRE 867-1081

Ani
Manzikert
R. Tigris
R. Euphrates
400 Km
300
200
100
0

Trebizond
Samosata
Damascus
Tephrike
Germaniceia
Aleppo
Jerusalem
Caesarea
Antioch
Sinope

B l a c k   S e a

Ancyra
Amorium

CYPRUS

Cherson

Constantinople

Smyrna
Ephesus

Pliska
Preslav
Adrianople

A e g e a n   S e a

Sardica
Philippopolis

Thessalonica
Ohrid
Prespa

CRETE

Thebes
Athens

R. Danube

Bari

Frontier of the Empire in 867
Frontier of the Empire in 1025
Frontier of the Empire in 1081
Coinciding frontiers of the Empire in 1025 and 1081

The accession of Basil I, however questionable the manner in which it was carried out, marked the beginning of a new epoch in the history of the Byzantine Empire in more ways than one. Basil founded a dynasty which occupied the throne for nearly two centuries and which numbered among its members some of the most able and dynamic rulers in the long history of the empire. He continued and developed with energy and brilliance the move from defense to expansion which had been cautiously and tentatively begun by his immediate predecessors in the mid-ninth century. The age of the Macedonian dynasty—the name is that used by modern historians—saw not only the reassertion of Byzantine military power and political authority but also the revival and flowering of Byzantine culture in all its aspects from philosophy to painting. It was as if, after two centuries of struggle merely to keep alive, Byzantine society was at last able to pursue more ambitious ends. Men appear to have reached back, at first hesitantly, over the long gap and to have made contact with the rich and brilliant world before the Arab and Slav invasions. They were consciously and deliberately engaging in a work of restoration—restoration of the world of Justinian. Like other restorations, their achievement contained more elements of originality than they themselves recognized.

Let us first look at the political history of the Macedonian age. The attempt to bring Bulgaria into the Byzantine sphere of influence, in which the conversion of the country played the central role, proved difficult to realize. King Boris, unwilling to see his country become a Byzantine protectorate, flirted with the German Empire and the Church of Rome. In the end the Bulgarian church was brought back to obedience to the Church of Constantinople, though with a certain measure of independence of action, while Boris himself avoided the dangers of hostility to the empire and subjection to it. While he lived, the problem could be left unsolved. But after his death, all the awkward consequences of the existence of a powerful Christian state within a few days' march of Constantinople were strikingly revealed.

In the early years of Basil's reign, the attacks of Arab raiding forces upon the cities of the southern Dalmatian coast were met by vigorous defensive measures. A new *theme* of Dalmatia was created, with its own local army and fleet. At the same time, combined missionary and diplomatic activity led to the conversion of the Serbs and the Slav principalities of present-day Hercegovina and Montenegro. In this way the hinterland of the Dalmatian cities was brought back into the Byzantine sphere of influence. Attempts to oust the Arabs from their toeholds in southern Italy at first met with failure, and provoked the Arab occupation in 870 of Malta, the last Byzantine outpost in the southwest. According to the chroniclers, the inhabitants of the island sided with the invaders and massacred the Byzantine garrison. But by the early 870s the Byzantine forces in Italy had been strengthened, and in 873 Bari was recaptured from the Arabs.

On the more important eastern front, the empire built up its forces and prepared for an assault on Arab positions that was no longer merely local. First of all the independent Paulician state had to be eliminated. A series of hard-fought campaigns ended in a decisive victory over the Paulicians in 872. Their capital, Tephrike (the modern Divriği), and a number of other strongholds were razed to the ground, and many of the captured Paulicians were resettled in Thrace. In the next year the Arabs were driven from Samosata (Samsat), and a long period of gradual advance and consolidation in the east began. As the enemy was driven back, new fortifications were built and new administrative districts set up. These were no mere tactical gains but permanent reconquests. The tide had at last turned. The learned patriarch Photios was involved in a missionary attempt to convert the Khazars, in the conversion of Bulgaria, and in the mission to win Moravia for the Church of Constantinople, the results of which far surpassed anything that Photios or any other Byzantine could have dreamed of, since it laid the foundations for the literature and culture of Slavic peoples.

On the accession of Basil I, Photios, who had been closely associated with the government of Michael III, was deposed. But as the architect of the conversion of Bulgaria and of missionary activities in the Crimea and elsewhere he shared the expansionist attitude of Basil, and before long he had returned to the capital as tutor to the emperor's sons. In 877, on the death of the Patriarch Ignatios, he was raised once again to the patriarchate and to a position of power and influence in the government of the empire. He probably played an important part in the drawing up of two practical handbooks of law, the *Procheiron* and the *Epanagoge*, which were issued by Basil I to replace the *Ecloga*. Though both books owed much to the *Ecloga*, their prefaces condemned it in harsh and vituperative terms as the "destruction of good laws," since it was tainted by its association with Iconoclasm. These handbooks were to be only the beginning of a drastic purification and recasting of Roman law, which was to embrace the corpus of Justinian supplemented by the enactments of later emperors. Basil evidently saw himself as a great legislator and a second Justinian. But he did not realize this project, for in 886 he died in a hunting accident. He was succeeded by his son Leo VI.

Leo, unlike his upstart father, was an erudite man, with a taste for preaching—some of his sermons survive—and a sharp eye for administrative problems, but little interest in foreign policy or military affairs. In particular he and his advisers do not appear to have realized, as Basil did, the importance of concentrating upon one enemy, the Arabs, and avoiding the danger of a war on two fronts by scrupulous maintenance of peaceful relations with Bulgaria. The caliphate was weak, no longer able to threaten seriously the great centers of population of the empire, and alien in faith. Bulgaria was now a Christian country, becoming more and more politically and ethnically united, and its army was within striking distance of Constantinople. But first let us look at internal affairs in the reign of Leo VI.

Leo brought to fruition his father's project of a new codification in Greek of the whole of Byzantine law, comprising elements of the canon law of the Church side by side with the civil law of the state. The *Basilica* or Imperial Code was largely based on Justinian's *Digest*, *Code*, and *Novels*, not in the original Latin, which was now scarcely known in Constantinople, but on the Greek translations and commentaries made in the time of Justinian and his immediate successors.

The commission of lawyers who drew it up drastically rearranged the order of exposition to make consultation easier. The vast work, in sixty books, was no mere mechanical compilation but the work of men with a clear grasp of the principles of jurisprudence. It became the foundation of all subsequent Byzantine legal science, and down the centuries a forest of commentaries grew up around it. Even today it is studied with interest by legal historians. The nineteenth century saw an edition in eight volumes, and a new critical edition of text and commentaries has been appearing since 1953, and has now reached thirteen volumes.

Leo VI also issued a number of new decrees, 113 of which he published in a collection. They dealt with many practical problems arising in the course of state or ecclesiastical administration, and tidied up a number of anomalies and anachronisms in the law. In particular they abrogated the independent rights of city councils and the legislative authority of the senate, on the grounds that the power of the state was now vested solely in the emperor, who was in his turn, of course, subject to the law. These rights had become vestigial survivals, but their formal abolition marked the culmination of a process of centralization which had been much accelerated during the empire's struggle for existence. The Roman Empire in its heyday had been a collection of civic and other largely self-governing communities, upon which was superimposed the authority of a monarchy concerned essentially with defense and foreign relations. The Byzantine Empire in its fully developed form knew only one center of political authority.

The system of *themes* had originally grown up in response to urgent problems of defense. For a time the military governors of the *themes* coexisted with the civil governors of the old provinces, which maintained a shadowy existence. Leo VI's legislation put an end to this vestigial survival and imposed uniformity upon the administrative system of the empire. At the same time he continued the process of dividing the original *themes*, often vast in extent, into smaller units which were both more manageable and less likely to provide the base for a successful military revolt. The various small administrative units established in territory newly conquered from the Arabs were more and more modelled on the *themes* in structure and organization.

Leo seems also to have tidied up the system of ranks and offices, and to have systematically distinguished between the two. His legislation concerning the trade guilds of Constantinople has survived. It shows a minute and bureaucratic control of the membership and commercial activity of these guilds of artisans and merchants under the close supervision of a high government official, the Prefect of the City. The guilds, which can probably be traced back to antiquity in some cases, doubtless originated as organs for the self-defense of their members by restricting entry to a craft or trade, fixing standards, prices, training and the like, and providing various elements of social security. As described in Leo's law, the so-called *Book of the Prefect*, they retained many of these cartel-like functions, but had superimposed upon them a whole series of obligations which transformed their nature. They now primarily served not the interests of their members but those of the community, or rather those of the state. The maintenance of supply at regular prices had become their prime function, to which they were legally bound.

In the military domain the process of attrition of Arab power on the eastern frontier went on. Soon, however, Leo and his advisers had more awkward problems to deal with. In 889 King Boris of Bulgaria abdicated and retired to a monastery near his capital of Preslav. His eldest son and successor, Vladimir, lacked his father's judgment and experience. He seems to have become the tool of a faction of Bulgar tribal leaders who resented the growing centralization of power in the kingdom and were hostile to Christianity, which they saw as an instrument of Byzantine interference in their country. There was much disorder in Bulgaria and the danger of a head-on clash with Byzantium. Fearing for the destruction of his life's work, Boris emerged from his monastery, imposed his will on a council of boyars, deposed Vladimir, who was soon afterwards put to death, and established on the throne his younger son, Symeon. Symeon had received a Byzantine education in Constantinople, where he had lived for many years, and was a monk at the time of his elevation to the throne. Boris had probably intended him to become Bulgarian patriarch. The close interpenetration of church and state—some might see it as subservience of church to state—made it advantageous to have a member of the royal family at the head of the church. Leo VI had on his accession deposed the powerful and independent-minded Photios and appointed his own brother Stephen as patriarch. Boris probably hoped that Symeon would follow his own policy of building a centralized, unified, Christian Bulgaria while avoiding any open conflict with the frighteningly powerful Byzantines. If so, he had misjudged his son. Or had he misjudged the situation? Perhaps it was not possible for two expansive and powerful states to coexist for long in the Balkan peninsula.

After some eighty years of peace, war broke out between Byzantium and Bulgaria in 894. The ostensible cause was the transfer of the market for trade with Bulgaria from Constantinople to Thessalonica. It may have been intended by the Byzantines as a provocation; more probably it was the outcome of muddle and corruption, since certain very high officials stood to gain by the change. It was no doubt a breach of a treaty between the two states, for all Byzantine foreign trade was regulated by treaty. In the days of Basil I and Boris, neither of whom wanted a conflict, it would have been cleared up by negotiation, but now it was allowed to escalate. Leo's government brusquely rejected Bulgarian protests, and Symeon reacted with suspicious precipitation by invading Byzantine territory. The Byzantines responded with their classic move. The army marched north up the Black Sea coast, the navy sailed to the Danube mouth to threaten the Bulgarian rear, and the Magyars, a confederation of pastoral nomads temporarily settled north of the Danube delta, were induced by Byzantine gold and promises to invade Bulgaria. Symeon hastily withdrew his army from imperial territory and signed an armistice, while Byzantine forces continued to occupy large tracts of Bulgaria. But Symeon's formidable army was still intact, and its commander was not a man to abandon his plans at the first contretemps. He too had a traditional strategy to follow. In 896 he fell on a major Byzantine army at Bulgar-

ophygon (ancient Burtudizum, near Adrianople) in Thrace and annihilated it. It was the most serious defeat the Byzantines had suffered
since the disastrous days of King Krum at the beginning of the century. The Magyars sensed the shift in the balance of power, withdrew
hastily from Bulgaria, and moved on with their ponies and their bul-
lock carts to Pannonia, the present-day Hungary, urged on from the
rear by the pressure of another pastoral people, the Pechenegs. Leo's
government negotiated a peace treaty with Bulgaria, restored the
trade market to Constantinople and contracted to pay an annual subsidy, probably in the guise of a war indemnity, to the Bulgarians.
Peace was restored in the Balkans, but it was an unstable peace, which
Symeon had in his power to break when he saw fit. The empire no
longer had one enemy, but two.

The caliphate and its half-independent feudatories soon began to
make local advances in the mountainous frontier area. But a few years
later—the date is uncertain—an expeditionary force under Nicephorus Phokas marched through the mountains of Cilicia and defeated
a major Arab army at Adana. Even with its striking force reduced,
the empire was a formidable military power, but it could not deploy
its strength on all fronts at once. In 902 the last Byzantine stronghold
in Sicily, the fortress of Taormina, fell to the Arabs, and in 904 an
Arab fleet raided Abydos at the mouth of the Dardanelles and went
on to capture and sack Thessalonica, the second city of the empire,
which had held out undefeated against the onslaughts of Slavs and
Avars in the past. The naval weakness of the empire which these
events suggest seems to have been quickly overcome. In 905 the admi-
ral Himerius defeated an Arab fleet in the Aegean. A few years later
a force under the same commander occupied Cyprus, which had been
a neutral no-man's-land since the late seventh century, and went on
to storm Latakiya in Syria. That the fleet was defeated by the Arabs
while sailing for home waters does not diminish the significance of
its exploit. However, an ambitious combined operation against Arab-
occupied Crete in 911 ended in failure.

A few years earlier, in 907, a Russian fleet under Prince Oleg of
Kiev had sailed down the Bosphorus. Unable to breach the defenses

of the city, the Russians had turned to negotiation. The resulting treaty not only established regular trading relations between Byzantium and Russia but enabled the empire to make use of Russian troops as mercenaries. Russian contingents indeed took part in Himerius's operations against Cyprus and Syria in 910 and in the expedition against Crete the following year. The de facto collaboration between Kiev and Constantinople represented a deterrent to Bulgaria so long as it lasted.

Leo VI had been married three times, but his three successive wives had died without bearing any sons. A third marriage was contrary to both canon and civil law, and Leo had by a decree of his own strengthened the prohibition against it. In 905 his mistress Zoë Carbonopsina (Coal-Black Eyes) bore him a son. Anxious to legitimize his heir, Leo married Zoë in January 906. This fourth marriage aroused a storm of opposition among laymen and clerics. The Patriarch Nicholas Mysticus repeatedly turned the emperor back from the gates of the church. Frustrated in Constantinople, Leo turned to Rome and obtained a dispensation from Pope Sergius III, who was overjoyed to find an emperor in Constantinople appealing to him over the head of his own patriarch. Thus fortified by papal support, Leo was able to dismiss Nicholas and replace him by a more pliable prelate. But the issue of the fourth marriage was not solved. It continued to divide the Byzantine church and Byzantine society and to provide a polarizing force around which factions gathered. The continuance of the dynasty was ensured, and the young prince Constantine was crowned co-emperor with his father in 908. But the unity of the governing class of the empire was broken, and its capacity to act decisively was weakened.

In 912 Leo VI died, and was succeeded by his two co-emperors, his brother Alexander and his seven-year-old son, Constantine. Alexander is described as a hedonist with no understanding of the problems of government. He had probably been kept deliberately away from them during his twenty-six years as titular co-emperor. Be that as it may, he soon showed himself unable to handle the situation. When the Bulgarian envoys presented themselves at his court to receive the subvention guaranteed by the treaty of 896, Alexander not only refused to pay the money, but treated the ambassadors insultingly, referring to them and their sovereign as savages clad in skins. Whether this was an act of policy or merely the bravado of an elderly pleasure-lover who found himself out of his depth is not known. But the result was immediate. Symeon reopened hostilities, and they continued without interruption till his death in 927. While the Bulgarian army was ravaging the European provinces of the empire, in the summer of 913, Alexander suddenly died. A council of regency for the boy Emperor Constantine VII was set up, headed by Patriarch Nicholas, who had been restored to office during Alexander's brief reign.

The dispute over the fourth marriage of Leo VI still sharply divided ruling circles in Constantinople. Nicholas himself was in the embarrassing position of acting as regent for a sovereign whose legitimacy he did not recognize. Leo VI's widow, the dowager empress Zoë, gathered round her a varied faction, united only by its hatred and distrust of the regent. To make matters worse, Constantine Dukas, the commander of the central army, rose in revolt and made a bid for the throne. For a time he held most of the Asiatic shore opposite the capital. Rumor and suspicion were rife in Constantinople, as men in positions of influence tried to reinsure against an eventual change of regime.

It was at this juncture that Symeon of Bulgaria appeared before the walls of Constantinople at the head of his formidable army. Powerful though it was, it could not hope to take the city by assault—the land and sea walls were impregnable. But two other possibilities must have been in his mind. The first was that Constantine Dukas might turn to him for help. After all, had not Justinian II been restored to his throne by Khan Tervel of Bulgaria two centuries earlier? The second was that one of the factions in the city might open the gates to him in order to score a point over its adversaries. The decision-making machinery of the empire was clearly in disarray, and Symeon was a Christian monarch, educated in the traditions of Byzantine culture, and a resolute and able man. There were worse ways out of this crisis paralyzing the ruling class of the empire.

The regent Nicholas decided that if anyone was going to invite Symeon into Constantinople it would be himself. He hoped to defuse the military threat to the capital and thereby strengthen the position of his own faction. He may also have sincerely believed that peace with Bulgaria was essential for the survival of the empire. Symeon was admitted to the capital and received with great ceremony by the regent, accompanied by the boy emperor. Once inside he was able to negotiate from a position of strength. One of his daughters was betrothed to Constantine VII. In a mysterious ceremony in the church of the Virgin at Blachernae the patriarch crowned Symeon with his own headdress. There has been much discussion of the meaning of this ceremony. One suggestion can be ruled out, namely that the astute churchman deluded the naive foreigner into thinking that he was being crowned as emperor while in reality some meaningless piece of mumbo jumbo was being performed. Symeon knew as much about ecclesiastical and court ceremony as did Nicholas, and must have been well aware that no unilateral action by the patriarch could make him a Byzantine emperor. Most probably what Nicholas did was to consecrate Symeon as ruler of Bulgaria and to give him the right to use the title of *basileus* in that country, as the western emperors had done in their territory since 800. In any case it was a matter of little importance. Symeon would soon find himself the father-in-law and natural protector of a reigning emperor, and in the fullness of time his grandson would be both Byzantine emperor and king of Bulgaria. The two states would become one.

Nicholas did not have sufficient support, however, to carry through his policy of concession to Symeon and "special relationship" between the empire and Bulgaria. The enmity of Zoë and her faction, the xenophobia of the citizens, and the disturbing threat of Constantine Dukas and his army on the Asian shore weakened his position, and before the summer was out Nicholas had been overthrown in a palace coup. A new regency council was set up headed by Zoë. The projected marriage alliance between the two states was repudiated. And the coronation of Symeon, whatever it may have signified, was declared invalid. Symeon, who had withdrawn to Preslav well satisfied, now returned at the head of his army and overran Thrace. As he ranged over the countryside he insisted that the populace should hail him as emperor. He had apparently abandoned the prospect of a peaceful settlement between Bulgaria and Byzantium, and was bent on taking over the government of the empire, by military force if no other means would succeed.

It is not the province of the historian to speculate on what might have been; there is enough trouble establishing what actually happened. But it is difficult to resist the impression that the summer of 913 saw one of the great missed opportunities of history. Had the Byzantine Empire and the Bulgarian Kingdom been able to overcome the rivalry imposed upon them by geography and, building upon a common religion and a largely shared culture, grow together into a polyethnic state without the narrow ethnic exclusivity which they both exhibited, they would have been able together to offer more effective resistance to attacks from west and east than either did separately, and the later history of Europe and the Near East might have taken a very different course. Whether Patriarch Nicholas had any such long-term perspective in mind, or whether he was merely reacting to challenges as they occurred, we do not know. During the subsequent years of hostility he certainly tried to keep a bridge open to Symeon, so much so that in the eyes of some of his contemporaries he was a traitor.

In the next few years the Bulgarians regularly invaded and plundered Byzantine territory. In 914 they took Adrianople, one of the key fortresses guarding the approaches to the capital. In subsequent years they operated in Macedonia and pushed forward the frontier of Bulgaria as far as the Adriatic. In 917 the Byzantines mounted a counterattack. It followed the usual plan of combined operations by army and fleet, and like so many such campaigns it ended in disaster. Symeon outmaneuvered the Byzantine army and defeated it with very heavy losses at Achelous, near Anchialus (in the vicinity of modern Burgas). This victory gave Symeon military mastery of the Balkans—he could move where he liked, when he liked. He did not waste time on futile demonstrations before the walls of Constantinople, but penetrated deeply into northern Greece, displaying the power of Bulgaria and the inability of Zoë's government to protect its citizens. What he could not do for the moment was to cross into Asia Minor, the economic and demographic center of the empire, since the Byzantine fleet controlled the sea. But he had partisans in the capital and he felt he could afford to wait.

Meanwhile within the capital dissatisfaction was growing with the ineffectual and rigid policy of the regency. The commander of the central army, Leo Phokas, had been discredited by the defeat at Achelous. In 919 Romanos Lekapenos, the commander of the fleet, a man who did not belong to the military aristocracy and who had not been closely associated with Zoë and her regency council, mounted a coup d'état. Zoë and her supporters were deposed. A new regency council was set up with Romanos at its head, and his daughter Helena was married to the fourteen-year-old emperor. In the next year Romanos was promoted to the rank of Caesar—reserved for members of the imperial family—and a few months later became co-emperor with his son-in-law and effective ruler of the empire.

For Symeon this meant the end of his expectation of establishing his influence in Byzantium by negotiation or dynastic marriage. Bulgaria and the empire were back on a collision course. The Bulgarians continued to build up their military pressure, in the slender hope that it might indirectly bring about a change of policy in Constantinople, while the new government of Romanos Lekapenos refused to make any concessions. The only promising course open to the Bulgarians was to win allies. Symeon began negotiations with the Fatimid rulers of Egypt and concluded an alliance by which the Egyptians would provide naval support to the Bulgarians. The quid pro quo was no doubt a share in the eventual spoils of victory. Had the plan come off, it might have enabled the Bulgarians to make a serious assault on Constantinople and it would certainly have permitted them to invade Asia Minor. But Byzantine diplomats were able to offer the Egyptians hard cash instead of promises, and they soon renounced their treaty with Symeon. The long, indecisive struggle continued on land, at a terrible cost to both sides in men and productive resources. In 923

Symeon again captured and plundered Adrianople. In 924 he once again appeared before the walls of Constantinople. Byzantines and Bulgarians alike had an interest in ending the war, but neither could afford to make the necessary concessions. A meeting was, however, arranged between Romanos and Symeon, and the Bulgarian monarch was received for the last time in the city in which he had been educated and where he had hoped to rule, if not to reign. Positions had hardened too much, and no agreement was reached, except on the diplomatic point that Byzantium henceforth recognized Symeon's imperial title in Bulgaria. Hostilities dragged on, and began to involve other Balkan peoples, whom the rival powers tried to play off against one another. The Byzantines had the longer purse. The question was whether their allies could stand up to the battle-tried Bulgarian army. The Serbs, who had become allies of Byzantium, were crushingly defeated by the Bulgarians, but in 926 Symeon suffered his first defeat ever at the hands of the Croats under King Tomislav. This setback did not prevent his making preparations for a campaign against Byzantium in the following year, but before it could be launched, in the spring of 927, Symeon suddenly died.

Bulgarian power collapsed with him. The strain on human and material resources imposed by the long years of war had been immense. Despair and demoralization were spreading among the common people, while the growing class of feudal proprietors, often the descendants of Slav or Bulgar tribal leaders, tended to put their own interests before those of the state. Only the dominating personality and daemonic energy of Symeon had maintained the unrelenting Bulgarian war effort. His son Peter succeeded him, and was soon married to a granddaughter of Romanos Lekapenos. Bulgaria became a docile Byzantine protectorate, serving as a buffer between the empire and the warlike steppe peoples who were once again on the move.

The disappearance of the Bulgarian threat left the empire free to develop its policy of reconquest in the east, which had been interrupted for more than a generation. In the very year of Symeon's death, operations began again on a major scale. The key city of Melitene

(Malatya), which guarded access to the upper Euphrates, was captured in 931, lost again to the Arabs, and retaken by the Byzantines, this time permanently, in 934. For a time the Hamdanid Emir Saif-ul-Dawla succeeded in reestablishing Arab overlordship over much of Armenia and making costly raids into Byzantine territory. But the weight of the centralized Byzantine Empire and the steady, professional generalship of John Kurkuas carried the day in the long run. By 943 Martyropolis (Mayferkat), Amida (Diyarbakir) on the Tigris, and Nisibis (Nusaybin) were in Byzantine hands. In the following year Kurkuas took Edessa (Urfa), a city famed for its holy relics, which included a letter written by Christ Himself and a cloth with His miraculous portrait. The latter, the so-called *Mandylion*, was brought to Constantinople with unprecedented ceremony and deposited in one of the churches of the city.

The campaigns of the 930s and early 940s had brought under Byzantine control a belt of country about a hundred miles deep, stretching from the high plateau of Armenia to the plains of Mesopotamia. Many Arab communities in this region came over to the Byzantines of their own accord and were baptized and resettled in other parts of the empire. The whole balance of military power in the Near East was now tilted in favor of Byzantium, while on the Moslem side dismay and disarray ruled. However, the Byzantine advance on the eastern frontier had not been uninterrupted by dangers elsewhere, in spite of the tranquillity of Bulgaria. In 941 a Russian fleet again devastated much of the north coast of Asia Minor. John Kurkuas and many units of the army under his command had to be temporarily withdrawn from the Tigris front. Swift movement and good logistics enabled him to catch the Russians before they departed—booty rather than conquest was the goal of their expedition—and defeat them both on land and at sea. Two years later the Russians offered a more serious threat. Prince Igor made a compact with the Pechenegs, and a joint Russo-Pecheneg force appeared on the Danube. Romanos was anxious not to get involved once again in a war on two fronts, and Igor was fearful of a direct conflict with the superbly trained and equipped Byzantine army. Negotiations began between Constantinople and Kiev. The outcome was a treaty which substantially repeated the terms of that of 911.

The very success of Byzantine arms strengthened the economic and political power of the military aristocracy of generals. Firmly based on their estates in the provinces, they began more and more to encroach on the tax-free holdings which were the economic basis of the *theme* armies, to turn the erstwhile soldiers into their own dependents, and in general to oppress the independent peasantry. The effects of this gradual feudalization of the Byzantine countryside were complex and far-reaching, and not all of them can have been evident in the early tenth century. What could not escape the notice of the imperial government in Constantinople was the loss of revenue as taxpaying peasants became quasi serfs, the ominous growth of the power and wealth of provincial magnates, and, perhaps most immediate of all, the shortage and poor quality of recruits to the army. Romanos Lekapenos was himself of humble origin, but this did not make him a social revolutionary or give him any particular sympathy with the downtrodden. Nevertheless he issued the first of a long series of laws aimed at limiting the encroachments of the "mighty" (*dynatoi*) upon the property of the poor. That so much legislation over so long a period had to be directed towards the same end suggests that it was not effective, and that it failed to stem the process of feudalization and the enserfment of the tough, egalitarian peasantry which had been the strength of the empire during its long struggle for survival. The process was one that was beyond the control of legislation. And the legislators themselves were concerned not so much with the radical social and economic changes that were taking place in the Empire, but rather with their fiscal, military, and political consequences. Romanos Lekapenos's first enactment may very well have been brought about by the disastrously severe winter of 927–28, when famine and distress were widespread and were exploited by the "mighty" to extend their land holdings at the expense of their less fortunate neighbors. But the changes which the emperor sought to bring under control were independent of good or bad weather, or of the wills of those involved in them.

During the years of victory, Constantine VII had been kept in the background by his energetic father-in-law, who proclaimed his sons co-emperors and was clearly trying to establish a dynasty of his own. Meanwhile Constantine devoted his enforced leisure to the pursuit of learning and the arts, not only as a munificent patron, but as a writer and painter. The activities of the group of scholars and men of letters around him will be discussed later.

By 945 Constantine was forty years old, and Romanos and his family had made many enemies. A plot, whose details are obscure, resulted in the deposition and imprisonment in monasteries of Romanos Lekapenos and his sons, and the assumption of sole rule by Constantine VII. Much of Constantine's immediate support came from the powerful Phokas family, one of the leading families of the military aristocracy. But the emperor was in no sense a tool of the provincial magnates; rather he played on the rivalry between families and factions among them, while continuing the policy of Romanos. The series of ineffectual laws limiting the encroachments of the "mighty" went on. In Bulgaria Byzantine overlordship was maintained, while a number of invasions by the aggressive Magyars were repulsed at the cost of Bulgarian rather than Byzantine lives. In southern Italy a low-keyed and indecisive struggle was maintained against the Arabs. The main thrust of Byzantine power was in the east. Germaniceia (Marash) was captured by the Byzantines and lost again several times. In 952 the imperial army crossed the Euphrates in force. By 957 the general Nicephorus Phokas was pushing south towards Membidj, east of Aleppo. About the same time a decisive success in Byzantine foreign policy was marked by the baptism of Princess Olga of Kiev and her visit to Constantinople, which was accompanied by all the refinement and splendor of Byzantine court ceremonial. Exactly when, where, and by whom Olga was baptized is a much-discussed problem, but that the baptism took place is beyond doubt.

Constantine VII died in 959 and was succeeded by his son Romanos II. His short reign—he died in 963—saw the expulsion of the Arabs from Crete by Nicephorus Phocas, who went on to capture a series of Moslem strongholds in eastern Cilicia and finally, in 962, to

Constantine VII being crowned by Christ; ivory relief of the mid-tenth century, now in the Museum of Fine Arts, Moscow. *Courtesy of Museum of Fine Arts, Moscow.*

take the great city of Aleppo. The reconquest of Crete put an end to the constant Arab raids in the Aegean and was followed by a great economic and cultural upsurge in the cities on its shores. Many of the most celebrated Byzantine churches and monasteries of Greece belong to the late tenth and early eleventh centuries.

Nicephorus Phocas's personal prestige and the influence of his family enabled him to marry Theophano, the widow of Romanos II, and become co-emperor with Romanos's infant sons Constantine and Basil and effective ruler of the empire. Nicephorus not unexpectedly continued the policy of reconquest in the east. In 965 he took Tarsus and Mopsuestia in Cilicia and reoccupied Cyprus after nearly three centuries of condominium and demilitarization. In 968 he was able to march far down the Syrian coast, giving an impressive display of Byzantine power to Moslem and Christian inhabitants alike. And in 969 he crowned his long career of military success by capturing Antioch, which, with its surrounding territory, he incorporated as a province of the empire.

On the northern frontier, however, a new and dangerous situation began to develop. Nicephorus had cut off the annual subsidy paid to the Bulgarian court since the death of Symeon in 927. This provoked protests from Bulgaria, which Nicephorus decided to stifle by calling on Prince Svyatoslav of Kiev, the son of the recently baptized Princess Olga, to threaten the Bulgarian rear. Svyatoslav appeared on the Danube in 968, and the cowed Bulgarians at once withdrew their protests. Svyatoslav, however, had realized that Bulgarian weakness gave him a great opportunity, and proceeded to establish his own authority on both sides of the Danube. This was more than the Byzantines had bargained for. A menacing Russian military presence within a few days' march of the capital was a threat which could not be ignored. Nicephorus was blamed for the disastrous turn events had taken. A palace conspiracy led to his assassination in 969. He was succeeded by a fellow general, John Tzimiskes, who had probably been the lover of Theophano. Once in power, he dispensed with her support and married her sister-in-law Theodora, the daughter of Constantine VII. The new regime did not meet with universal acceptance, and several revolts by members of the military aristocracy had to be put down. Meanwhile Svyatoslav's confidence grew day by day. Tzimiskes attempted to negotiate with him, but the Russian insisted that the Byzantines abandon Constantinople and withdraw to Asia Minor. Byzantium faced a major war on the northern frontier, a danger which its rulers had avoided since the days of Symeon, nearly half a century earlier.

The new challenge called for a switch of the military effort from Syria to Bulgaria. It was not until 971 that John Tzimiskes was able to march into Bulgaria at the head of a powerful army, take Preslav, drive Svyatoslav back to the Danube, and bottle him up in the fortress of Silistria, where he soon surrendered. Bulgaria was brought under direct Byzantine control and virtually ceased to exist as a state, although some centers of resistance still held out in the far west. The Bulgarian church lost its patriarch and its independent status and became a province of the Church of Constantinople. John Tzimiskes' reaction to the threat by the prince of Kiev was an impressive display of Byzantine organization and Byzantine military power, and left the empire in a more dominant position than before. One immediate result was the opening of friendly relations with the western Emperor Otto I.

In the next year Tzimiskes was back in northern Mesopotamia, and in the three years that followed took Emesa (Homs), Baalbek, Damascus, Beirut, Acre, Sidon, Caesarea, and Tiberias, and came within striking distance of Jerusalem. It was an astonishing display of strength and military skill. But the centers of Moslem power in Iraq, Iran, and Egypt were left untouched. In spite of the heady rhetoric of chroniclers, Byzantium was not on the point of recovering the rich eastern provinces it had lost in the seventh century.

In January 976 John Tzimiskes died, probably of typhoid fever. As had happened at the death of Nicephorus Phokas, several military magnates rose in revolt and tried to seize the throne for themselves. Meanwhile the two sons of Romanos II, Constantine VIII and Basil II, who had been kept in the background during the reigns of Nicephorus Phokas and John Tzimiskes, were able to assume power. Con-

The Virgin and Child, mosaic in the apse of the Katholikon, one of the monastery churches of Hosios Lukas in central Greece, c. 1020. *Courtesy of Sonia Halliday.*

stantine was a weak and pleasure-loving character who took little interest in the exercise of imperial power. For Basil, an austere and forceful man, a lifelong bachelor with no cultural interests, power was the very breath of life. His first few years were taken up in the long struggle against a rebellious general. It was only after Prince Vladimir of Kiev had responded to his appeal and sent a force of 6,000 men, the nucleus of the later Varangian guard, that he was finally able to crush him in 989.

The close relations which Basil II built up with Kiev culminated in the baptism of Vladimir and the official "conversion" of Russia in the same year. The agreement was cemented by the despatch of Basil's sister Anna, a princess born in the purple, to be Vladimir's bride.

Russia now became a spiritual and cultural dependency of Byzantium, its church headed by a Greek metropolitan appointed by Constantinople. But the facts of geography meant that this vast land never came under Byzantine political control in the way that Bulgaria had. Byzantine rulers always had to treat Kiev with respect mingled with mistrust.

In the meantime Basil had launched a punitive expedition to Bulgaria, where a nucleus of independence in the west was rapidly expanding. His efforts met with little success and taught him the difficulty, and the importance, of finally subduing Bulgaria. It was to this end that most of the rest of the emperor's life was devoted. A long series of hard-fought campaigns, in which all the forces of the empire were engaged, led to the capture of Pliska, Preslav, and Vidin in 1001, of Skopje in 1004, and of Dyrrhachium (Durazzo) in 1005. The Bulgarians, under their new ruler Samuel, showed unexpected resilience and readiness to counterattack. In the very year that Basil took Vidin on the Danube, Samuel captured and sacked Adrianople. But the empire's resources in money, men, and skill told. Gradually Samuel became bottled up in the far west of his kingdom. In 1014 the main Bulgarian army was overwhelmingly defeated on the upper reaches of the river Struma. Basil had the 15,000 prisoners blinded, leaving every hundredth man with one eye to guide his companions back to the royal capital at Prespa. He was determined not merely to win battles but to eliminate Bulgaria as a military power. When the ghastly cortège reached Prespa, Samuel died of shock. A few of his kinsmen and followers held out for a year or two, but in 1018 the Bulgarian state was finally destroyed, and its territories reincorporated in the empire, which now stretched from the Danube to the Euphrates and Tigris.

Bitter experience had taught Basil the danger of leaving too much power in the hands of the great provincial military families. Throughout his long reign he strove implacably to assert the authority of the centralized state and to hinder the encroachment of the magnates on the property of free peasants and soldiers. His two immediate predecessors had abrogated some of the laws defending the poor against the "mighty." Basil reinstated the old laws and ordered all property illegally acquired by the "mighty" to be restored to its original owners without compensation. How far the restoration was actually carried out is not known. But Basil II was not a man to be trifled with, and his measures must have hindered the development of feudal relations in the Byzantine countryside. In absorbing conquered Bulgaria into the empire he wisely exempted the new Bulgarian provinces from paying taxes in gold, and permitted them to continue paying in kind as they had done under Bulgarian sovereignty. Bulgaria had not yet developed a money economy—the Bulgarian kings struck no coins— and the disruptive effects upon Bulgarian society of its introduction would have been disastrous both economically and politically. The Bulgarian church became an autonomous archbishopric, and continued to enjoy many privileges, including that of direct appointment by the emperor. Basil wished neither to provoke a desperate rebellion nor to let Byzantine magnates enrich themselves at the expense of his new Bulgarian subjects.

The long Bulgarian war successfully concluded, the emperor turned his eye westward. The whole of the Balkans to the Adriatic was now either Byzantine territory or ruled by clients of the empire. The Arabs were being slowly edged out of Byzantine Italy. Beyond the Straits of Messina lay the rich province of Sicily, ruled for more than a century by Arabs. It was while he was preparing a grandiose amphibious expedition for the recovery of Sicily that Basil II died, in 1025, having reigned for sixty-two years and exercised sole power for forty-nine. He was not an attractive character, but he had succeeded in his aims of reasserting and restoring Byzantine power from the Straits of Messina to the Tigris and from the Danube to Syria, and of maintaining and reinforcing central power against the centrifugal tendencies of the great military magnates. To the historian Niketas Choniates, writing in the aftermath of the Fourth Crusade, there were two Byzantine emperors whose greatness was beyond question. One was Heraclius, the other was Basil II.

After Basil's death a period of rapid change began, which in the first place took the form of disintegration and decline, however much

hope it may have contained for the future. Basil's long series of decisive victories ensured the maintenance of peace on the frontiers for a
time. And when that peace was broken, as it was by Arab operations
in Syria and Mesopotamia in the early 1030s, Byzantine military
power and organization were able to restore the situation rapidly, and
even to improve it, as when the general George Maniakes recaptured
Edessa (Urfa) in 1032. But the days of Byzantine military supremacy
were numbered. In the countryside the growing power of the military
magnates was no longer restrained by the heavy hand of Basil II.
His successors were men whom the magnates neither respected nor
feared. Ironically the military aristocracy were from a long-term point
of view sapping the roots of their own power by taking over the property of free tax-paying peasants and of peasant-soldiers. But in the
meantime they made the most of the opportunity to increase their
holdings and their wealth. In the capital the civilian aristocracy of civil
service families mistrusted the army and misunderstood problems of
defense, while they enriched themselves by corruption and an elaborate system of perquisites. Both parties pursued their own short-
sighted interests. The result was a rapid collapse of the military and
financial power of the state, accompanied by an intellectual renaissance.

Basil II was at first succeeded as ruling emperor by his brother
Constantine VIII. Three years later, in 1028, Constantine died, leaving two middle-aged, unmarried daughters, Zoë and Theodora. Theodora had been for some time a nun, but Zoë discovered a late voca-
tion for matrimony and married a series of leading members of the
civil aristocracy, raising them in turn to the imperial throne. None
were men of high capacity; but by now the course which events were
taking could not have been diverted by the most able ruler. Zoë's first
husband Romanos III was murdered in his bath in 1034 with the
complicity of his consort. Her second, Michael IV, inaugurated a policy of harsh taxation of the Bulgarians, to make up the revenue lost
by the growth of the estates of the military magnates. This was a clear
reversal of the policy of Basil II. Within a few years it led to a revolt
in Bulgaria, where one Peter Deljan was proclaimed emperor, and

to widespread rebellion elsewhere in the northern Balkans. Deljan's revolt was put down in 1041. But further west the Byzantines were defeated by Stephen Voislav of Zeta (an area coinciding with the later Montenegro). Voislav established the independence of his principality and thus made the first breach in the system established by Basil II.

When Michael IV died, in 1041, he was for a time succeeded by his nephew, Michael V, whom he had prevailed upon Zoë to adopt. In the following year the emperor, wishing to have a free hand to rule, tried to banish his obstructive stepmother to a monastery. But Zoë, now experienced and resourceful, had him deposed and blinded. After a brief and disastrous joint rule with her sister Theodora, whom she extracted from her convent, she married another leading member of the civil aristocracy, Constantine IX Monomachos, and had him proclaimed emperor. During Constantine's reign, which lasted until his death in 1055, the breakdown of the Byzantine army developed at headlong speed. Mercenary forces, including both the Scandinavian and Russian Varangians and bands of Normans from southern Italy, replaced the former peasant-soldiers of Asia Minor. For a time the army retained local effectiveness when well led. George Maniakes recovered Messina and went on to reconquer Syracuse and much of eastern Sicily from the Arabs in 1042. In 1047 the Armenian kingdom of Ani was annexed, completing Byzantine control of the mountainous land to the east of Asia Minor. But the disunity of the army and of its leaders was displayed in a series of military revolts. Meanwhile the Arabs recaptured the territory which Maniakes and his men had won in Sicily.

Apart from the change in the composition and effectiveness of the Byzantine army, the whole military situation in eastern Europe and the Near East was being rapidly transformed by the advance westwards of the peoples of the steppe. As the Pechenegs, Cumans, Uzes, and others pressed forward into the Ukraine, they drove a wedge between the Black Sea and the Kiev state. In this way Russia, for all its immense resources in manpower, ceased to be an effective ally of the empire. The crossing of the Danube and invasion of Bulgaria by the Pechenegs was symptomatic of the new situation. On the eastern

The crown of Constantine IX, believed to have been a gift to the King of Hungary.
The central plaques in cloisonné enamel portray the Emperor, and the Empresses
Zoë and Theodora. It is now in the National Museum, Budapest. *Courtesy of Magyar
Nemzeti Museum, Budapest.*

frontier a new power appeared, that of the Seljuq Turks, who from
their homeland in central Asia swept through Persia and Mesopotamia and captured Baghdad in 1055. The annexation of the kingdom
of Ani removed a buffer state between the Seljuqs and the Byzantines,
who now faced one another along the whole length of the frontier
from the Caucasus to Syria. In the west the Normans of southern Italy
had created an aggressive, expansionist kingdom whose thrust was
directed as much against the Byzantines as against the Arabs of Sicily.
These dramatic changes undermined the whole basis of the Byzantine

supremacy established by the earlier Macedonian emperors, and above all by Basil II.

In 1054 a state of schism was formally declared between the eastern and western churches, when Cardinal Humbert deposited a Bull of Pope Leo IX excommunicating Patriarch Michael Kerularios on the high altar of Hagia Sophia in Constantinople. Relations had nearly reached breaking point in the patriarchate of Photios in the previous century, when King Boris of Bulgaria had been able to play the two churches one against the other. Peace had been patched up, but had now broken down again. The overt differences between the two churches concerned points of theology, such as the Procession of the Holy Spirit (the "filioque" clause), liturgy, such as the use of leavened or unleavened bread in the Eucharist, and ecclesiastical discipline, such as the celibacy of the secular clergy. But underlying these more technical differences were two more fundamental disagreements. The first was that between the pliable, optimistic, sometimes Pelagian outlook of the eastern Church, which was always ready to compromise between the ideal and the possible, and which at bottom believed that men could perfect themselves by their own will, and the more sombre, Augustinian attitude of the Latin Church, with its developed doctrine of original sin and grace. Communication between the two churches often became a dialogue of the deaf which separated them farther instead of bringing them nearer. The second disagreement concerned papal supremacy. Since the Council of Chalcedon in 451 the eastern Church had given precedence to the bishop of Rome over the four eastern patriarchs of Alexandria, Antioch, Jerusalem, and Constantinople. But it had not recognized any right of the pope to interfere in the other patriarchates in matters of ecclesiastical discipline. And on questions of doctrine it recognized only the decisions of an ecumenical council of the Church. The pronouncements of the pope carried no more weight in its eyes than those of any other bishop. Disagreement on the question of papal supremacy was exacerbated by the menacing attitude adopted towards Byzantium by certain of the pope's subjects, and in particular the Normans of southern Italy. Thus the dispute between the clergy of the two churches was drawn into the wake of a political, and eventually a military, confrontation between the empire and the Latin west.

In spite of these radical and threatening changes in the surrounding world, Constantinople in the reign of Constantine IX remained the center of an intellectually and artistically lively activity. Constantine established and endowed higher schools of philosophy and law, sometimes loosely referred to as the Imperial University. There had been several such initiatives in the previous century, notably by Michael III, Basil I, and Constantine VII. But apart from the fact that more is known about Constantine IX's foundations than about those of his predecessors, his activity in this sphere does appear to have had less of an ad hoc character than theirs did. It was evidence not merely of the state's need to train specialists for its own services, but of a dawning realization that one of the elements in the empire's superiority over its neighbors—which no eleventh-century Byzantine doubted for a moment—was precisely its direct access, through the Greek language, to the treasures of ancient thought, and the ability to develop this intellectual tradition fruitfully.

In 1055 Constantine IX died. Zoë had preceded him to the grave, and the now extremely elderly Theodora was acclaimed sole ruler, apparently without serious dispute. She was the last of the Macedonian dynasty, a great-granddaughter of Constantine Porphyrogenitus and a great-great-great-granddaughter of Basil I. This sentiment of loyalty to a dynasty was something new in Byzantine life, and it was destined to remain an important political factor for the next four centuries. It was doubtless connected with the emphasis laid by the Macedonian emperors on central power, and the long reigns enjoyed by some of them, in particular Constantine VII (forty-six years) and Basil II (sixty-two years).

Theodora soon felt death to be imminent, and nominated as her successor Michael VI, a retired civilian official. In 1056 she died. The next year saw a military revolt in Asia Minor headed by Isaac Comnenus, a member of one of the families of the military aristocracy. He succeeded in ousting Michael VI and had himself proclaimed emperor. But by 1059 the combined hostility of the civilian aristocracy of the capital and of the leaders of the Church, who often sprang from the same families, made Isaac's position untenable. He abdicated, and was succeeded by Constantine X Dukas, a pawn of the civilian aristocracy and of its leader, the philosopher, scholar, and statesman Michael Psellos. The old régime of corruption, tax farming, and neglect of defense was restored to power.

The empire's enemies were not slow to exploit its military weakness. In 1064 the Hungarians took the key Danube fortress of Belgrade, while the Uzes invaded the Balkans en masse. In 1065 the Seljuqs broke into Byzantine Armenia and took Ani. Two years later they swept into Asia Minor and captured Caesarea in Cappadocia. In the same year Constantine X died, leaving juvenile sons under a council of regency. Faced with the imminent danger from the Seljuqs, in 1068 his widow married Romanos Diogenes, a Cappadocian magnate with some military experience, and had him proclaimed emperor. Romanos assembled an army consisting largely of Pecheneg, Turkish, and western mercenaries and marched into Asia Minor in the hope of ousting the Seljuqs from the territory which they had occupied. At first he enjoyed some local successes, and penetrated into the mountains of Armenia. But in 1071 a combination of careless strategy and desertion in battle by some mercenary contingents led to a crushing defeat for the Byzantines and the capture of Romanos. It was more than two and a half centuries since a Byzantine emperor had been taken prisoner in battle, and the shock felt in Constantinople was immense. To make matters worse, Bari, the last Byzantine possession in Italy, was captured by the Norman Robert Guiscard in the same summer.

The disarray in Constantinople led to civil war. Michael VII, a son of Constantine X, was proclaimed emperor by a faction of the civilian aristocracy, while Romanos Diogenes, released against promise of ransom by the Seljuq sultan, tried to reassert his authority in Asia Minor. The outcome was the defeat and blinding of Romanos by his rival. Michael VII, the pupil of Michael Psellos, was a poor advertisement for the philosophy professed by his teacher and chief minister. Unable to cope with the difficult situation in the empire, he chose to do nothing. Soon the Bulgarians began a national revolt, which was quelled with the greatest difficulty. The Croatian kingdom seized the opportunity to establish its independence. The whole structure of sovereignty established by Basil II was now in ruins. A series of military revolts in the mid-1070s underlined the dissatisfaction of the military magnates with the corrupt and ineffectual government in Constantinople, and the readiness of many of them to risk the integrity of the empire in order to establish their own personal power. In 1078 one such magnate, Nicephorus Botaneiates, had himself proclaimed emperor and gained possession of the capital with the aid of a faction within the walls. Michael VII abdicated and sought refuge in a monastery. Nicephorus's seizure of power was not welcome to many of his fellow magnates, and a complex struggle for power between provincial military commanders ensued. As what remained of the Byzantine army was engaged in tearing itself to pieces, the Seljuqs advanced still farther westwards and established their Sultanate of Rûm, with its capital at Iconium (Konya) in Phrygia. In this desperate situation Alexios Comnenus, nephew of the late Emperor Isaac Comnenus and head of one of the most powerful military families of Asia Minor, began to build up an alliance of aristocratic clans and to make careful preparations for a march on Constantinople. His preparations bore fruit in 1081, when he forced his way into the capital with scarcely any bloodshed, made Botaneiates abdicate, and had himself proclaimed emperor. Alexios's proclamation marked the beginning of a long period of rule by the provincial military aristocracy, and the end of an epoch which had seen the empire reach the apogee of its power and then plunge into headlong collapse. When Alexios mounted the throne he faced a complex of problems unprecedented in the earlier history of Byzantium.

CONFIDENCE AND CLASSICISM

If the watchword of the years 641–867 was defense, that of the ensuing period was expansion and conquest. The long, slow work of strengthening the empire militarily and of giving it a social cohesion unknown to the late Roman Empire now began to bear fruit. The organization of the *themes*, provinces defended by soldiers who were also landholders and whose younger sons joined a free peasantry of taxpayers and settlers on waste land, the settlement and absorption of countless Slavs, Arabs, Armenians, and others in the depopulated territory of the empire, the sense of solidarity engendered by a long struggle against an infidel foe, had all contributed to a gradual improvement in the military and economic situation of the empire. In the late ninth and early tenth centuries that improvement reached its climax, and the balance of power in the Near East was dramatically changed. Internal dissension and political fragmentation in the Moslem caliphate contributed to the sudden reversal of roles. But the main factor was the internal development of the empire, which had now become a formidable military power.

It was a power which was fatally flawed, for the system of *theme* armies which provided the striking power of a highly centralized empire also gave rise to an ever more ambitious, hereditary aristocracy of military commanders, whose interests clashed with those of the central government. That clash of interest, never successfully resolved, led by the end of the period to the erosion of the military strength of the empire and to a dangerous devolution of its political authority. But these were not dangers which the men of A.D. 900 could foresee. And had they foreseen them there was probably little they could have done to forestall them.

And so, confident in their new power, the rulers of the empire pursued an aggressive policy of expansion, particularly in the east. In their own eyes they were not aggressors—they were only recovering that which was rightly their own. When they conquered their enemies and occupied their territories, they were merely exercising an indisputable right. A sense of superiority to other states and peoples, which often turns to arrogance or downright chauvinism, pervaded much of the "official" literature of the period. Often it took on a racist tone. It was no longer enough to identify one's society as Christian. Since the conversion of Bulgaria there was another Christian state on the very doorstep of the empire. And from the beginning of the tenth century, Christian Bulgaria became a more dangerous foe of the empire than the Moslem Arabs. Later other Christian enemies appeared, in particular the Normans. The Byzantines could no longer see themselves simply as the defenders of Christendom against the infidel. They became in their own eyes both the Chosen People—the New Israel, as they termed themselves—and the heirs and restorers of the Roman Empire.

This conception of their own role often led them to look with disdain on other peoples. The manual of statecraft which Constantine VII composed for his son—known to scholars by the modern title *De Administrando Imperio*—contained many comments on the vices and shortcomings of foreign peoples. "For just as each animal mates with its own tribe," observed the imperial author, "so it is right that each nation also should marry and cohabit not with those of other race and tongue but of the same tribe and speech." In another passage he warned his son:

> If any nation of these infidel and dishonorable tribes of the north shall ever demand a marriage alliance with the emperor of the Romans, and either to take his daughter to wife, or to give a daughter of their own to be wife to the emperor or to the emperor's son, this monstrous demand of theirs also you shall rebut, saying: "Concerning this matter also a dread and authentic charge and ordinance of the great and holy Constantine is engraved upon the sacred table of the universal church of the Christians, St. Sophia, that never shall an emperor of the Romans ally himself in marriage with a nation of customs differing from and alien to those of the Roman order . . . unless it be with the Franks alone."

There had clearly been a great change from the days when Justinian II and Constantine V married princesses of the Khazars. The fact that Constantine VII's own niece by marriage was the wife of King Peter of Bulgaria is dismissed with the remark that the Emperor Romanos Lekapenos, who arranged the marriage, was a "common illiterate fellow, and not from among those who have been bred up in the palace, and have followed the Roman national customs from the beginning; nor was he of imperial and noble stock, and for this reason in most of his actions he was arrogant and despotic."

Liudprand of Cremona, who visited Constantinople several times in the mid-tenth century as ambassador of the German Emperor Otto I, complains of the contemptuous treatment he received at the court of Nicephorus Phokas. The emperor told him:

> Your master's soldiers can fight neither on horseback nor on foot, because of the size of their shields, the weight of their armor, and the length of their swords. Their gluttony hinders them too, since their stomach is their god. They are courageous only when they are drunk, and cowards when they are sober. Neither has your master a fleet worth mentioning. I alone have naval power, and I will attack him with my ships, destroy his coastal cities, and reduce to ashes those on the banks of rivers. And who, tell me, has the forces to resist me on land?

It is in the light of this arrogant self-confidence and this contempt for foreign peoples that one can understand such atrocities as the wholesale blinding of the defeated Bulgarian army by Basil II, which was utterly contrary to the theory and practice of medieval warfare.

Most of the twenty or so great families of the military aristocracy were of foreign origin, largely Armenian, since the mountainous area of eastern Asia Minor was a reservoir of manpower. They had in the course of time become hellenized, and if they belonged to a heretical Church, as most Armenians did, converted to Orthodoxy. Yet some of them retained a sense of ethnic identity and a feeling of resentment towards the dominant Greek culture, which they had themselves embraced. Thus Gregory Pakourianos, a soldier who had risen to the rank of Domestic of the West, or commander-in-chief of the imperial forces in Europe, in his retirement founded a monastery at Bachkovo, in present-day Bulgaria. In the deed of foundation of his monastery he proclaimed that he belonged to "the glorious people of the Georgians," he insisted on his monks knowing the Georgian language; and he forbade any "Roman" ever to become a monk there on account of their violence, their tittle-tattle, and their greed. The chance survival of this document reveals the almost schizophrenic state of mind which must have been shared by many Byzantine officers of non-Greek origin.

For the lower ranks in the army and for ordinary civilians, the situation was even more difficult. They were discriminated against in a variety of ways. There was bitter religious strife between the predominantly Greek Orthodox Church and the countless Armenian immigrants who flocked into Byzantine territory after the annexation by the empire of the four Armenian kingdoms—Taron in 968, Taiq in 1000, Vaspurakan in 1021 and Ani in 1045. In the early eleventh century the Byzantine government tried to force ecclesiastical union upon the Monophysite Armenians and Syrians. The Jacobite patriarch of Antioch was arrested and deported to Macedonia. His successor fled to Moslem territory. In 1040 the Constantinopolitan church issued pronouncements restricting the right of intermarriage between Orthodox and Monophysite citizens and the right of Monophysites to give evidence in court. In the 1060s all who did not accept the Chalcedonian faith were ordered to be expelled from the city of Melitene, and their religious books to be burned. Armenian and Syrian prelates and clergy were arrested, imprisoned, and exiled. Many of the now numerous non-Greek non-Orthodox subjects of the empire were treated as second-class citizens, and it is no wonder that they sometimes responded in kind. When Romanos Diogenes led his army to meet the Seljuqs, the Greeks in eastern Asia Minor complained that they suffered more at the hands of the Armenians than at those of the Turkish invaders, and the emperor had to take special security measures to protect the army against the citizens whom it purported to defend. At the crucial battle of Manzikert, Armenian contingents were the first to break ranks and flee, according to one chronicler.

Thus Byzantine society, in identifying itself no longer simply as Christian (as opposed to infidel), but rather as Greek Orthodox Christian, undermined that social cohesion which had been built up in the years of resistance against Arab onslaught. In the end this contributed to the crisis in which the empire found itself in the second half of the eleventh century.

Contempt and mistrust for foreigners extended to the foreign mercenaries and their leaders, who played so important a role in the defense of the empire. Kekaumenos, a retired general, wrote a kind of *vade-mecum* for his sons after the mid-eleventh century, which included an imaginary speech of advice addressed to the emperor. He warned the sovereign of the danger which foreign forces represented, and quoted many examples from history of their unreliability and treachery. He was particularly indignant at the way in which foreign *condottieri*, men of no account in their own country, had high Byzantine dignities conferred upon them. This, he declared, diminished the prestige of the empire and gave the foreigners so rewarded an inflated idea of their own importance. "If foreigners serve you, Sire, for their uniform and their rations, they will serve you loyally and wholeheartedly, looking to you for a handful of coins and their food. But if you promote a foreigner above the rank of *spatharocandidatus*, he at once begins to despise you and will not serve you as he should." In fact, many Byzantines sought to blame foreigners for the decline in their own society which had become visible since the death of Basil II in 1025, but whose roots stretched much further back. This left a heritage of xenophobia to later generations, and colored in particular Byzantine attitudes towards the Catholic Latins.

Another crucial feature of this period was the struggle between the military and the civilian or bureaucratic groups for control of central power. The military aristocracy sought to make the soldiers a privileged group within the state. The Emperor Nicephorus Phokas insisted that they and their families must be exempt from taxation, must not be "at the mercy of the civil jurisdiction, to be arrested and scourged like slaves," but subject only to the jurisdiction of their own officers, must be treated with respect, and not looked down on or despised. The soldiers mistrusted the refinements of the court and the capital. "Do not wish to be a bureaucrat," Kekaumenos warned his sons, "for it is impossible to be both a general and a comedian." The civilians in their turn despised the soldiers as boorish and uncultured. Psellos recognized something of the greatness of Basil II, but complained of the austerity of his reign and the lack of esteem for culture which he encouraged. The difference between the civilian and military schemes of values is brought out strikingly in two characterizations of the Emperor Michael VII Dukas, the former pupil of Psellos. Psellos's own description of his imperial pupil was too long to be quoted in its entirety. But it made him out to be a paragon of all the virtues—except courage and decisiveness. He combined the words and deeds of a monarch with the profundity of a philosopher, the persuasiveness of a rhetorician, the skill of a mathematician and man of science. He knew all that was to be found in books, and could improvise a poem—although his command of classical meter was not quite perfect. His laughter brought joy, his tears pity. He rarely displayed anger. He enjoyed hunting up to a point, but preferred his prey to escape. He was unmoved by the panoply of imperial power, but sought rather the perfection of a philosopher. Thus far Psellos. His contemporary, the historian John Skylitzes, reflected in general the view of the military aristocracy. This is what he had to say about Michael VII: "He busied himself continuously with the useless and unending study of eloquence and with the composition of iambics and anapaests; moreover he was not proficient in this art, but being deceived and beguiled by the consul of the philosophers [Michael Psellos], he destroyed the whole world, so to speak." The same historian, speaking of the disintegration of the army in the middle of the eleventh century, wrote, "The soldiers themselves, abandoning their weapons and the army, became lawyers and keen followers of legal questions and problems . . . The army was unarmed and depressed because of the lack of pay and provisions: and only the barest section of it was present, for the bravest part of the army had been removed from the military rolls."

Such is the background against which the literature, thought, and art of the period must be seen. Both groups in the ruling class had their own reasons to lay emphasis upon the cultural tradition of the Byzantines and to seek to recreate something of the intellectual world of late antiquity, of which they felt themselves to be the heirs. The process of reaching back to revive Hellenic tradition began at the end of the previous period. Photios, the future patriarch, sought out and read a vast number of books, including classical, Hellenistic, and patristic works which no longer survive, and included summaries and/or critical discussions of them in his *Bibliotheke*, written about the mid-ninth century. He seems to have been at the center of a group of officials and others interested in widening and deepening their knowledge of their literary heritage. Among their aims was that of restoring the use of atticizing literary Greek, which had been virtually forgotten during the seventh and eighth centuries. To this end they compiled lexica of rare and unusual words, no longer familiar in the spoken language of their own time.

An important factor in the incipient revival of classical literary culture was the introduction of a new book hand, based on a stylization and regularization of the cursive hand used for letters and documents. The new hand was developed about the beginning of the ninth century, probably in response to the needs of theological controversy. It could be written more quickly and took up less space than the old majuscule, in which each letter was written separately. (The material normally used for books at this time, parchment, was expensive. A manuscript of Plato, copied in 895 and now in the Bodleian Library in Oxford, cost twenty-one gold nomismata, of which thirteen were for the wages of the calligrapher and eight for the parchment. The supply of parchment could not be increased to meet demand, since it was made from the skins of animals slaughtered for food. There was a close correlation between the supply of parchment and that of meat.) The new hand soon became the normal hand for books, while the old majuscule, now used only for the liturgical books of the Church, became more and more ornate and fussy. As books long lost or forgotten were recovered by searching in monastic and other libraries, they were recopied into the more convenient new style of writing, and excerpts from old commentaries, lexica, and other reading aids were often added in the wide margins provided for this purpose.

The ninth-century scholars and copyists seem to have confined themselves largely to prose works. This was not because they did not know or did not appreciate poetry: they recorded countless poetic words in their lexica. It was rather because poetry often dealt with the world of imagination and emotion, a world in which these men, trained by the study of Aristotelian logic, felt ill at ease. It was also a world which was traditionally the domain of the Church. To venture into it could lead to suspicion of heresy or crypto-paganism. But by

Book cover decorated with jewels, and portraits of saints and the Crucifixion in the fine cloisonné enamel; late ninth century. *Courtesy of Biblioteca Marciana, Venice.*

the early tenth century these inhibitions were overcome, and Homer, Pindar, the Attic dramatists, and the Hellenistic poets were being transcribed into the new hand and equipped with marginal commentaries to aid readers in understanding them. Probably none of the surviving manuscripts is the first transcription of a classical or patristic text from the old majuscule hand. But there are many which can be only a few removes from the original transcription, and which give some idea of what it looked like. Among these are some of the survivors from the library of Arethas, archbishop of Caesarea in the first half of the tenth century. A cold, calculating ecclesiastical politician, Arethas was also a passionate bibliophile and lover of literature, who sought out rare books and had them copied on the finest vellum by the most elegant penmen. Another manuscript of the same kind is the splendid Venetus A of the *Iliad* now in the Biblioteca Marciana in Venice.

By the mid-tenth century virtually all the surviving texts had been transcribed into the new hand and made available, in the capital at least, to a generation of readers eager to learn to handle its incomparable heritage. For these men the literature of antiquity provided models to be copied. The art of writing occasional poetry in classical meters—dedications, epitaphs, descriptions of works of art, genre pieces and the like—was revived. Constantine Kephalas, an ecclesiastic and teacher, compiled c. 900 a great anthology of epigrams, reaching from the earliest beginnings of Greek poetry to his own day, and equipped with notes on the authorship and occasion of the various poems. Kephalas's anthology no longer survives in its original form, but a shortened version exists in a mid-tenth-century manuscript. The writing of short poems in the simple iambic meter was taught to schoolboys, though the more difficult hexameter and elegiac meters were beyond their capacity. The occasional poem in classical meters continued to be one of the most frequently practiced literary genres throughout the later Byzantine period and beyond. There was a lively production of poetry in classical meters in the tenth and eleventh centuries. Leo VI himself wrote some colorless occasional poems side by side with his sermons, liturgical hymns, and other works. John

Geometres (active second half of the tenth century) wrote hymns, religious poems, and epigrams, some of which display real poetic feeling as well as technical virtuosity. Constantine the Sicilian (first half of the tenth century) was a far from negligible minor poet, and John Mauropous and Christopher of Mytilene (both mid-eleventh century) occasionally rose above the limitations of their medium in their poetic addresses and descriptive poems. Mauropous's little poem in which he called on God to spare from damnation Plato and Plutarch was not only a masterpiece of form, but also indicates a new attitude to pagan literature and thought.

> If you are willing to spare any pagans from your punishment, my Christ, may you choose Plato and Plutarch for my sake. For both clung closely in word and in deed to your laws. If they did not know that you are Lord of all, only your charity is needed here, through which you are willing to save all men for nothing in return.[2]

In the same way Byzantine men of letters passed from the study of classical Greek historians to imitation of their methods and style. Side by side with the chronicle, which was concerned essentially with recording events in order, we begin to find a new interest in the character of the participants in those events, their motives and their understanding of what they were doing. The important was distinguished from the trivial, and the causes and effects of events were explored. The earliest historical works which show this new humanist approach are two histories of the recent past commissioned by Constantine VII during the years when real power lay in the hands of his father-in-law, Romanos Lekapenos. The authors of these works—and one of them was probably composed in part by Constantine himself—had clearly studied the historians and biographers of antiquity, in particular Polybius and Plutarch, and learned from them how to go beyond a simple chronological narrative and to seek understanding of the why and the how of history. They set a pattern which was followed with increasing confidence and skill by a succession of historians, culminating in those who recorded the final collapse of the Byzantine Empire in the fifteenth century and the fall of Constantinople to the Ottoman Turks.

The rhetorical theory of antiquity—which was really a theory of literature as a whole—was revived and studied. Men began by composing commentaries on the great textbooks of the past, to make them accessible to Byzantine students. The earliest, by John of Sardis, probably belongs to the early ninth century, and it was followed by many other longer and more comprehensive commentaries, which included more and more original observations. These commentaries gradually took on the character of independent textbooks, and were often accompanied by collections of model compositions in different genres and styles which replaced or supplemented those surviving from antiquity. Writers schooled in this tradition learned to handle literary Greek with ever-growing assurance, sense of style, and clarity. To see the results of two centuries of the study and practice of rhetoric one need only compare the prose of Photios—awkward, strained, and tortuous—with that of Michael Psellos—lucid, exciting, varied, and sophisticated. In the former case one has the impression that a powerful intellect is struggling with an imperfect medium of communication. With Psellos, medium and message are perfectly adapted to one another.

The correct—or near-correct—use of the archaizing literary language and acquaintance with its world of allusion and reference became a mark of social distinction in a metropolitan society dominated by highly literate bureaucrats. The unconstrained language of the seventh and eighth centuries was rejected with expressions of contempt and disgust. It could be used for works of popular edification or for technical writing. But serious writing called for imitative, archaizing language. Writers were highly conscious of the choice of linguistic forms open to them, and often motivate or excuse their choice in a preface. For instance Constantine VII, in his manual of statecraft addressed to his son—which was of course not a public document— observed that he had chosen "not to make a display of fine writing or of atticizing style, swollen with the sublime and the lofty, but rather by means of everyday conversational narrative to teach you that of which you should not be ignorant." Theophanes Nonnos, the compiler of a tenth-century medical encyclopaedia, pointed out that it

Miniature of Basil II from his Psalter made in Constantinople between 1017 and
1025. The prostrate figures in the foreground represent conquered Bulgarians. *Courtesy of Biblioteca Marciana, Venice, and Scala/Art Resource, New York.*

was not through ignorance that he made use of "nouns and verbs taken from the market-place and the cross-roads and barbarous and corrupt expressions." The retired general Kekaumenos, distrustful of the culture of the capital, wrote to his sons: "I have no part in letters; for I never studied Hellenic culture to acquire well-turned speech and learn eloquence. I know that some will censure me and cavil at my ignorance. But I have not composed this as a work of literature for others, but for you, my sons, flesh of my flesh."

The extent to which the use of language served as a mark of social distinction is astonishing. It underlines the fact that the society of the Macedonian age was much more "high-pitched" than that of the preceding Dark Age. Both in the capital and in the provinces the distance between those at the top and those at the bottom was increasing and was more regularly marked. The diplomatic correspondence of Leo Choirosphaktes in the early tenth century is an extraordinary pastiche of the Greek of the Roman Empire, full of rare words, obsolete constructions, and recondite allusions. Yet these letters are not the amusements of a quirky scholar but state papers of the utmost importance. A manual of court ceremonial by a certain Leon Katakylas was rejected by Constantine VII because its author was "lacking in Hellenic culture." In the second half of the tenth century Symeon the Logothete rewrote the corpus of lives of saints used for liturgical purposes. Many of these texts were of provincial origin and couched in easygoing or downright popular Greek. Symeon redrafted them in what he felt was language worthy of the subject, with obsolete words, classical constructions, and high-flown circumlocutions. Much of the concrete detail of the original texts was replaced by elegant statements of doctrine and pompous injunctions to virtue. Symeon's "modernized" texts were adopted for liturgical use, and their more unpretentious originals have often been lost. The constant repetition of these precious texts must have helped to direct popular taste towards the archaic and away from the simplicity of living speech.

Another feature of the classicizing renaissance of the period was the production of encyclopaedic works, purporting to summarize the knowledge of the ancients on this or that topic. Many of these were compiled under the direct patronage of Constantine VII. Thus it was in the library and scriptoria of the palace that the material was found for the *Book of Ceremonies*, which preserves records of imperial ceremonial going back to the age of Justinian and earlier, for the treatise on foreign affairs addressed by Constantine to his son, and for a handbook on the provinces of the empire. Another work originating in the palace was the so-called *Constantinian Excerpts*, a vast collection of lengthy extracts from Greek historians from Herodotus to the ninth century, arranged by subject-matter—On Embassies, On Virtues and Vices, On Ambushes, etc. As the imperial sponsor naïvely remarked, this arrangement saved the reader the trouble of reading the original works. A collection of excerpts on natural history and others on agriculture, on medicine, and on veterinary science can with some confidence also be attributed to the initiative of Constantine VII. The same is true of a synopsis of the great legal corpus of his father, Leo VI. There is, however, no direct connection proven between the emperor and the great tenth-century dictionary of literature, the *Suda*. The *Suda* is a very long alphabetical dictionary of authors, noteworthy words, and literary topics, based on similar compilations of late antiquity and on the lexica and commentaries composed in the ninth century. It preserves, often in garbled or ambiguous form, a great deal of priceless information on classical antiquity.

This encyclopaedism of the mid-tenth century stands in sharp contrast to the search for classical texts so prominent in the two preceding generations. Men felt that they had recovered the Hellenic heritage. What mattered now was to make it readily accessible, particularly to those who had neither the opportunity nor the inclination to peruse the original texts. That in breaking up so much ancient literature into convenient snippets they were destroying much of its value does not appear to have occurred to the self-confident encyclopaedists. How far their work contributed to the loss of the original texts which they epitomized or excerpted is an open question. Books were costly objects in the Middle Ages, and a man would not copy or have copied lengthy texts if he was persuaded that the gist of them could be found in more compendious works. The case of the *Constantinian Excerpts* is an interesting one, as, once their excerpting was done, the excerptors may have simply thrown away the unique collection of historical texts from which they worked. Of the *Excerpts* themselves only three and a half sections survive of the original fifty-eight.

Some of these encyclopaedic works were compiled for the private use of their authors, but others bear witness to the existence of a literate, reading public which wanted easy access to knowledge. In lives of saints and other documents of the period, one regularly meets the young man who learns to read and write and studies the Psalms in his native town in the provinces, and who then goes on to the capital to pursue the literary education which would enable him to handle the literary language and make a career in the bureaucracy of state or church. Education provided a channel of social mobility in a society which had become much less egalitarian, and the encyclopaedic compilations made this social mobility easier.

Language and rhetoric were not the only features of the high culture of late antiquity which the age of the Macedonians sought to imitate and absorb and make its own. For centuries all that was readily available of Greek philosophy was the logic of Aristotle, often accompanied by a commentary by the Neoplatonist Porphyry. Some acquaintance with Aristotelian logic was necessary for the conduct of theological argument, and crude epitomes seem often to have been attributed to prestigious names of Church Fathers. Now the texts of the great philosophers themselves were more readily available. Splendid manuscripts of Plato were copied at the end of the ninth century—one of them at the behest of Arethas of Caesarea. Men began to study not only Plato and Aristotle, but also the Neoplatonist philosophers of late antiquity—Plotinus, Porphyry, Iamblichus, Proklos, and others. Philosophy was probably still looked on by most Byzantines who concerned themselves with it as the handmaiden of theology. But others began to see it as an autonomous intellectual discipline, with its own aims and its own rules. This was a somewhat difficult position to maintain, since many of the late Greek philosophers were pagans with a firm anti-Christian stance, and since the philosophical speculations of the ancients often led them to conclu-

Portrait of Michael Psellos (on the left), philosopher, historian, and statesman, from a twelfth-century manuscript on Mount Athos. *Courtesy of Patriarchal Institute, Vlatadon Monastery.*

sions at variance with Christian dogma on such matters as the nature of the soul or the eternal existence of the universe. Nevertheless such was the prestige and attraction of philosophy by the mid-eleventh century that an imperially sponsored school of philosophy was set up in the reign of Constantine IX Monomachos, with Michael Psellos at its head. Psellos himself was steeped in the Neoplatonism of Proklos, towards which he often adopted a somewhat uncritical attitude. He was convinced that philosophy was a method of arriving at the truth which was neither opposed to nor subservient to revealed religion, the dogmas of which he never challenged. But it was easy to attack him as a crypto-pagan, and attacked he often was. The protection of his imperial patrons saved him from what might have been unpleasant consequences. But a clearly defined zone of conflict between the classicizing intellectuals of Byzantium and the Church was beginning to appear. A certain woolliness of thought on Psellos's part and his own skill as a controversialist helped him to avoid a direct confrontation with the authorities of the Church. He was rebuked as a Platonist by the patriarch John Xiphilinos and defended himself in a spirited and courageous letter, in which he staked out a claim for philosophy as an autonomous science, which could in the end only confirm the truth of true religious beliefs.

Psellos was a many-sided man of letters, as much rhetorician as philosopher, and he played a dominant role in the government under several emperors. Of relatively humble origin, he provided an example of the social mobility conferred by education in the metropolitan society of the eleventh century. His successor as head of the imperial school of philosophy was a man of very different character. John Italos was born in Italy, the son of a Norman mercenary and a Greek woman from southern Italy. When he came to study philosophy under Michael Psellos he seems to have been already about thirty. He had none of the literary graces of Psellos and little of his personal charm and pliability. His enemies said he had an Italian accent and never really learned to speak Greek, by which they meant the archaizing, learned tongue. But John Italos was a brilliant dialectician and a man with a passion for truth which would tolerate no compromise. The young flocked to his lectures, attracted by the boldness and clarity of his thought. A faction in the Church accused him of heresy and paganism, alleging that he was teaching youth to undermine the Christian faith. He was acquitted in 1076, but he still had many enemies, and he did not know how to bend before the storm. After Alexios Comnenus seized power in 1081, John Italos was open to attack on several grounds—as an adherent of the deposed Dukas dynasty, as a Norman at a time when Norman armies were invading Byzantine territory, as a diplomat who had conducted negotiations with the papacy resulting in damage to Byzantine interests, as the intellectual leader of the younger generation of that civilian aristocracy which the new emperor was determined to oust from power. He was again hauled before the ecclesiastical courts, and this time convicted, in a trial whose political character could not be hidden. Found guilty, he was dismissed from his post and vanished, a broken man.

The condemnation of John Italos, occurring at the very end of the period under consideration, marked the end of what the French Byzantinist, Paul Lemerle, has called *"le gouvernement des philosophes."* The new régime, while encouraging literature and the arts, was careful not to provoke conflict with any important group in the Church, and speculative philosophy was frowned upon. However, as we shall see, the study of Hellenic philosophical tradition was not abandoned. The Pandora's box, once opened, could not be closed again. Much as the cultures of the eleventh and twelfth centuries in Byzantium have in common, the sudden change in the attitude of the authorities towards Greek philosophy is one indication among many that the closing decades of the eleventh century marked an important break in the history of Byzantine society. A new foreign environment, with new enemies; a new social structure in the countryside; a new political régime: all these were reflected in new attitudes towards the heritages of Hellenism and Christianity.

In the rich and varied intellectual life of the Macedonian age flowed many different currents, of which one of the most interesting is the revival of religious mysticism. Some believers, and in particular monks, had always sought and occasionally attained the kind of exaltation which they interpreted as the direct experience of the presence of God. But since the days of St. John Climacus few had tried to describe their mystical experiences or to give systematic help to others on how to attain them. In the last decades of the tenth century and the first part of the eleventh, Symeon the New Theologian, monk and later abbot of the monastery of St. Mamas in Constantinople, explored anew the theory and practice of contemplation leading to union with God. Directly or indirectly he drew on the works of the great mystics of the age of the fathers, and through them on the Neoplatonist mysticism of the late pagan world. He set out his theory and practice in a corpus of fifty-eight hymns, in which passion, theological insight, and a vivid, direct style, full of striking and original images, are combined. His hymns are not composed in classical quantitative meters but in simple accentual meters, above all in the fifteen-syllable "political verse" in which most Greek popular poetry has been couched up to the present day. Symeon was the first writer to make extensive use of this meter. The origin of the "political verse" has been the subject of much dispute. It seems likely, though not proven, that it was the meter of the rhythmical acclamations chanted in the Byzantine court, and ultimately goes back to the meter in which Roman soldiers hailed their triumphant generals, often in scurrilous Latin verses. At any rate Symeon's use of it for serious subjects was a break with a long literary tradition, and an attempt to speak to simple people in a metrical form which they could understand and remember and which owed nothing to classical models. The sureness of Symeon's touch is borne out by the extraordinary success of the "political meter" throughout the succeeding centuries. Symeon's language is literary Greek, though without the archaism and affectation of the atticists. The spoken language of the people was still too fluid to be the vehicle of his passionate message, which was often intellectually challenging.

Symeon had no immediate successors. But his ideas dominate all later mysticism in the Orthodox church and came to the fore again in the fourteenth century, when another great contemplative movement swept through the monasteries of the Byzantine world. Though utterly different in aim and method from philosophers like Michael Psellos, he was nevertheless part of the same upsurge of intellectual and emotional exploration. Where Psellos sought his inspiration in the thought of the Neoplatonists, Symeon turned for his to another part of Hellenic tradition, that embodied in the great ascetics of the patristic age. For all their differences, they have in common a bounding and confident curiosity.

So far Byzantine culture has been discussed as if it were coextensive with Constantinopolitan culture. Byzantine society in this period was certainly very highly centralized, but it would be rash to assume that

The rock-cut churches of Cappadocia. These extraordinary rock formations in the Göreme Valley had dwellings and churches carved into them in which a provincial style of art remained unaffected by metropolitan influences. *Courtesy of Josephine Powell.*

there was no literature of provincial origin. A case in point is the epic poem of Digenis Akritas, which is in fact a rather mechanical juxtaposition of two poems, perhaps by different authors. It survives in a number of distinct Greek versions, some of which show clear traces of having passed through a stage of oral transmission, and in an Old Russian version probably made about the thirteenth century. Both the original poems deal with life in the border areas of eastern Cappadocia and Armenia, where Byzantines and Arabs lived to- gether in a strange mixture of hostility and cooperation, and where individuals and groups easily passed from one side to the other. The first poem recounts how a border emir, himself a Byzantine taken prisoner in childhood and brought up in the Moslem faith, kidnaps the daughter of a Byzantine grandee of the Dukas family. The girl's brothers defeat the emir in battle and force him to return with them to Byzantine territory. There he is converted and marries his captive. A son is born to them whom they call Basil Digenis Akritas (=Twain-born Borderer). After various adventures the emir goes back to Arab territory and returns, bringing his mother, his family, and many Arab followers, all of whom are converted and settled in Byzantine lands. The poem has a clear storyline which reflects the realities of life in the borderlands and avoids the marvellous or supernatural. The second poem is full of folktale motives and magic. It describes the childhood and education of the young Basil, his adventures with marauding bands of cattle rustlers, and his courtship of Eudokia, the daughter of a border grandee. She elopes with him, and they live in the wild borderlands, where Basil kills bandits and imposes law and order. In a second section of the poem Basil recounts a series of adventures, including the rescue of Eudokia from a dragon, a curiously erotically colored combat with an Amazon, and an affair with the daughter of an emir. A third section describes the great castle which he built near the Euphrates and the life he and Eudokia pursued there. Finally he dies at the age of thirty-three—like Alexander the Great, Julian the Apostate, and Jesus—and his wife drops dead of grief beside him.

This composite poem is known only in later manuscripts. But many factors suggest that both sections of it were composed in the ninth or tenth century. It is not popular poetry; there are echoes in it of Homer, Pindar, Arrian, and other classical writers, which point to a learned author or editor. And though some of the later versions are in vulgar Greek, the original seems to have been couched in literary, though not atticizing, Greek. The location of the events narrated, the almost total neglect of the capital and the emperor—who appears once briefly and rather impersonally—and the whole romantic, ballad-like tone of the narrative suggest the work of a poet or poets who knew and understood the life of the eastern borderlands; perhaps a man of education in the service of one of the border barons. Whether he drew on earlier ballad literature is an open question. The surviving later ballads concerning Digenis Akritas derive from the epic and not vice versa. In the later Byzantine period the poem enjoyed popularity, and the adventures of Digenis were even depicted on painted pottery. There are also traces of an illustrated manuscript of the poem, now lost. How much other material of this kind may have existed it is impossible to say.

A large number of churches probably built during the Macedonian age survive in various regions of the Byzantine Empire. Athens has at least five. They are mostly quite small buildings, and are almost without exception of the cross-in-square pattern, with a small central dome raised on a drum. There are sometimes secondary domes either on the arms of the cross or on the corners of the building between the arms. Many of these churches were adorned with pictures either in mosaic or in the less expensive fresco, but few examples of this monumental decoration survive. Two such churches were built in the reigns of Basil I and Leo VI within the vast complex of buildings forming the Great Palace at Constantinople. Neither is still standing. But from a surviving sermon of Patriarch Photios, probably delivered at its inauguration, we learn a good deal about one of them, the Nea or New Church. It was on a considerably larger scale than most of the surviving churches, as befitted an imperial foundation. It was of the cross-in-square pattern, with subsidiary domes over the spaces between the arms of the cross. The interior walls were decorated in mosaic. In the central dome was a bust of Christ Pantocrator (Ruler of All), in the apse a full-length portrait of the Virgin, flanked by saints who intercede for the sins of mankind; along the walls were narrative pictures of events in the Gospel story and of saints, and so on.

It is clear that after the final rejection of Iconoclasm, a standard iconographical scheme for the decoration of churches evolved in the course of the ninth century and was repeated from building to building over the centuries with little change—Christ Pantocrator in the dome, the Virgin, usually accompanied by saints, in the apse, saints of special importance (perhaps those to whom the church was dedicated) in the pendentives of the dome, where they existed. Along the walls of the nave the upper register was filled with representations of stages in the Incarnation, sometimes supplemented by events in the life of the Virgin, while the lower register was reserved for portraits of saints, stiffly and frontally depicted, each with his own traditional iconography, and recalling the repetitive procession of martyrs in the sixth-century church of St. Apollinare Nuovo in Ravenna. Where there was a portico or narthex, it was reserved for the prophets, sometimes arranged in a kind of family tree, the so-called Tree of Jesse, in whose branches in later churches strange pseudo-prophets sometimes lurked, such as Plato and Aristotle, and even Aristophanes. The church thus became a kind of microcosm of the universe, a constant reminder of the scheme of salvation of mankind. There was little scope for innovation or for the infiltration of classical motifs here. And so far as can be discovered, the monumental art of the period was little influenced by the classicizing tendencies of the age. But we may well be wrong, since so little has survived.

There are, however, plenty of surviving works of portable religious art. Regrettably these do not include many icons, but book illustrations and carved ivories exist in abundance. There are several senses in which a return to the study and imitation of classical models can be seen. By "classical models" is meant mosaics, paintings, and above all illustrated manuscripts dating from the fourth century A.D. and later, many of which, in their turn, were copied from Hellenistic models. The first and most superficial sense was the introduction of architectural backgrounds of classical inspiration, and in particular those derived from the Roman stage. The most obvious example was the decorative arch, sometimes with stage curtains attached, which was used as a frame for everything from Easter tables to illustrations in medical textbooks. Evangelists were often portrayed seated in a kind of niche in a long decorative wall, in the position sometimes occupied by statues of poets in the Roman theater. Similar classical architectural backgrounds, often of quite inappropriate character, can be

David seated on a rock playing his harp, from a tenth-century Paris Psalter. The illustration is an example of the adoption of classical iconography for religious themes.

Courtesy of Bibliothèque Nationale, Paris (Hirmer Fotoarchiv).

found in manuscript pictures of all kinds. Another kind of superficial classical borrowing was the bucolic or idyllic background, which was also inappropriately introduced into religious pictures.

A more important type of classical borrowing was represented by the introduction of personifications and allegorical figures, often clearly modelled on classical originals. Reclining river gods frequently appeared in biblical and other religious scenes. The portrait of Isaiah in a tenth-century Paris Psalter[3] is flanked by a draped female figure with a billowing hood over her head, and labelled "Night," and by a child carrying a torch and labelled "Dawn." The picture of David[4] in the same manuscript shows the Psalmist seated on a rock amidst bucolic scenery, playing upon his harp. In the foreground a reclining half-draped male figure reminiscent of a classical river god is labelled "Mount Bethlehem." Seated upon the rock beside the Psalmist, with her left hand resting lightly upon his shoulder, is a draped female figure of classical aspect, labelled "Melody." Another female figure, unlabelled and so far unidentified, peeps from behind a column to the right of David. The background to the picture is formed by lightly-drawn classical architectural motifs. These examples could be paralleled many times from illuminated psalters, Gospel books, and patristic texts of the period.

A further stage in the classicizing of religious pictures takes place when the figures in them are modelled on exemplars from classical art. Thus the figure of David seated upon a rock, surrounded by animals and playing his harp, was an adaptation of the iconography of Orpheus. The portraits of the evangelists in Gospel books were often closely modelled, down to the details of their drapery, on classical portraits of philosophers. For instance the splendid seated Matthew in a Gospel book now on Mount Athos[5] was copied directly or indirectly from a statue of Epicurus, of which a Roman copy is preserved in the Palazzo Margherita in Rome. The picture of the reception of David and Saul in Jerusalem in the Paris Psalter,[6] in which the two figures in armor stand at the right side, while one Israelite woman dances in the foreground and another stands somewhat indifferently in the background beside a columned structure which represents Jerusalem,

The reception of David and Saul in Jerusalem from the Paris Psalter. The scene is based on a Greek painting of the meeting of Iphigenia with Orestes and Pylades.

Courtesy of Bibliothèque Nationale, Paris (Hirmer Fotoarchiv).

Ivory statuette of the Virgin and
Child—the only free-standing Byzantine ivory statue that has survived.
Dating from the eleventh century, it is
now in the Victoria and Albert Museum, London. *Courtesy of Victoria and Albert Museum, London.*

is modelled in all its details except the dancer in the foreground on a painting illustrating the meeting of Iphigeneia with Orestes and Pylades in Euripides' *Iphigeneia in Tauris*. The original painting, perhaps a Hellenistic work, does not survive. But two fresco copies were found in Pompeii. These examples too could easily be multiplied.

Perhaps the most important effect of the increased interest in classical models was the general tendency to replace the flat, frontal, abstract, spiritualized representations of the human figure so common since the seventh century by rounded, solid, naturalistic representations, which reflected the real, spatial world. Not that there is much evidence of artists going back to nature. What they copied and adapted was, as usual, the work of other artists. This rebirth of naturalism affected the monumental art of church decoration relatively little. Its effect was most striking in the self-contained pictures of the book illustrator. Such magnificent specimens of tenth- or early eleventh-century art as the Paris Psalter,[7] the Paris Gregory of Nazianzus (in particular the Vision of Ezekiel),[8] the Psalter of Basil II,[9] and the Menology of Basil II[10] are remarkable for the naturalism of figures and drapery, their relation to other objects in a real three-dimensional space, and the expressiveness of pose, gesture, and facial expression. The same may be said, *mutatis mutandis*, of many ivory sculptures of the period, such as the Harbaville Triptych, now in the Louvre, or the Virgin Hodegetria, now in Liège Cathedral, or the Virgin and Child in the Victoria and Albert Museum in London.

Imperial portraiture, of which many examples survive from this period, though more rigid and stylized than illustration of biblical themes, often shows the same classical influences. The mosaic portrait of Leo VI prostrate before Christ in the gallery of St. Sophia is still flat and abstract. The same is true nearly two centuries later of the enamel of Irene Dukaina, consort of Alexios Comnenus, in the Pala d'Oro in St. Mark's in Venice, and even truer of the miniature of Nicephorus Botaneiates and his consort Maria of Alania in a Paris manuscript of John Chrysostom,[11] though here there is some discrepancy between the flat, disproportionate, symbolic bodies and the naturalistic faces. With the graceful ivories of the coronation of Constantine VII or of his son Romanos II (Moscow, Municipal Museum of Fine Art, and Cabinet des Médailles, Paris) we are at once in a different world of natural representation of the human body, its movement and its draperies. The mosaic imperial portraits in the galleries of St. Sophia—Alexander in the north gallery, Constantine IX and Zoë in the south gallery—though constrained by rigid iconographical traditions, still show signs of the new tendency, especially in the treatment of the faces.

Classicism in literature and classicism in the visual arts were no doubt both part of a single movement, in which the leading circles of Byzantine society turned to modes of expression more appropriate to their sense of power and their feeling of superiority to other communities. But they differed in a number of ways. First of all, literature, and particularly classicizing literature in archaizing atticist language, was produced by and for a very limited section of society, which had enjoyed a literary and rhetorical education. It was, to use a modern term, inherently élitist. The visual arts carried their message to much more extensive sections of society. For the illiterate—and most Byzantines were illiterate—the paintings on church walls, the icons in their churches and houses, the mosaics and frescos in public places, and the portraits and devices on coins provided a means of communication from which they learned the ideas and attitudes deemed desirable by the leaders of their society. Those leaders took care, too, that they did not learn the wrong ideas. The iconography of church decoration was controlled by the ecclesiastical authorities, and the dogmatic significance of changes in it was well understood. In secular matters too, art was taken seriously. Each time the much-married Empress Zoë took a new husband, she had the head on the mosaic portrait of herself and her consort in Hagia Sophia changed accordingly. Unfortunately for her, the artists did not always make a perfect job of the change. When we bear in mind the role of art as a medium of communication, we realize why it was above all in book illustrations, the most restricted medium, that classicizing tendencies were most visible. Classicism was essentially an elitist taste, which spread from the top down—but perhaps not very far down.

Nevertheless, the renaissance of the tenth century was a notable achievement, to which later generations owe much. Paul Lemerle called it *"le premier humanisme byzantin*," and analyzed with sensitivity and learning the part played in it, not only by the notables who wrote books and patronized art, but also by countless schoolmasters and humble scholars, most of whom remain nameless. He might have added a mention of the artists who looked with fresh eyes at the works of their predecessors in late antiquity and adapted their vision of the world and their techniques to the demands of their patrons and the spirit of the times. For painters and sculptors and mosaicists in the Byzantine world enjoyed none of the prestige and glamor of men of letters. They were mere craftsmen in the eyes of their contemporaries, and they rarely, if ever, signed their works. The humble and nameless, as much as the distinguished and powerful, were seeking new intellectual and aesthetic expression for the bounding confidence and the grandeur of their society. They naturally turned to an earlier age when Roman power and authority, Roman literature and art, Roman science and law held an unchallenged place in the then-known world, and sought to reproduce the spirit of that age, insofar as they could understand it.

In the middle decades of the eleventh century, the growing power and independence of the provincial magnates and the short-sighted policy of the aristocracy of officials in the capital undermined the military and financial basis of Byzantine power with headlong rapidity. The centralized authoritarian state no longer appeared to work. Political instability was the order of the day at home, as emperor succeeded emperor in answer to the maneuvers of factions of officials or the erotic whims of an elderly princess. Beyond the frontiers, new enemies appeared as old ones vanished, the Byzantines lost sight of who were their friends and who their foes; they were in any case incapable of facing the latter with their own resources. The idea of Byzantine superiority no longer corresponded with the facts of the situation; a discrepancy arose between the ideal and the real. Exaggeration of classicism and a kind of empty, windy rhetoric replaced the confident command of a millennial cultural tradition. The justified

feeling of the excellence of Byzantine society, which always had a tone
of arrogance about it, turned into systematic xenophobia. History was
explained in terms of the perfidy and cruelty of foreign peoples, who
were blamed for the shattering collapse of Byzantine power. This
interpretation made more intense the distrust and contempt in which
strangers were held, and more wildly unreal the Byzantine claims to
innate superiority. All this took place in a world in which the defense
of the empire's territories was more and more entrusted to foreigners,
either mercenaries from outside the empire or contingents of Bulgarians and Armenians who resented the domination of a state which
could no longer absorb them as equal citizens. Many, perhaps the
majority, of the twenty or so military families who dominated the
provinces and from time to time tried to seize control of the central
power were themselves of Armenian or Georgian origin. They had
long ago adopted Orthodoxy and Hellenism and been completely
absorbed into Byzantine society. But it may be that the ideas and
methods of statecraft which they brought from their mountainous
homelands, where political power was dispersed among local clan
chieftains, reinforced the feudal and aristocratic attitudes of the military leadership and their unwillingness to act as agents and servants
of a powerful central authority.

The defeat of the Byzantines at Manzikert in 1071 and the consequent loss of most of Asia Minor, the seizure of imperial power by a
faction of the provincial nobility, the growing unreality of the concepts expressed in literature and art, and the repression of freedom of
thought and expression symbolized by the condemnation of John
Italos were all aspects of a deep crisis in the life of Byzantine society.
Under the leadership of a new governing elite, it had to face a variety
of new and unprecedented challenges, not the least among which
were the crusades (on which see pp. 161ff.).

4

FROM FALSE DAWN
TO CATACLYSM
1081–1204

Portraits of six emperors from a fourteenth-century manuscript: (top row) John II,
Manuel I, and Alexios II; (bottom row) Andronikos I, Isaac II, and Alexios III. *Courtesy of Biblioteca Estense, Modena.*

When Alexios Comnenus, with the support of a coalition of provincial aristocratic families, established himself in power in Constantinople, the problems he had to face were at first sight not unlike those which confronted the successors of Heraclius four and a half centuries earlier. Asia Minor, the richest and most populous region of the empire, was almost entirely in the hands of the Seljuq Turks. The armies of the state were defeated and demoralized and its coffers empty. The Seljuqs, it is true, lacked the fanatical drive which carried the Arabs in less than a century from Medina to the banks of the Loire and the Jaxartes. They had already conquered more territory than they could readily administer and exploit, and the political unity which had held them together on their journey from central Asia was weakening. On the other hand, the Byzantines in 1081 had to face a dangerous attack from the west as well as from the east. The Normans in southern Italy were pressing forward with the same aggressive impetus that had recently led their kinsmen at home to conquer England. In the late 1060s they had mopped up one by one the Byzantine possessions in Apulia and Calabria, and finally taken Bari in 1071. One of their leaders, Roger Guiscard, crossed the Straits of Messina, overthrew the Moslem rulers of Sicily, and set himself up as king of a polyethnic and multicultural state in which Greek, Latin, and Arabic were all currently spoken. His elder brother, Robert Guiscard, aimed to conquer a kingdom for himself too. His purpose was no less than to seize Constantinople and establish himself on the throne of Constantine and Justinian. Accordingly he crossed the Straits of Otranto in 1082 and gave siege to Dyrrhachium (Durazzo), the great Byzantine fortress guarding the gateway to the Balkans. The threat posed by the Normans was more immediate than that of the Seljuqs in Asia Minor.

Unlike his predecessors in the seventh century, Alexios Comnenus could count neither on a native army of peasants nor on the enthusiasm of defending Christianity against the infidel. The social basis of the old *theme* armies had been destroyed and their principal recruiting grounds overrun. And many of the enemies facing the Byzantines

157

were themselves Christian states. Mercenary troops and diplomacy were the only weapons available to the new emperor. Mercenaries, however, cost money, so one of Alexios's first acts was to confiscate the treasures of the churches of Constantinople, the only reserve of readily negotiable wealth available to the government. Though he pawned these treasures rather than selling them, his action roused the opposition of ecclesiastical circles and somewhat tarnished the reputation he sought as the champion of Orthodoxy against the dangerous heresies of the intellectuals. With the money so raised, Alexios got together a motley army of soldiers of fortune—including many Englishmen who had left their native land after the Norman conquest—and marched west to face Robert Guiscard. He was too late to save Dyrrhachium, which the Normans captured in October; after their victory they fanned out to pillage and plunder in Epirus, Macedonia, and Thessaly.

Alexios needed allies. The Venetians—who were still theoretically subjects of the empire—were not eager to see an aggressive ruler established on both sides of the entrance to the Adriatic and able to interfere with their lucrative eastern trade. They welcomed Alexios's overtures and promised the aid of their own notable fleet—but at a price. The treaty signed early in 1082 granted a high Byzantine dignity to the Doge of Venice and lavish subsidies to the Venetian church. More important, it gave Venetian merchants unrestricted right to trade free of customs dues throughout the empire, except in the Black Sea. The Byzantines had never sought or enjoyed a monopoly of foreign trade within their own territory, but they had always restricted foreign traders to certain ports and markets and insisted on their paying the same customs dues as citizens of the Empire. The special position now granted to the Venetians enabled them to undercut Byzantine merchants in every market and inevitably led to the transfer of much long-distance trade to, from, or through the empire into their hands, with the consequent grave loss of revenue to the Byzantine state. But it was the price that had to be paid to keep the formidable Normans out of the Balkans and to give Alexios the breathing space he needed to establish some kind of order in the chaos which his

feckless predecessors had bequeathed to him. The Venetians cut the
Normans' supply routes, and recaptured Dyrrhachium in the summer of 1083, while the Byzantines gradually built up their military
pressure and forced the invaders to withdraw from the Balkans. In
the meantime, however, the Slav principalities of the northwestern
Balkans profited by the Norman war to establish their own independence from Byzantium.

By 1085 Robert Guiscard had been succeeded by his son Bohemond, who shared his father's hostility to the empire and was not
likely to accept the status quo for long. Alexios, in his turn, had guaranteed his own power by appointing to key positions members of his
own family and of those military families to which it was allied. At
first these had included the house of Dukas, and Alexios's eldest
daughter, Anna, had been betrothed to Constantine, the son of Michael VII and Mary of Alania, whom he designated as his co-emperor
and heir presumptive. But relations with the Dukas clan were tense,
and when his own eldest son, John, was born in 1092, Alexios dismissed Constantine, broke off the betrothal, and relied more and
more on his own network of family relations. A radical reform of the
whole administrative system was undertaken. Old ranks and offices
were devalued or abolished and a new hierarchy set up. The coinage
was further debased and a number of supplementary taxes imposed,
many of which had to be paid in the old, heavy coinage. In this way
revenue was raised to meet the cost of a growing army of mercenary
contingents, which included westerners, Bulgars, Turks, and others.
Alexios also tried to lay the foundations of a genuine native army,
both by settling conquered enemies on Byzantine territory with an
obligation to military service and by grants of land to citizens in return for service. In the changed world of the late eleventh century,
however, these land grants did not maintain a private soldier, as they
had under the Iconoclasts. They were rather great estates granted as
pronoiai to feudal magnates. The *pronoia* estates were inalienable,
though they could in theory be withdrawn. They rapidly became heri-
table. The holder of a *pronoia* was obliged to serve himself, or provide
a substitute, as a heavily armed knight and to furnish in addition a

certain number of mounted and foot soldiers. In return he collected the taxes and dues from the estate, while the peasants who cultivated it became in effect his serfs.

These reforms were far from completed when a new military danger appeared. The Pechenegs, who had for long dominated the plains of the southern Ukraine and Wallachia, and had often in the past been used by the Byzantines to bring pressure to bear on the Bulgarians or the Russians, decided to exploit Byzantine military weakness in the Balkans. After a series of raids from 1087, they swept over the Balkan range and through Thrace and reached the walls of Constantinople in early summer 1091. The Pechenegs could do little about the walls of the city, but they could and did seek an ally who could challenge the imperial navy—Tzachas, the Seljuq emir of Smyrna. Tzachas had built up a considerable fleet, which was manned by Greek sailors from the coastal towns of western Asia Minor. In 1091 his fleet sailed into the Sea of Marmara to support the Pecheneg army, and during the winter of 1090–91 Constantinople was besieged by land and sea, as it had not been since the great Arab sieges of 684 and 717.

Alexios negotiated an alliance with a Turkic people who had only recently appeared in the steppe north of the Black Sea, the Cumans. By skillful strategy he succeeded in drawing the Pecheneg army away from Constantinople and in joining forces with the Cumans, who marched south from the Danube delta. On 29 April 1091 a decisive battle took place at Levunion near the River Maritsa. The Pecheneg army was shattered and its men killed or captured. Strengthened by this victory, Alexios began punitive measures against the Serbs, who had defected from their alliance, but with little effect. The empire's new allies, the Cumans, were dissatisfied with their treatment—they wanted land to settle on—and were encouraged by elements in Constantinople hostile to Alexios's clean sweep of the old régime to revolt. In 1094 they invaded Byzantine territory, led by a pretender who made himself out to be the son of the Emperor Romanos Diogenes. They got as far as Adrianople before Alexios was able to defeat them.

In the first fifteen years of his reign, the emperor had succeeded in reasserting Byzantine authority in the Balkans and in defeating two powerful foes. He was now ready to turn to Asia Minor, where the Seljuqs had been left to rule undisturbed for a quarter of a century and into which there had poured band after band of half-nomadic Turkish tribesmen, each under its own leader. But before he could undertake the formidable task of regaining Asia Minor, at least in part, he was confronted by a new and unprecedented challenge.

The establishment of Seljuq power in Palestine had put difficulties in the way of pilgrims proceeding to the Holy Land. Leading clerics in the west called for an expedition to liberate the Holy Places. At the same time Alexios was appealing for mercenaries to help reconquer Asia Minor for the empire. In the west a growing population created a hunger for land in a society where power and possession of land went together. Impoverished knights, who may have won their spurs in the fight against the infidel in Spain, were ready for further adventures. The explosive expansion of Norman power in southern Italy and Sicily was an indication of the readiness of northwest European society to seek new worlds to conquer in the Mediterranean. When a religious motive was added to the already existing drive towards expansion, a movement of uncontrollable power was set on foot. This is not the place to enquire further into the deeper causes of the crusades, which, though in the end they failed totally to realize their original aim, marked an irreversible change in the political, military, and economic relations between eastern and western Europe.

At the Council of Clermont, Pope Urban II called on rich and poor to take up the struggle to liberate their enslaved Christian brothers in the east. The response was something that neither the pope nor Alexios expected or wanted. A kind of mass hysteria seized western Christendom, throwing up half-mad charismatic leaders like Peter the Hermit, in whose wake tens of thousands of common people set off, ill-armed and unprovided for, on the long trek across Europe to Constantinople. At the same time the great feudal lords, scenting conquest, mobilized their followers and prepared to undertake a well-organized military expedition. Among their number were Godfrey of Bouillon, the duke of Lorraine, the count of Toulouse, brother of the king of France, the son of William the Conqueror, and Alexios's old enemy Bohemond the Norman. The army they mustered numbered 4,000 to 5,000 knights plus 20,000 to 25,000 infantry men, doubtless accompanied by thousands of camp followers.

The Byzantines and the crusaders saw the liberation of the Holy Land in two quite different perspectives. For the crusaders it was a religious duty, transcending the bonds of political society; for the Byzantines it was simply a matter of reasserting legitimate political authority in their former provinces. The feudal lords of the west and their followers wanted to carve out independent principalities for themselves; the Byzantines assumed that reconquered territory belonged to them, and that the soldiers who fought for it would be rewarded in the same way as any other mercenaries. These were the principal points of misunderstanding. But there were others. Accustomed to the centralized exercise of power, the Byzantines saw the crusader armies, in which each man owed allegiance only to his own lord, as a disorderly rabble. And they were horrified by the sight of members of the clergy bearing arms, which was in flagrant contradiction of canon law as it had developed in the Orthodox church. To the crusaders the Byzantines appeared arrogant, devious, cowardly—and rich. Seldom in the course of history has an enterprise which was at least in part common engendered so much misunderstanding and mistrust.

It was in August 1096 that the first wave of crusaders reached Constantinople. They were the remnants of the ill-armed and unorganized followers of Peter the Hermit. Alexios arranged to feed them and ferry them across to Asia as quickly as he could. Most of them were soon captured or killed by the Turks. By the autumn the well-armed and orderly contingents of the great feudal dignitaries began arriving. They had already gained an evil reputation in Byzantine eyes by treating the empire as occupied territory and living off the land. Alexios, alert to the danger of this foreign army encamped outside the capital, tried to regularize the situation. On the one hand, he offered supplies, transport across the Bosphorus, guidance, and advice once in Asia. On the other, he demanded that the crusading leaders take an oath of allegiance to him, which, he hoped, would bind them to act as agents of the imperial government. Negotiations dragged on until early 1097. Most of the crusading leaders gave their oath of allegiance, but often only in return for a large bribe. In the spring Alexios ferried the crusaders across to Asia and operations began with some semblance of collaboration. In June the crusading army took Nicaea and advanced along the military route through Dorylaeum and on to the Cilician gates, while the Seljuqs fell back before them. The Byzantines were able to reoccupy a number of cities in western Asia Minor. By early summer of the next year, 1098, the crusaders reached Antioch. Here, what unity of policy there had been broke down. The crusading leaders were now eager to establish themselves as rulers in Syria, and they no longer heeded the interests of Alexios. They even began to quarrel among themselves over the spoils of victory, as Raymond, count of Toulouse, and Bohemond the Norman squabbled over Antioch. In the end Bohemond succeeded in establishing himself as an independent ruler there, while the count of Toulouse followed the main army southwards. In July 1099 the crusaders took Jerusalem. Godfrey of Bouillon was elected ruler of the kingdom of Jerusalem, while other crusading leaders set themselves up in ephemeral principalities in other parts of the newly conquered territory.

The immediate effect of the First Crusade, so far as Alexios was concerned, was that his subjects had been mishandled and pillaged by a foreign army, a few cities in Asia Minor had been recaptured—and many of them lost again—a number of unreliable westerners had set up illegitimate political communities on the territory of the empire, and his old Norman enemy could now threaten him not only from across the Adriatic but from Antioch, which had once been the third city of the empire. Relations between Alexios and Bohemond were tense. But the Norman was soon involved in hostilities with the Turks and was defeated by them in 1104. His defeat enabled the Byzantine army to recapture Tarsus and Adana, while the fleet seized the north Syrian ports of Laodicea (Latakia) and Tripoli. In 1105 Bohemond returned to the west to mount a full scale operation against the Byzantines as his father had done twenty-four years earlier. By

1107 the Normans had landed at Valona and were once again besieging Dyrrhachium. This time the empire had the military resources to meet and defeat them. In 1108 Bohemond undertook to recognize Byzantine sovereignty. It was a great victory for Alexios and immensely strengthened the Byzantine position in the Balkans.

But as the political map of Europe changed and new states came to the fore, a fresh challenger to Byzantine power in Europe appeared. The Magyars, long settled in Hungary, had abandoned the marauding habits that made them the terror of western Europe in the tenth century. Now a Christian state, Hungary had been tempted by the weakness of Byzantium to expand its influence southwards, into Croatia and Dalmatia. Unable to restrain the Hungarians by military means, Alexios came to terms with them by negotiation. A treaty was signed, and the emperor's eldest son, John, was married to a princess of the Hungarian royal house. The empire was no longer in the predominant position it had enjoyed under the Macedonian emperors, when its allies became in effect protectorates. The conflict between Byzantium and Hungary was not settled by the treaty, but was to continue, with interruptions, throughout the twelfth century. The alliance of 1108 was not pleasing to the empire's other ally, Venice, which regarded Dalmatia as its own preserve. The ensuing coolness led Alexios in 1111 to grant trading privileges to Venice's rival, Pisa. If the emperor hoped that the two Italian city states would mutually restrain one another, he was mistaken. The Pisan treaty merely hastened the takeover of Byzantine long-distance trade by Italian merchants and the consequent loss of revenue to the empire. Alexios Comnenus never really had time or opportunity to deal with the situation in Asia Minor. Had he been able to put an effective force in the field against the Seljuqs from the beginning, they might have lost interest in Asia Minor, which in their eyes had originally been of secondary importance; their main aim had been to conquer the rich Moslem lands to the south and to take over the caliphate. But as things were, they were left virtually undisturbed for two generations, during which the whole social structure of the Greek population of Asia Minor broke down and there were mass conversions to Islam. Over

Mosaic of the Emperor John II Comnenus and the Empress Irene on either side of
the Virgin, in the south gallery of Hagia Sophia, Constantinople. *Courtesy of Hirmer
Fotoarchiv, Munich.*

most of that vast land, so long the economic and military heart of the
empire, Byzantine power was never to be established again. Alexios
did carry out some successful minor campaigns in Asia Minor, but
they were never of more than local significance.

When he died in 1118 he was succeeded by his eldest son, John II,
though not without a determined attempt by John's formidable sister
Anna to put her own husband, Nicephorus Bryennius, on the throne.
Alexios Comnenus was a man of almost superhuman energy, great
tenacity of purpose, unflinching courage, and clear intelligence. And
he represented in his person and through his family perhaps the only
social force capable of imposing order on the chaos left by immediately preceding governments. He accomplished a great deal, and the
empire on his death was more confident and more powerful than it
had been since the great days of Basil II. Yet neither he nor the class

of which he was a representative was able to foster military power and social solidarity as the great Iconoclast rulers had done. Internally, the growth of great estates and the diminution in the numbers of the peasantry had diverted too much of the social productivity into private hands. The state was chronically short of money and of men. Alexios was often forced to buy time by pledging the future of his country. The world in which he had to conduct his policy was changed, too. The west was no longer remote and powerless. The German Empire, France, the Normans and the Hungarians were now independent forces to be reckoned with, as were some of the Italian city states. From being a unique superpower, which could in large measure determine the course of events, Byzantium was reduced to the situation of being merely one European state among many. But old habits of thought and action die hard, and in 1118 few in Constantinople can have realized that Europe, and with it they themselves, were entering a new epoch. They were like sailors trying to navigate a strange new ocean with old charts.

John II seems to have faced little internal opposition on his accession. There is no evidence that the conspiracy against him by members of his own family enjoyed any popular support. And even the man who was to take his place, his brother-in-law Nicephorus Bryennius, was notably lukewarm in his support of the plot, and continued to be a trusted servant of John Comnenus until his death many years later. The international situation, however, was menacing. The Normans were hostile as always, both in Sicily and in Antioch. The Hungarians had ambitions to extend their power into the Balkans, and supported the Serbs and other south Slav peoples in their efforts to break free from Byzantine tutelage. John used his position as a member by marriage of the Hungarian royal house to build up a pro-Byzantine party at the Hungarian court and among the upper clergy, as well as to influence the succession to the throne of Hungary. But he was unable to put an end to the clash of interest between the empire and Hungary. Most of Asia Minor still remained under Turkish control. An Armenian kingdom established in Cilicia in the aftermath of Manzikert by a family of Armenian notables was following a con-

sistently anti-Byzantine policy and cooperating closely with the crusader states of the Levant. And the Venetians continued to put a stran-
glehold upon the foreign trade of the empire. It was essential for John
II to prevent the potential enemies of the empire from making common cause against him, and to establish priorities between them. His
diplomatic activity was directed to these ends from the beginning of
his reign. That we cannot always follow it in detail is due to the lack
of contemporary narrative sources such as exist for the reigns of his
predecessor and his successor.

From the outset of his reign John was under pressure by the Venetians to ratify the treaty which they had signed with his father nearly
forty years earlier. John was not in the desperate situation that Alexios
had been in, and he had seen the economic and social effects of a
generation of Venetian trading privileges. For a long time he delayed
ratification, putting the Venetians off with various excuses. Venice
replied by diplomatic pressure and veiled threats. Finally, in 1126, the
Venetian fleet began raiding Byzantine islands in the Aegean to show
the seriousness of its intentions. John was obliged to ratify all the
terms of the treaty of 1082, and thereby to condemn the empire to an
unending economic drain.

Successful military operations by John to bring the Serbian principalities back under Byzantine control led to a breach with Hungary.
About 1128, King Stephen of Hungary declared war on the empire
and took the Danubian frontier fortresses of Belgrade and Braničevo
(near the confluence of the Morava and the Danube). But Byzantine
pressure forced him to withdraw, leaving his Serbian protégés unde-
fended. In the first ten years of his reign John II had succeeded in
asserting Byzantine authority in the northern Balkans and in discouraging any attempts by the Normans to gain a footing on imperial
territory. He was now ready to turn eastwards and attempt the much
more difficult task of reestablishing Byzantine power in Asia Minor
and Syria. But before he could do this, he had to face an unexpected
turn of events in the west. In 1130 the Norman King Roger II united
Sicily and southern Italy under his rule. The threat offered by a united
and powerful Norman state in the central Mediterranean concerned

not only the Byzantines but also the German Empire, which had a long-standing interest in northern and central Italy. The two empires were thrown together. John II signed a treaty of friendship with the Emperor Lothair and later with his son Conrad III. The German-Byzantine alliance kept Norman ambitions under control and enabled John II to proceed with an active eastern policy without fear of an attack from the west.

The sultanate of Rûm had broken up into a number of more or less independent principalities. John II's first task was to subdue the Danishmend emir of Melitene (Malatya), whose territory straddled the route to Cilicia and Syria. This he achieved in a series of successful campaigns, culminating in a crushing defeat of the Danishmend prince in 1135 and the annexation of Melitene and its territory. The next obstacle on the route to Syria—for the crusader states and not the Seljuq principalities of Asia Minor were the prime objectives—was the Cilician Armenian kingdom. In 1137 John marched into the Taurus Mountains on what turned out to be almost a triumphal procession. City after city, fortress after fortress surrendered at the mere approach of the chillingly efficient Byzantine forces, and the Armenian Prince Thoros was driven into exile. Tarsus, Adana, and Mamistra were taken, and by the late summer John was encamped before the walls of Antioch. Its Norman ruler, Raymond of Poitiers, son-in-law of Bohemond, who could not trust his largely Greek and Orthodox subjects, soon surrendered the city and swore allegiance to the Byzantine emperor. In the following year John made a state entry into Antioch which was stage managed with all the Byzantine talent for ceremonial. It was a demonstration to the people of Syria and to the rulers of the crusader states not only that John II was the only legitimate ruler of the territory, but also that the empire was once again able to field a major army adequately supported and brilliantly led. The heady rhetoric of Byzantine panegyrists, some of which survives, uses all the stock motifs of Byzantine superiority to other peoples and the "manifest destiny" of the empire to rule over them.

But things were not to be so simple. From 1138 onwards tensions grew between the empire and the crusader states. The Latin clergy supported the anti-Byzantine stance of many of the local Christian communities who often professed the monophysite faith. It proved increasingly difficult for the Byzantines to maintain what was in effect an army of occupation in Cilicia and northern Syria. Finally, in 1142, the prince of Antioch repudiated his oath of allegiance to the empire and put an effective end to Byzantine influence south of the Taurus Mountains. John II looked on the defection of Antioch as a momentary setback and planned a further campaign against Antioch, perhaps with the ultimate intention of reestablishing Byzantine rule throughout western Syria and Palestine   it is difficult to distinguish between empty rhetoric and genuine policy. In 1143 he was once again in the field in Cilicia. On 8 April, while hunting, he was wounded by a poisoned arrow and died shortly afterwards. He had time only to name as his successor his youngest son, Manuel, who was with him at the last. There are enough unsolved problems about the death of John II to lend some plausibility to the view that he was the victim of a plot in which Manuel was involved. But we shall never know with certainty.

   John II Comnenus was a successful soldier and a tireless monarch. Clearly an upright and kindly man, he won a reputation for fairmindedness and incorruptibility among his contemporaries. We are unfortunately too ill informed on the internal history of his reign to know whether he actually tried to remedy any of the notorious abuses of the period, such as the regular extortion by tax farmers. He built up an effective military force out of mercenaries, feudal levies, and prisoners of war, and led it with brilliance and caution, but he probably overstretched the military capacity of the empire towards the end. And the very possibility of taking offensive action in the east depended upon neutralizing the danger in the west by means of the German alliance, which could not be counted on to last indefinitely. The Byzantine empire was still living on borrowed time.

   The new emperor, Manuel I, was, like his father and his grandfather, a ruler of outstanding ability and energy. But both his character and his policies were marked by glaring contradictions. He was a convinced believer in the special role of the empire as a superpower, with legitimate claims to all territory that had ever belonged to his predecessors. At the same time he was deeply influenced by the western world and an admirer of western ways and the western lifestyle. He tried, and for a time succeeded, in reasserting Byzantine authority, not only in the Balkans, but also in the Levant and even in Italy. But he was able to do this only by depending on alliances with western powers which made an absurdity of his claim to restore Byzantine universalism. His program for the restoration of the Roman Empire in the west could only have been achieved at the price of Church union. But this had long been a virtual political impossibility, and the anti-western feeling aroused among the Byzantine people by Manuel's promotion of westerners, by the misconduct of the armies of the Second Crusade, and by the arrogant self-assurance which many western powers displayed in their dealings with the Byzantines made it utterly unrealizable. Manuel concentrated too much of the dwindling resources of the state upon building an army which was unable to defend the society off which it lived. And in his preoccupation with the western world he neglected the danger posed by Turkish control of most of Asia Minor. His reign was marked by a series of brilliant successes, none of which proved to be lasting. It ended in a disaster as great as that of 1071, or perhaps greater, as the empire no longer had the resources nor the will to rise above it.

Manuel returned at once to Constantinople from Cilicia after the death of his father, and he abandoned the proposed campaign against the crusader states. Not only did he have to arrange to fill the vacant patriarchate in order that he might be duly crowned himself, but also he had to deal with his elder brother Isaac, who had hoped to succeed to the throne. Manuel at first imprisoned Isaac in a monastery in the capital, though later the brothers were reconciled, and Isaac was even appointed to command armies. A contemporary historian records, however, that, so long as Isaac lived, Manuel always wore a breastplate for fear of assassination.

Manuel saw the aggressive Normans as the most immediate threat to the empire. Accordingly the alliance with the German Empire remained at first the cornerstone of his foreign policy, an alliance which was symbolized by the marriage of the young emperor to Bertha of Sulzbach, sister-in-law of the German Emperor Conrad III. However, the outbreak of the Second Crusade frustrated this simple policy. The crusade, if it won any successes, could only strengthen the crusader states of the Levant, which in Byzantine eyes were illegal squatters upon imperial territory. And insofar as it led the Emperor Conrad to concentrate on the Holy Land, it left the empire without an effective ally in the west.

When the crusading armies reached imperial territory in 1146, their passage was marked by disorders and excesses which contributed to the growing anti-Latin feeling among the Byzantine people. Like his grandfather Alexios I, Manuel demanded and obtained from the leaders of the crusade an oath of allegiance and an undertaking to hand over to the empire any former Byzantine territory which they might reconquer. He was probably less optimistic than Alexios had been that such an undertaking would be fulfilled. Anxious to be rid of his unwelcome guests as quickly as possible, Manuel arranged for the crusading armies to be given supplies and ferried across to Asia. He does not appear even to have met his brother-in-law Conrad. The German contingent, the first to arrive, was roundly defeated by the Seljuq sultan near Dorylaeum in Phrygia on 25 October, and ceased to be an effective military force. The French contingent under Louis VII had already reached Constantinople by early October. Relations between the king and the emperor were outwardly correct but somewhat frigid. Perhaps Manuel knew of the advice given to Louis by a French bishop, that he should ally himself with the Sicilian Normans against the treacherous Byzantines, who had actually made a truce with the Seljuqs. At any rate, the French were rapidly transported to Asia and provided with supplies and guides. They marched down the military highway to Attaleia (Antalya), their journey marked by much violence against the local people and by constant squabbles between the French and the surviving Germans, who hated each other much more than either hated the infidel. From Attaleia, Louis and his barons took ship for Syria, leaving the hapless Germans—and much of their own infantry—to the mercies of the Turks and the

Byzantines. Conrad, who had been wounded, soon recovered, and with the remnants of his shattered army returned to Constantinople, where he was received with honor, since he was still a valued ally and all the more valued now that he had abandoned the crusade.

In return for this kindly treatment, the German emperor promised to lead an expedition against the Normans in Sicily. But King Roger II had profited by Manuel's preoccupation with the Crusaders and the absence of Conrad to make a pre-emptive attack across the Adriatic in 1147. He not only took Corfu but marched through central Greece and sacked Thebes and Corinth. He carried off many of the inhabitants of these cities, including skilled silk weavers, whom he settled in his own domain. In 1149 Corfu was recaptured by the combined efforts of Byzantines, Germans, and Venetians, and preparations went ahead for an expedition against Sicily by the German and Byzantine emperors. However, the Normans were able to frustrate this project by building up an anti-German alliance in western Europe with French help, and by instigating the Hungarians and Serbs to hostile action against the Byzantines, which led to the first of a series of wars in the Balkans between the empire and Hungary. In this way Europe became, perhaps for the first time, divided into two grand alliances. On the one side stood Byzantium, Germany, and Venice. On the other stood the Sicilian Normans, France, many of the north Italian cities, Hungary, and the Serbian principalities, with covert support from the papacy. Nothing could reveal more clearly that Byzantium was now in reality merely one among the states of Europe, in spite of its pretensions to universal sovereignty. Both coalitions tried to extend their influence to Russia, where they supported rival claimants to the throne at Kiev. In the outcome it was the Byzantine candidate who won, but his victory brought little accretion of strength to the empire. Manuel also engaged in a long and lively correspondence with Henry II of England, the long-standing enemy of the king of France, but to no practical effect.

By 1152 the Emperor Conrad was at last ready to undertake operations against the Normans with Byzantine and Venetian aid, but his death brought a sudden change of policy. His successor, Frederick

Barbarossa, was unwilling to underwrite Byzantine claims to Sicily and southern Italy. So the alliance between the two empires, which had originally been prompted by Byzantine weakness, was abandoned and replaced by rivalry which soon became hostility. Manuel had now built up a powerful army of his own, in large measure composed of mercenary contingents and maintained by ruthless requisition and taxation. He was able without foreign aid to reestablish Byzantine control of the Balkans.

In 1154 Roger II of Sicily died and was succeeded by his son, William I. With a new and untried ruler in Palermo, Manuel felt that the moment had come to restore Byzantine power in Italy. His fleet besieged and captured Ancona, and with that port as a base, his army began marching southwards. Many vassals and dependants of the Normans espoused the Byzantine cause, whether from conviction or expediency, and soon the whole east side of Italy from Ancona to Taranto was under Byzantine control. Contemporary rhetoric exalted Manuel's successes. Manuel himself may have conceived a program of restoring the Roman Empire in the west as Justinian had done. If this was more than rhetorical fantasy it suggests a profound lack of realism on Manuel's part. Justinian had dealt with the Vandal and Ostrogoth kingdoms one by one and had no need to look beyond them. In the twelfth century powerful states like Germany and France would certainly oppose so radical a change in the balance of power, and Venice, as usual, would resist control of the Adriatic by any single state. The Byzantines would need at least the passive support of the Italian cities and the population of the countryside. This they could not obtain without the approval of the papacy. And the price of such approval would be union of the churches on papal terms, which would never have been acceptable to the Byzantine clergy and people. The anti-Latin feeling current in Constantinople and elsewhere meant that any rapprochement with the western Church would arouse fierce opposition among the laity also. The Italian expedition, and the absurd hopes which it raised, were disastrous for Byzantium. In 1156 William I of Sicily, now fully in control of his father's heritage, defeated the Byzantines at Brindisi and soon expelled them entirely from Italy. The German Emperor Frederick Barbarossa was alarmed at the implications of Manuel's operations in Italy, and from being a cool ex-ally of the Byzantines became their open enemy. Manuel had to reassess the situation in the west and cut his losses. In 1158 he signed a treaty with William I which marked the end of Byzantine hopes in the west.

Manuel now turned east to deal with the crusader states. Here, where the enemies he faced were weak, at variance with one another, and constantly harassed by the Turks, his success was spectacular. In 1158 he set out at the head of a huge army. The Cilician Armenian kingdom, which had revived after its defeat by John II, was easily reduced to vassal status. Reynold, the prince of Antioch, hastened to accept Byzantine sovereignty with a remarkable display of humility. Barefoot and in penitent's garb, he marched at the head of his suite from the town of Mamistra to Manuel's camp and threw himself in the dust before the emperor, who at first pretended not to notice him. Finally the prince was dismissed on condition that he allowed a Byzantine garrison to be installed in the citadel of Antioch, that he supplied a contingent to the imperial army, and that he replaced the Catholic patriarch of Antioch by an Orthodox prelate. King Baldwin of Jerusalem, who was no friend of the prince of Antioch, was glad to put himself under Byzantine protection.

In the spring of the following year, 1159, Manuel made a ceremonial entry into Antioch which was clearly intended to symbolize the new relationship between the empire and the crusader states. Preceded by his Varangian guards with their double axes, Manuel entered the city on horseback, wearing a purple robe over his gold coat of mail and with a jewelled crown on his head. The prince of Antioch walked beside him, holding the bridle of his horse. Behind, uncrowned and unarmed, rode the king of Jerusalem, followed by the dignitaries of the empire in their ceremonial robes. The glittering procession wound through the streets strewn with tapestries and flowers to the cathedral and the palace. There followed a week of festivities, celebrations, and tournaments, during which Manuel won the admiration of all for his lavishness, his personal charm, and his commanding authority. It was magnificent, for the Byzantines had a fine sense of ceremony, but it was not war. When the festivities were over, the emperor advanced to the Turkish frontier, where the sultan's envoys awaited him, and signed a truce. The western leaders felt that they had been tricked. There was to be no great campaign to roll back the tide of Islam. Yet the crusader states were forced to depend on the empire for protection against the Moslems.

Manuel was not eager to precipitate a conflict with the formidable Seljuq Turks. He had other frontiers to guard. That with Hungary was the most sensitive, and the scene of continuous incidents, any one of which might escalate into war. When King Géza of Hungary died in 1161 Manuel supported his brothers against his son, Stephen III, and succeeded in gaining many adherents among the Hungarian leaders and in particular the clergy. In this way he made Hungary for a time incapable of aggressive initiative, and in 1164 he was able to sign a treaty which gave the Byzantines considerable advantages. It was during these years of relative tranquillity that the Seljuq Sultan Kilidj Arslan paid a prolonged visit to Constantinople, where he was treated with every mark of respect and consideration. This public display, with all the refinement of Byzantine ceremonial, of the friendly relations between emperor and sultan must have seemed to the rulers of the crusader states and their hard-pressed barons the final proof of Byzantine duplicity. To the Byzantines it was rather a symbol of their own power.

In 1167 Manuel allowed war to break out between Byzantium and Hungary, which brought Dalmatia, Croatia, and Bosnia firmly under Byzantine control. At this moment of the apogee of Byzantine authority in the Balkans, Manuel seems to have conceived the idea of bringing Hungary itself into unity with the empire. He married his daughter Maria to the brother and heir presumptive to the Hungarian king, Béla-Alexios, who was a hostage in Constantinople, and proclaimed him his heir and successor. Whether this was a serious attempt to transform the empire by uniting it with one of the new states of Europe, or merely a tactical maneuver to increase Byzantine influence in Hungary, we shall never know. For in the following year a son was born to Manuel by his second wife Maria of Antioch, and Béla-Alexios was ousted from the Byzantine succession. However he did in the end succeed Stephen III on the throne of Hungary and made his court a center of Byzantine influence.

One of the Serbian princes, Stephen Nemanja, had profited by the hostility between the empire and Hungary to unite the divided Serbian principalities and create a Serbian state. Now that Hungary and Byzantium were at peace, he fought hard militarily and diplomatically to retain the independence of his country, but in vain. By 1172 he had been forced to recognize Byzantine sovereignty, though his kingdom was never transformed into a province of the empire as Bulgaria had been a century and a half earlier.

The effective ending of the Byzantine-German-Venetian alliance had brought to the fore again the ruinous effect on Byzantine trade and revenue of the privileged position enjoyed by Venetians in the empire. Manuel tried to undercut Venetian privileges by making alliances with Genoa in 1169 and with Pisa in 1170. Neither of these cities was able to offer serious competition to the Venetians. What they did do was pick up the scraps left by the Venetians and so further damage the Byzantine economy. Manuel tried to harass Venice by a series of minor measures against her citizens, and relations between the empire and its erstwhile subject grew extremely tense. Finally, on 12 March 1171, all Venetian citizens throughout the empire were arrested and their movable property confiscated. It was a beautiful demonstration of the efficiency of the Byzantine civil service, and one quite beyond the capacity of any western state to emulate. But it did little to help Byzantium. The Venetians retaliated by sacking the islands of Chios and Lesbos. The Byzantine navy had been allowed to run down since the days of the capture of Ancona, and it was unable to offer any serious resistance to the galleys of the *Serenissima Repubblica*. Relations between the two states remained broken off until after Manuel's death, and anti-western feeling in Constantinople and the other cities of the empire grew intense. Partly as a result of the conflict with Venice, Manuel began to support the league of Lombard cities which had been formed to resist the interference in Italian affairs of Emperor

Frederick Barbarossa, the ally of Venice. But the days were long past when the empire could exercise any significant influence in Italy. In fact Byzantium was finding itself now increasingly isolated among European states, a circumstance which further exacerbated anti-western feeling in the empire. Men no longer distinguished between one Latin and another. All were seen alike as arrogant, untrustworthy, and malicious. The westerners in their turn became more convinced of the inherent perfidy and deviousness of all Byzantines.

In the meantime Sultan Kilidj Arslan realized that the isolation of the empire was the Seljuqs' opportunity. He was urged by Frederick Barbarossa to attack Byzantium, doubtless in the hope that this would lessen Turkish pressure on the crusader states. In 1175, after many years of virtual peace with the empire, Kilidj Arslan invaded Byzantine territory in Asia Minor. Manuel prepared for the major conflict which he had so long managed to avoid, and in 1176 he led what was virtually the total fighting force of the empire into Asia Minor. He hoped to expel the Turks from western Asia Minor for good, and his goal was the Seljuq capital of Konya. As his huge army, encumbered with baggage and siege engines, climbed from the Meander valley towards the Sultan Dagh, it had to traverse a pass, at the end of which stood an abandoned Byzantine fort known as Myriokephalon. The Turkish army was stationed on the hills overlooking the pass, clearly visible to the Byzantines. There was some debate whether it was prudent to take the Byzantine forces through such a defile in full view of the enemy. The hotheads prevailed, flank guards were posted, and the army pressed on into the pass, brushing aside the Turks who tried to resist them. When they were well into the defile the enemy moved round them through the hills and charged into their flank and rear. For a time the Byzantines held on, pressed close together into a dense mass. Then Manuel, whether because he hoped to outflank the Turks or because his nerve failed, rode back out of the pass, followed by most of his army. They found themselves entangled with the baggage train, which blocked the narrow road. There the Turks were able to cut them down without mercy until nightfall. Finally Manuel accepted the sultan's offer of terms and withdrew with the remnants of his army. Kilidj Arslan may not have realized the extent of his victory—in any case his interest lay in the east and south, and Byzantium was of secondary importance. But Manuel knew what he had lost, and himself compared his defeat at Myriokephalon with that of Romanos Diogenes at Manzikert a century earlier. The formidable army built up by the sacrifices of the Byzantines had been annihilated. For the time being the empire was without military protection and surrounded by enemies, and Manuel's dream of making Byzantium once again a superpower was over. The last few insignificant Byzantine garrisons were expelled from Italy. The Hungarians began probing the northern frontiers, and the Serbs tried to shake off Byzantine control. There was little that Manuel could do about it. He had overstretched the empire's resources. The wealth accumulated by his father's careful husbandry he had spent on costly contingents of mercenaries. He had created a military ruling class—many of whose members were the hated westerners—which was divided from the rest of the population. The army had swallowed up the resources of the state and had in the end proved unable to protect it.

Manuel survived for four more years after the disaster of Myriokephalon and died in 1180. He left as his successor his twelve-year-old son Alexios II, under the regency of his widow, Maria of Antioch. The regent was detested as a westerner and was forced to rely more and more on the support of westerners in Constantinople. Many members of the imperial family were hostile to her and eager to challenge Manuel's will. Apart from their anti-Latin sentiments and their personal ambitions, they believed that the empire needed experienced and resolute leadership, not that of a boy and a foreign woman. Collectively they had plenty of military and political experience, since all three Comnenian emperors had regularly appointed members of their family to key military and civil positions. But they lacked effective leadership—perhaps years of subordination to so strong a personality as Manuel had made them unable to exercise leadership—and they failed to agree among themselves. It was left to one who was far from Constantinople, and who was in a way the black sheep of the family, to seize the reins of power which had fallen from Manuel's dying hands.

The enemies of the empire, who had been hovering like vultures over a dying beast since the destruction of the Byzantine army at Myriokephalon, swooped down upon their prey on the news of Manuel's death. In 1181 King Béla of Hungary seized Dalmatia, a large part of Croatia, and the key fortress of Sirmium guarding the old Roman military road to Constantinople. Stephen Nemanja wrested Serbia once again from Byzantine control. Most of the western half of the Balkan peninsula was thus lost to the empire. Two years later, in 1183, the Hungarians and Serbs launched a major invasion. Their army marched unopposed down the military highway, capturing and virtually demolishing the cities on the way. Belgrade, Braničevo, Niš, and Sofia fell. (Fortunately, the early Byzantine churches in Sofia were spared, whether from piety or haste.) In the west the Normans made preparations that were more leisurely but all the more menacing. Not until summer 1185 did their fleet cross the Adriatic. Soon Dyrrhachium had been taken by storm, and the ungarrisoned islands of Corfu, Kephallonia, and Zakynthos were occupied without opposition. The Norman fleet then sailed around Greece and by August anchored off Thessalonica. After a nine days' siege—during which the garrison and its commander displayed neither competence nor courage—the second city of the empire fell. The entry of the Normans was accompanied by violence and rapine on a terrifying scale, and many citizens were put to death with brutal and random cruelty. The wealth of the city and the priceless treasures of its churches were a temptation which the soldiers could not resist, and the Normans were probably simply unable to cope with the problems arising from the size of the city and the numbers of captives. The man who began negotiations with the Norman leaders and succeeded in persuading them to establish some kind of order was the archbishop of the city, Eustathius, a former teacher in the Patriarchal School in Constantinople and a notable scholar. The eyewitness account which he wrote of the siege and its aftermath reveals unsparingly the breakdown of the Byzantine administrative system, and indeed of the bonds of Byzantine society, as well as the increasingly arbitrary brutality of an army of occupation.

From Thessalonica the bulk of the Norman army set out by land for Constantinople. Demoralized by loot and plagued by epidemics, they rapidly lost their discipline and became a rabble rather than a military formation. They were easily defeated by a Byzantine force from Constantinople and soon broke up in disorder. A major land campaign in the east was clearly beyond their capacity.

Meanwhile events were moving fast in Constantinople. The opposition to the Regent Maria of Antioch, led by her step-daughter Maria and her western husband, Rainier of Montferrat, went so far as an attempt to murder the regent, which failed. The conspirators began quarrelling among themselves, and the regent appealed to her brother-in-law, Béla III of Hungary, for help, an invitation which the Hungarian monarch was delighted to receive.

Andronikos Comnenus, the son of Manuel's uncle Isaac, and a nephew of the historian Anna Comnena, was a few years younger than Manuel. Like his cousin, he was a man of daemonic energy, sharp intelligence, and captivating charm. But he had never known for long the discipline of power and was by temperament incapable of self-discipline. His relations with Manuel had been marked by a mixture of cordiality and mistrust. The two men were too alike, and Andronikos never hesitated to speak his mind to his imperial cousin. He had displayed great bravery and panache in Manuel's Turkish campaigns at the beginning of his reign, and in 1151 had been given command in Cilicia with responsibility for relations with the crusader states, but he behaved there with a certain lack of prudence. A year or two later he was in charge of the two key provinces of Niš and Braničevo. There he let himself be enticed into clandestine negotiations with the king of Hungary, which came perilously near to treason. In early 1154 he was arrested and imprisoned in the capital. He escaped, was recaptured, escaped again, and made his way in secret to Galicia, where he was hospitably received by Prince Jaroslav. Jaroslav was glad to harbor such an unexpected guest, as it enabled him to bring pressure on Byzantium by threatening to support with arms Andronikos's return. In due course, however, in 1165, Andronikos went back to Constantinople peacefully, pardoned by his cousin Manuel. Once again he was appointed governor of Cilicia. Rather than using his personal charm to reconcile the sullen Armenians to Byzantine rule, he exploited it to seduce a series of crusader princesses. First it was the turn of Philippa of Antioch, the sister of Prince Bohemond, who complained furiously to her brother-in-law Manuel. Andronikos was recalled from Cilicia but found it prudent not to return to Constantinople; rather he set out on an extensive tour of the crusader states, taking with him much of the revenue from his former province. In Acre he captivated the widowed queen Theodora of Jerusalem, who openly lived with him as his mistress. When Manuel, at the request of the scandalized King Amalric, sought the extradition of his errant cousin, the pair of lovers slipped across the Moslem frontier to Damascus, where they were welcomed by the Emir Nur-el-Din. After some years of wandering in Moslem lands as far as Tbilisi and Baghdad, Andronikos and Theodora settled down in a castle in Paphlagonia, near the Byzantine frontier. There he lived, half pensioner of the local emir, half brigand. In the last years of Manuel's reign things got too hot for him, and he returned to Constantinople, throwing himself on the emperor's mercy in a beautifully stage-managed scene—for he was a consummate actor. Manuel pardoned him and sent him to be governor of Pontus on the Black Sea coast. It was there that the news of Manuel's death and of the tense situation in the capital reached him.

Andronikos saw his chance. He was both a member of the imperial family and an outsider. He had become a legend in his lifetime, and unparalleled glamor surrounded his personality. As the news from the capital told of continuing squabbles among the opposition to the regency, he decided to seize his chance and set off in 1182, at the head of such troops as he could muster, on the long march to Constantinople. As he progressed through Asia Minor more and more men rallied to his cause, for to the downtrodden peasantry he offered an escape from their wretchedness and to the soldiers a chance of glory and booty. When he reached Chalcedon in May 1182 he had a significant force at his command. In the city the news of his approach had an electrifying effect. All the pent-up resentment against the Latins—now the only supporters of the empress-regent—came to a head. Andronikos no doubt had agents in the city working for his return. In particular, he enjoyed the support of the commanders of what remained of the Byzantine navy. Spontaneously or not, the people of Constantinople suddenly fell on the numerous Latins in the city and massacred almost all of them. Only those lucky enough to find a ship ready in the harbor escaped. The gates of the capital were thrown open, and Andronikos made his solemn entry through streets lined by the cheering populace and running with the blood of the butchered Latins.

At first Andronikos appointed himself regent and protector of the young Alexios II. The dowager empress and former regent Maria was charged with treasonable correspondence with the king of Hungary, found guilty and sentenced to death. Her portraits in public places were painted over, to make her appear a hideous hag rather than a beautiful young woman. In September 1183 Andronikos was crowned co-emperor. In November the boy Emperor Alexios II was put to death, and a little later Andronikos married his former ward's thirteen-year-old fiancée, Agnes-Anna, the daughter of Louis VII of France.

The new emperor had a clear-cut policy. He believed that the military aristocracy who had enjoyed power for the last century had ruined the empire, and he wanted to return to what he felt to be a more just and egalitarian society; and he rejected the involvement of the empire in the politics of the Latin world. With these ends in view, he dismissed many aristocratic officeholders and replaced them by men of humbler origins. He put an end to much corruption and suppressed many irregular payments which had in the course of time become official perquisites. He put a stop to the sale of offices. He did much to reduce the abuses of the tax collectors. He insisted that officials should be paid an adequate salary and severely punished if they took bribes. He took measures to suppress the piracy which had sprung up in the Aegean. All these were admirable reforms in themselves, but they would not be lasting unless accompanied by radical changes in the economic and social structure of the Byzantine community, which it was beyond Andronikos's power to carry out. He sought support both among the merchants, whose livelihood had been threatened by the Latin monopoly of foreign trade, and among the peasants, who were oppressed and exploited by the feudal landlords. Andronikos was something of a populist. He had himself depicted in one of the churches of Constantinople, not in the jewelled robes or gilded armor of an emperor, but in the garb of a peasant, and with a sickle in his hand. But neither the merchants of Constantinople nor the peasants of the great estates were an effective political force in the twelfth century. And Andronikos was in a hurry. He had never learnt the art of playing one group off against another, and of waiting for the favorable moment. The ousted aristocrats formed conspiracy after conspiracy, and there were many attempts on the emperor's life. Andronikos met violence with violence, and a kind of underground civil war developed, in which the plots and risings of his enemies were answered by a reign of terror which grew more and more indiscriminate. Ultimately Andronikos's unpredictable acts of repression alienated the very groups which had welcomed his accession to power, in particular the people of Constantinople, who were often the first to suffer from the Emperor's paranoiac cruelty. The wholesale execution of the military aristocracy left the empire even less able to meet the threats of aggressive neighbors than it had been before. It could not even deal with acts of dissaffection by its own citizens. In 1183 Isaac Comnenus, grandson of Manuel's elder brother Isaac, seized Cyprus and set up an independent state. All that Andronikos could do was to arrest and execute Isaac's friends in Constantinople. In the end Andronikos was left with no support in the capital except that of his bodyguards, and probably very little in the countryside. What precipitated his downfall was the approach of the Norman army. The people of the city, whether from a spontaneous outburst of hatred or because they were instigated by members of the military aristocracy, suddenly turned against Andronikos in autumn 1185. He was seized and put to death before the eyes of his subjects with the most barbaric cruelty.

Andronikos provided for a time a means of expression for the pent-up dissatisfaction of many members of Byzantine society. He was able to discern much of what was going wrong but quite unable to provide any lasting remedy for the ills of the empire. His political ineptitude, his impatience, and his readiness to resort in any moment of difficulty to brute force prevented him from providing even the kind of temporary respite from crisis which a wiser and less arrogant ruler might have provided.

The mob who butchered Andronikos was unable to govern the empire, and turned at once to the military aristocracy for a leader. Isaac Angelos, a member of an obscure family which had risen to great power and wealth under the Comnenus dynasty, was proclaimed emperor. All of Andronikos's reforms were repealed or allowed to lapse. The old abuses became more flagrant than before, and open corruption became the order of the day. There is no need to recount in detail the melancholy history of the empire in the last two decades of the twelfth century. Immediately after the accession of Isaac II there was a rising in Bulgaria, headed by two landowners who had been slighted by the new emperor. The whole of the Bulgarian provinces joined in the revolt, and an independent state was set up which proclaimed itself the heir and successor of the Bulgaria of Boris, Symeon, and Samuel. In spite of two campaigns in Bulgaria by Isaac II, in 1186 and 1187, he was quite unable to restore Byzantine rule but had to accept the fait accompli and recognize by treaty the new Bulgarian kingdom. This marked the final end of Byzantine domination in the Balkans, where only peninsular Greece, southern Macedonia and eastern Thrace remained in Byzantine hands.

The Third Crusade in the late 1180s presented the usual problems to the empire, which was less able to deal with them than it had been in 1096 or 1146. By the Treaty of Nürnberg of 1188 Isaac guaranteed passage through Byzantine territory for the crusading armies. In the event the French and English crusaders took the sea route, and scarcely impinged upon the empire's territory or interests, except that in 1191 Richard I of England, to avenge a slight to his betrothed, Berengaria of Navarre, seized Cyprus from the rebel Isaac Comnenus, and a little later handed it over to Guy de Lusignan, the former king of Jerusalem. The German crusading army, which came overland, was a different matter. Its leader, the Emperor Frederick Barbarossa, was no friend of Byzantium. When he entered the Balkans in 1189 he was welcomed by Serbia and Bulgaria, with whom he began to negotiate an anti-Byzantine alliance. Whether he merely wished to frighten Isaac II and so facilitate his passage to the Holy Land, or whether he was anxious to eliminate what he regarded as a tiresome survival of the remote past, is still an open question. Be that as it may, Frederick occupied Philippopolis as if it were enemy territory, and took Adrianople by force when the citizens refused to open the gates to him. As the German army advanced towards Constantinople, its approach caused great alarm.

Isaac at first arrested the German ambassadors when they reached the capital, and he refused to negotiate with Frederick. The German emperor responded by seizing Didymoteichum in Thrace and ordering his son Henry to prepare a fleet and obtain the pope's blessing for a crusade against the Greeks, whose prevarication and double-dealing, he said, made them the de facto allies of the infidel. Faced with this threat, Isaac released the ambassadors and apologized humbly to Frederick. An agreement was patched up by which the Byzantines gave hostages to the Germans, who in their turn agreed to keep away from Constantinople and to cross to Asia by the Dardanelles rather than the Bosphorus. Until they made the crossing, in the spring of 1190, the Byzantines waited with apprehension in case the German emperor should change his mind. The public humiliation which had been inflicted upon Byzantium could scarcely have been greater and was hardly compensated by the relief with which the Byzantines learned in the following summer that Barbarossa had fallen from his horse and been drowned in the river Kalykadnos in Cilicia.

After the grim old German's death, Isaac tried to reestablish Byzantine influence in the Balkans. In 1190 he defeated Stephen Nemanja of Serbia and forced him to yield some territory but was in turn de-

feated by the Bulgarians. In 1194 he met a further and more serious
defeat at the hands of the Bulgarians at Arcadiopolis. Discontent at
his ineffective rule mounted among the very class who had raised him
to power. Some sought to disengage themselves from the collapse
of imperial power by what amounted to unilateral declarations of
independence in the regions they controlled. In April 1195 Isaac II
was deposed by a palace coup, blinded, and thrown into prison. The
choice of the conspirators fell upon his elder brother, Alexios III, who
always called himself Comnenus, after his grandmother, rather than
by the less distinguished name of Angelos. If Isaac was an ineffectual
ruler he was at least a courageous and energetic soldier. Alexios III
was a pleasure-loving nonentity, dominated by his headstrong but
injudicious wife, Euphrosyne. Euphrosyne's brother-in-law, Michael
Stryphnos, the commander-in-chief of the imperial fleet, distinguished himself by selling the ships and pocketing the money in 1203,
when the Venetian fleet had already set sail to attack Constantinople.

The eight years of Alexios III's reign are a melancholy chronicle
of failure. In 1196 Stephen Nemanja, the founder of the Serbian kingdom, abdicated and retired to a monastery, leaving as his successor
his younger son Stephen, who was married to a daughter of Alexios
III. But the empire and its ruler were too feeble to seize upon the
opportunity of enlarging Byzantine influence in the Balkans. When
Stephen's elder brother Vukan rose in rebellion against him, it was to
Hungary and not to Byzantium that the Serbian monarch turned for
support. Alexios's attempts to end the war with Bulgaria by negotiation ended in total failure. The hostilities dragged on for several years,
with Bulgarian armies regularly marching unopposed through Macedonia, burning and pillaging as they went. Finally, after complicated
diplomatic maneuvers, including Byzantine support of two Bulgarian
rebels who set up principalities of their own, much of Macedonia fell
to Bulgaria. In the west the situation was ominous for the Empire.
Henry VI, the new German emperor, was also heir to the Norman
kingdom of Sicily. He was an ambitious ruler who dreamed of world
conquest. His brother, Philip of Swabia, was married to a daughter of
the former Byzantine Emperor Isaac II, a relationship which Henry

made use of to justify his hostile intention towards Byzantium. Alexios III had no stomach for a fight with the new superpower to the west, and tried to gain time by concessions. These included the payment of an enormous tribute of 1,600 pounds of gold annually. This money was raised by a special tax, the *Alamanikon*, which bore heavily on all classes in the empire. Even the tombs of former emperors in the church of the Holy Apostles were despoiled of ornaments to meet Henry's demands.

In 1197 the German emperor suddenly died, and the structure of alliances built up by Henry and his father began to disintegrate as the various princes pursued their own separate ends. Alexios III was able to abolish the hated *Alamanikon*, but even so he could not undertake any diplomatic initiative to improve the situation of the empire. Instead he proposed an alliance with the papacy, which he rightly took to be the dominating force in Italy after the crumbling away of the German régime. But the price would have had to be Church union, which in the state of anti-Latin feeling that prevailed in Constantinople was inconceivable. The Patriarch John Kamateros denounced any concessions to the western Church, and Alexios's proposed union had to be quietly abandoned. By 1198 Pope Celestine III had been succeeded by the energetic and unyielding Innocent III. Ideas of a further crusade were abroad, and were given clear and strong support by the new pope. Innocent viewed the Byzantine Empire as an asset which could be taken over by Church union and integrated into his crusade, which was to drive the Moslems once and for all out of the Holy Land. The Doge of Venice, Enrico Dandolo, who had long smarted under an insult, real or imagined, which he had received in Constantinople years before, was not in the least interested in ousting the Moslems, with whom Venice carried on a lively and profitable trade. But he was eager to eliminate the empire, which he saw as the last obstacle to securing Venetian supremacy in the eastern Mediterranean. He was in a strong position, as the crusaders owed him money. Philip of Swabia, the brother of the late German Emperor, felt himself obliged to overthrow the man who had deposed and blinded his father-in-law, and was in any case not averse to fishing in troubled waters. The coming together of these various interests made it almost inevitable that the proposed crusade would turn out to be an instrument for the conquest of the Christian east, and that the Moslems would be quietly forgotten.

The Byzantine government was well aware of the danger in which it stood, but could do little to ward it off. The least move towards Church union, which would have put the empire under the powerful protection of the pope, was greeted with unbending hostility by the leaders of the Church, who in this instance really did reflect the almost paranoiac anti-Latin feelings of the common people.

In 1201 the crusaders assembled at Venice. The Venetians refused to provide ships unless they first used their arms to capture the port and fortress of Zara (Zadar) from Christian Hungary, which the crusaders duly did. In the meantime Alexios Angelos, the son of Isaac II Angelos, had succeeded in escaping from his prison and fleeing westwards. He turned first to Pope Innocent, who gave him a courteous but discouraging reception. He then went to his brother-in-law, Philip of Swabia, who began to negotiate support for him from Venice and the crusaders. Alexios had nothing to lose, so he readily promised not only vast sums of money but also Church union in return for his establishment on the imperial throne. By May 1203 the crusaders agreed to take Constantinople *en passant*, establish Alexios on his father's throne—as a blind man Isaac II was now unfit to rule—and then go on to the Holy Land. In June the Venetian fleet, with the crusading army aboard, appeared off Constantinople, captured Galata on the other side of the Golden Horn, and began a siege of the city. On 17 July the city fell, in spite of courageous resistance put up by the Varangian guard and a handful of Byzantine troops. Alexios III fled with the crown jewels. Isaac II was released from prison and restored as titular emperor, while his son Alexios IV became co-emperor and effective ruler.

The new emperor was from the first powerless, caught between the Venetians, who demanded payment for services rendered, and the people of the city, who would have nothing to do with an emperor who owed his throne to the Latins. While the crusaders encamped outside the walls, subversive forces stirred within the city. In January 1204 there was a popular revolt. Alexios IV was killed and his father returned to his prison, where he soon died. A new leader had to be found. For want of anyone better, the leaders of the revolt proclaimed as emperor Alexios Dukas Murtzuphlus (=Bushy-Eyebrowed), the son-in-law of Alexios III. For a brief period he reigned as Alexios V. The crusaders were now faced with a problem. Were they to go on to the Holy Land leaving a declared enemy of the Latins in power in Constantinople, or were they to take the city a second time? Gradually the view prevailed that the Byzantine Empire must be eliminated. A plan was drawn up for the partition of the territories of the empire between the various crusader groups and the establishment of a western emperor and a Latin patriarch in Constantinople.

On 13 April the city fell to the crusading armies for the second time. For three days the soldiery were permitted to pillage freely. Impoverished though Constantinople now was, it was still the richest city of the western world, and to the eyes of rough soldiers from France and Germany its streets were paved with gold. In the words of a modern historian, they fell upon Constantinople as savages might fall upon a watch. No one can calculate what was removed or destroyed in the three days' sack of the city. Only the sack of Rome by the Vandal King Gaiseric in 455 caused comparable destruction. Apart from the looting, many citizens were killed, and many more fled the capital, never to return. Once some semblance of order was restored, the crusader leaders met to elect an emperor. Their choice fell on Baldwin of Flanders, who enjoyed the support of Venice. On 16 May 1204 he was crowned in Hagia Sophia as the first Latin emperor of Byzantium. Meanwhile the crusading army marched westward through Thrace, all thought of the Holy Land abandoned. The marquis of Montferrat established himself as king of Thessalonica. Other crusading leaders turned southwards into peninsular Greece. A Burgundian baron, Othon de la Roche, received Athens and Boeotia as his fief. Other little Latin states were established in central Greece. The Peloponnese fell to Geoffrey of Villehardouin. The Venetians took Crete and Euboea and other islands. Virtually the whole territory of the empire was partitioned among the crusading leaders. Only in Epirus, in northwestern Asia Minor, and in distant Pontus did large territories remain under the rule of Greeks. The Byzantine Empire no longer existed.

TRADITION AND INNOVATION

The period from the accession of Alexios I in 1081 to the death of Andronikos I in 1185, and indeed to the capture of Constantinople by the Fourth Crusade in 1204, was one full of paradoxes. An apparently brilliant revival of Byzantine power after the anarchy and weakness of the mid-eleventh century was followed by rapid collapse and disintegration. Although it was the Seljuq Turks who occupied the old heartland of the empire in Asia Minor, the military effort of Byzantium was for most of the time directed against various western powers and coalitions. Power appears to have been in the hands of an aristocracy which owed its position to its military prowess and devoted the economic resources of the empire to military goals, yet Byzantium ended up unable to defend itself. Centralized rule was the order of the day, yet towards the end of the period many territories were independently governed by local magnates, and it was precisely these regions that were able for a time to offer effective resistance to the Latin conquerors. Older historians sought to explain the course of events by the psychological or moral qualities of the successive rulers. There was little agreement among them on what these qualities were; for some Alexios was a cruel tyrant, while John and Manuel were enlightened monarchs, for others Alexios and John had the interests of their subjects at heart, while Manuel was a weak and selfish ruler. Their disagreement over the enigmatic figure of Andronikos was even greater. Gradually it was realized that the fate of the empire was not wholly determined by the will of the ruler, and historians began to ask in what groups and classes of society each of them found support. The next step was to enquire what were the changing economic interests of these groups and classes, and to supplement the information in the narrative sources by that provided by documents. Lastly some historians went on to seek the actual links between economic interests and political action, and to pose such questions as how Venetian economic privilege really worked and whether it favored or hindered the economic growth of provincial towns; what elements in Byzantine society supported Andronikos Comnenus, and why, and what it was that lost him their support; whether the military magnates acted as a single group, or whether the conflicts which divided them were not perhaps more significant than the common interests which united them. It becomes clear that it is not enough to seek an explanation of the collapse of the empire in the feudalization of Byzantine society. After all, the westerners who destroyed the empire also belonged to a feudal society. What we want to know is how feudal relations actually developed in Byzantium, and in what ways they differed from feudal relations in the west. These are diffficult questions to answer, not least because of the wholesale loss or destruction of Byzantine archives, apart from those of a few monasteries. But it is not impossible to attain a deeper and more fundamental understanding of the changing dynamics of Byzantine society in the twelfth century than historians have had in the past. Perhaps the time is now ripe for a new exhaustive study of the Age of the Comneni. The last such study, published by F. Chalandon in the early years of the present century, is now in many respects out of date, and in any case was concerned almost exclusively with political and military history.

In the previous section, explanations have been suggested for some of the paradoxical features of the period. They are no more than working hypotheses. In a way the cultural history of the age offers fewer problems than its political, economic, and social history. Twelfth-century texts exist in great number and variety. Works of art of the period are well represented. There are many detailed descriptions of Byzantine society by outsiders, ranging from the chroniclers of the crusades to the Jewish traveller Benjamin of Tudela, from Russian pilgrims to Arab geographers. We must always remind ourselves that we may be wrong in our interpretation of those works of literature and art because so much is still unclear about the social and economic development of the community which produced them, and the ways in which it was reflected in the culture of Byzantium.

Some things, however, are clear about the climate of thought and feeling of the period—first of all, the picture which the Byzantines formed of western society and of their own relationship to it. The schism between the two churches in 1054 had been on points of theology, ritual, and church discipline, and had gone unnoticed by the mass of laymen. However, it did give rise to a new literary form, the anti-Latin treatise. The earliest of these confined themselves to such matters as the use of leavened or unleavened bread in the Eucharist and the celibacy of the clergy, and were addressed to the clergy. Soon, however, polemicists began to seek the cause of the westerners' theological errors in their alleged moral and social weaknesses. A kind of stereotype of the westerner as ignorant, barbarous, and malign began to be spread in Byzantine society, clerical and lay alike. For the Church had an extremely efficient chain of communication, which led from the deliberation of synods and the decisions of patriarchs to the pastoral activity and predication of the humblest priest or monk in the provinces. In earlier ages Byzantines had looked upon western Christians with patronizing pity, as people who would have been Byzantines if they could. Now they began to see them as alien in thought and motive and potentially hostile.

Consequently, when the south Italian Normans attacked the empire in 1089, their behavior appeared to be a confirmation of what Byzantine theologians had been saying about western Christians in general, and it added a further element to the stereotype. The aggressiveness of the Normans was taken to be characteristic of western Christians as a whole, including above all their spiritual leader, the pope. When the crusaders arrived in Constantinople they provided further confirmation of the stereotype, and added new elements to it. Their divided leadership and apparent lack of a common discipline was contrasted with the centralized control and uniform discipline of Byzantine armies. To Byzantine eyes the crusaders seemed to neglect the essential distinction between civil and ecclesiastical authority, which had been clearly set forth in the legislation of Justinian and repeated many times thereafter. The conquest of territory was a matter for the emperor and for the emperor alone. The duty of the leaders of the Church was to define correct belief and maintain the spiritual welfare of the community. Yet in the crusaders they saw a great military movement which had no lay authority in command of it but was directed, it seemed, by the pope. When the Byzantines looked more closely at the crusading armies they were not reassured. The historian Anna Comnena, who was well informed about the world in general, was horrified to find that the pope had an army of his own. The sight of members of the clergy bearing arms and using them on the field of battle was profoundly disquieting to the Byzantines, whose own canon law forbade absolutely the shedding of blood by a person in religious orders. Centuries earlier a village priest in Cappadocia had been excommunicated for taking up arms against Arab invaders, and the incident was recalled by twelfth-century historians.

When the leaders of the First Crusade set up their own independent states in the territories reconquered from Islam instead of handing them over to their rightful sovereign, the emperor, the Byzantines interpreted their conduct as evidence of unreliability and perjury. Had they not undertaken to restore to the empire any imperial territory they might recover, in return for the transport and supplies furnished by the empire? The Byzantines began to ask themselves whether the crusades were not a gigantic make-believe to cover the real intentions of the crusaders and their pseudo-Christian leader, the pope, which were to conquer and occupy the lands of eastern Christians. After all, they had shown little disposition to help when the imperial forces in the Levant were hard pressed by the Fatimids of Egypt—who incidentally had also hindered the passage of pilgrims to the Holy Places—or when the greater part of Christian Asia Minor was occupied by the Moslem Seljuqs and the property of the Church there seized.

To these criticisms of the crusades in principle there was added the ill feeling caused by the behavior of the crusaders, who often treated those parts of the empire through which they passed as if they had been occupied territory. To the Byzantine peasant or citizen whose property they pillaged and whose women they violated, the crusaders were no better than the infidel Turks, who at least did not pretend to be defending Christendom. The events of the Second and Third Crusades only confirmed the impression formed by those of the First Crusade.

Then there was the matter of the Venetians, and later of the Genoese and Pisans. Their freedom from imperial taxation gave them an advantage over Byzantine traders which they were quick to exploit. Many small commercial and industrial enterprises must have been ruined by their privileged competition. Furthermore, the treaties which regulated trade with foreigners in the past had not allowed the permanent settlement of foreign communities on Byzantine soil. When Russian or Bulgarian merchants had sold the goods they brought with them and bought what they wanted, they returned to their native lands. But the Venetians settled in Constantinople and other cities, brought their families and their clergy with them, set up their own administrative and judicial organs, and in general behaved as if they were quite independent of Byzantine sovereignty. There must be more than a little truth in Byzantine stories of the arrogance and contempt with which they treated the Orthodox subjects of the empire, who were after all the new Chosen People.

The combination of ecclesiastical, military, economic, and social confrontation with the Catholic west led in time to a growth of anti-Latin feeling which became almost paranoiac. This was something quite distinct from the general xenophobia of the days of Byzantine greatness. It was the product not of strength, but of weakness. It led to endless conflict in the streets of the capital and other cities, and in 1182 to a bloody and mindless pogrom in Constantinople in which thousands of Latins were massacred. The situation was complicated by the growing dependence of the empire on Latin mercenaries and their leaders, and on the consequent promotion of westerners to positions of dignity and responsibility in the empire. Such cases may not have been all that numerous; we do not know. But they were noted and resented. A bishop of Ephesus in the mid-twelfth century, writ-

ing to a grandson of Anna Comnena who was in command of a province in the north, congratulated him on being a true Hellene and not
a Latin interloper. The westerners were in the empire to stay, and their
influence was considerable in the higher ranges of society. Manuel I
liked western ways, married successively two western princesses, and
exchanged the stiff formality of the Byzantine court, which had so
impressed and annoyed Liutprand of Cremona two centuries earlier,
for a more relaxed western style. The Hippodrome, where the chario-
teers of the Blues and the Greens had raced against one another since
the days of Constantine, was now the scene of the western sport of
jousting, in which—horror of horrors!—even the emperor himself
took part. The influence, real or alleged, of westerners at court was a
further source of discontent among the common people. It undermined in some degree their loyalty to their own legitimate government. And it fed the current of anti-Constantinopolitan feeling which
ran strong in the provinces and which in the closing decades of the
twelfth century enabled local magnates to establish virtually independent governments in their own regions.

Some features of the general anti-western feeling in Byzantium are
worthy of special note. Though Byzantine emperors and officials were
well aware of the differences between the various peoples and states
of western Europe, maintained regular diplomatic relations with
many of them, and often tried to play them off one against the other,
in the popular imagination they were all lumped together without
distinction as "Latin." What marked them off from the Byzantines
was their obedience to the Church of Rome, and it mattered nothing
whether they were French or German or Italian. The vices of each,
be they real or imagined, were attributed to all. The only significant
exceptions to this general rule were the Hungarians (who were often
thought of as *sui generis* and not merely as a species of Latin) and,
curiously enough, the English, many of whom served in the Varangian
guard. Here, incidentally, is another paradox: a society permeated by
hatred for the Latins entrusted the security of its leader to a body of
largely Latin mercenaries. But the Varangian guard had been formed
by Basil II, when the relations between Byzantium and foreign peo-

ples were on a very different footing, and it had originally consisted of Russians, who had in theory been converted to Orthodoxy.

While hostility might be expressed against the Norman kings of Sicily or the crusader princes in the Levant, the main butt of Byzantine hatred was the pope. The discovery that the bishop of Rome was Anti-Christ was made and proclaimed by Byzantine clergymen centuries before seventeenth-century Englishmen or twentieth-century Ulstermen had given the matter a thought. Though in fact different popes pursued different policies, no account was taken of this in the popular stereotype. All popes were enemies of the Chosen People and master-minded the military onslaughts of their enemies. This meant that any policy involving a *rapprochement* with the papacy, even if the question of Church union was never raised, aroused the fiercest opposition among clergy and people and could not be long maintained even by the most resolute of governments.

In the tenth century Constantine VII warned his son that no marriage alliance between the imperial house and any foreign royal family—except that of the Franks—was to be tolerated. This was at a time when there were no major disputes between the eastern and western churches. Two centuries later, long after the mutual excommunication of the leaders of the two churches, Latin princesses regularly married into the imperial family and Byzantine princesses became the consorts of western monarchs. John II married a Hungarian bride, and Manuel I married successively a German and a Norman from the Levant. Manuel's sister Maria married a Norman mercenary, John Roger; nieces of Manuel were married to Henry II of Austria, to Baldwin III of Jerusalem, and to William of Montpellier. Isaac II's daughter married successively King Roger of Sicily and Philip of Swabia. Nothing could illustrate more strikingly the change in the "official" attitude towards foreign potentates since the heyday of the Macedonian dynasty, and the curiously ambivalent attitude towards westerners in the twelfth century.

Though there is no doubt that the commercial privileges accorded to the Venetians and others did irreparable harm to Byzantine trade and to the revenues of the Byzantine government, yet their effects were not wholly negative. In particular they appear to have stimulated economic life in a number of provincial towns, which were for the first time drawn into a wider network of trade which gradually came to embrace the whole Mediterranean region. The economic growth of these towns in turn led to increased prosperity in the regions to which they belonged. It was a prosperity doomed to be short lived. But while it lasted it was real enough. These are some of the contradictions in the complex Byzantine relationship with the western world, which in the age of the Comneni became no longer remote and peripheral, but entered into direct contact with Byzantine society and penetrated throughout its fabric.

By constantly setting themselves in their imagination against the Latins, the Byzantines redefined their own identity. The conversion of Bulgaria and the ensuing military conflict with the Bulgarians had made it impossible simply to identify Byzantium with Christendom. The new conflicts with the Latins in the military, the economic, and the religious plane made the old identification even less apt. Two possibilities were open. One was to deny that the westerners were really genuine Christians. Some of the more frenzied outbursts of rhetoricians and polemicists in the last decade of the twelfth century come very near to such a denial. And the feeling was widespread that the Latins were somehow second-class Christians, though the Roman Church was never treated as heretical in the strict sense, but only as schismatic. The other possibility was to develop the classicizing trends of the culture of the Macedonian age and to declare the Byzantines to be Greeks, superior to other peoples because their possession of the Greek language gave them direct access not only to the basic texts of Christianity but to the whole literary and philosophical heritage of Hellas, which the Latins could approach only through a handful of translations, many of them made through Arabic intermediaries. This was more and more the course taken, not only in intellectual circles, but by wider sections of the people and often by the rulers themselves. There is a very real sense in which the prehistory of Greek nationalism can be traced back to the long and traumatic confrontation with the Latin west in the twelfth century.

However there were dangers in such a course. In particular, if pursued to its logical conclusion it could lead not merely to conflict between state and Church authorities, but to the breakdown of the synthesis between Christianity and Hellenic culture made in the age of the Fathers of the Church. And quite apart from the personal religious convictions of individual rulers, such a breakdown would have been unacceptable to any Byzantine government, because it would have undermined its legitimacy, made its exercise of authority accidental rather than essential, and reduced it to the level of those western Christian governments over which it claimed superiority. And of course it would have run counter to the deeply felt religious conceptions of the mass of the people of the empire. So we find that on the one hand the tradition of writing philosophical commentaries on Aristotle, which had lapsed since the early seventh century, was taken up again and developed by a group of scholars, some of whom enjoyed the patronage of Anna Comnena, the daughter of Alexios I. And the study of Proklos, the last of the great pagan Neoplatonists, was actively pursued in Constantinople, to judge from the number of manuscripts written in the late eleventh and twelfth centuries. Yet on the other hand there was often a curious reluctance to be seen to be seriously interested in Greek philosophy. Michael of Anchialos, the future patriarch, was appointed professor of philosophy by Manuel I in 1165 or 1167. In his inaugural lecture he declared that he would confine himself to teaching Aristotle, and implied that Plato had better be given a wide berth because his doctrines were contrary to Christian dogma. About the middle of the twelfth century Nicholas of Methone, one of the leading theologians of the period, wrote a long refutation of Proklos in which he displayed a surprising mastery of the techniques of philosophical argument. He complained that many of his contemporaries were being misled into heresy by their study of Proklos. Nicholas's refutation was completely different in quality from the kind of nihilistic anti-intellectual attack on secular learning which was made from time to time throughout Byzantine history in monastic circles. It was important enough to be copied and studied four centuries later in connection with the Council of Trent.

Though there was no repetition of the affair of John Italos, when a prominent figure of Byzantine intellectual life was tried and condemned for heresy, there was throughout the twelfth century a long series of heresy investigations in which teachers were involved. These were concerned not so much with traditional sectarian heresies like Montanism or with new "popular" heresies, like the dualist Bogomilism, which had an obvious appeal to those who were dissatisfied with established political and social order, but dealt with "intellectual" heresies, which had a philosophical basis but little mass appeal. They are probably to be interpreted as a sign of the continuing tension between the bold exploration of the tradition of Hellenic thought and the need to remain within the framework of the Hellenic-Christian synthesis. It is noteworthy too that higher education came under more direct control by the Church authorities than it had been in the previous century. The schools of philosophy and law founded by Constantine IX in 1054 may have continued in being or may have been revived from time to time. But the predominant educational institution was now the Patriarchal School, with which very many writers and scholars of the twelfth century were connected. The Patriarchal School carried out in an institutionalized way the teaching duty incumbent upon all bishops. Some such arrangements may well have existed earlier, but it was not until the very end of the eleventh century that there was any trace of a regular and continuing organization, with a hierarchy of teaching posts not only for theology but for grammar and rhetoric as well, fixed places of instruction in churches of the capital, regular salaries and a regular system of appointment and promotion, in which the emperor as well as the patriarch were involved. Successful teachers in the Patriarchal School could expect to end their careers in one of the prestigious metropolitan sees of the provinces. Such an educational institution—which seems to have taught laymen as well as future clerics—could be relied on to maintain the emphasis on Greek intellectual tradition as something peculiar to the Byzantines, and at the same time not to allow the emphasis to be carried too far.

Nevertheless, in spite of these limitations, the literature, thought

Ivory plaque showing Adam and Eve working in the fields, a fine example of Byzantine carving from the eleventh or twelfth century. *Courtesy of The Metropolitan Museum of Art (Gift of J. Pierpont Morgan, 1917).*

and art of the Byzantine world continued to draw upon and to develop classical tradition in a most lively fashion throughout the period. Sometimes the anxiety to imitate classical models—and to be seen to be imitating them—led to preciousness and turgidity. But some Byzantine writers succeeded in surmounting the difficulties of classicism and made of it rather a rich and flexible instrument for the expression of original observation, feeling, and thought. Scholars were no longer concerned to piece together the broken fragments of ancient learning. They displayed a confidence and sometimes an originality which suggest that they felt themselves to be the equals and colleagues of the ancients rather than feeble epigones, and a great deal of the literature of the period is in some measure scholarly. It is the literature of an intellectual élite, but an élite which is open, and which, in medieval terms, was probably quite large. Classicizing literature of this kind is always in danger of becoming totally disconnected from the life of the society within which it is produced. The Byzantine literature of the twelfth century did not entirely escape this danger, especially in the closing decades of the century when Byzantine society was in manifest crisis. Many of the panegyrics, funeral orations, and the like, with their constant repetition of grandiose comparisons, their almost hysterically declamatory tone, and their wild exaggeration of the most trivial and fleeting successes, are distasteful to the modern ear. Yet their sometimes almost zany exaggeration is itself a symptom of the growing discrepancy between the Byzantines' picture of themselves and the sorry reality. The discerning reader can often crack the code in which they are composed and find in them genuine expressions of the political, moral, and intellectual controversies of the times.

To enumerate even the principal twelfth-century Byzantine writers and their works is beyond the scope of this book. It is better to dwell on certain genres or types of literature and incidentally to give some account of the major figures. Let us begin with philosophy and theology, which are closely connected. Long, analytic, philosophical commentaries on the works of Plato and Aristotle were one of the principal types of philosophical literature in late antiquity, and reflected the way in which philosophical problems were studied. Proklos and other leading Neoplatonists produced such commentaries on the dialogues of Plato. Aristotle's works were the subject of commentaries by representatives of many schools, from the Peripatetic Alexander of Aphrodisias around A.D. 200 to the Neoplatonists and to Christian scholars like John Philoponus (sixth century) and David and Elias (early seventh century). In the period of the great Arab conquests and the loss of the northern Balkans, comment upon Aristotle ceased, presumably because regular study of his work ceased. Only his logical works remained of interest—some acquaintance with them was necessary for the pursuit of theological argument. Now, quite suddenly, in the early twelfth century, the tradition is taken up again. Eustratios, bishop of Nicaea, wrote a long commentary on Aristotle's *Ethics*, while Michael of Ephesus wrote on the *Ethics*, the *Organon*, and the zoological works. These commentaries naturally embodied much traditional material, but they also contained many original and penetrating observations. Though Eustratios was, and Michael may have been, a churchman, they made no attempt to square Aristotelian doctrine with Christian dogma. Philosophy was for them a serious and autonomous pursuit. Eustratios was a pupil of John Italos, and Michael had studied either with Italos or with Michael Psellos. Eustratios was the author of several anti-Latin theological treatises and was chosen by Alexios I to defend the Orthodox point of view in a debate in Constantinople in 1112 with a Latin prelate, Pietro Grossolano. In his theological writings Eustratios used well-constructed logical arguments, rather than compilations of quotations from the Bible or the Church Fathers, torn from their sources. He was much concerned with the relations between the persons of the Trinity, and in particular between the Father and the Son, which he saw as largely a philosophical problem, soluble by rational argument. This approach aroused the wrath of the more traditionally-minded leaders of the Church, and in 1117 he was charged with heresy and condemned, in spite of strong support from the emperor and from the patriarch, John Agapetos. The case of Eustratios reminds us of the progress of rationalism resulting from the teaching of Psellos and Italos, of the close links between the study of Hellenic philosophy and theology, and of the interplay between enlightenment and repression characteristic of the age.

In the middle of the century there was a dispute concerning the sacrifice of the Eucharist. If the Son was sacrificed to the Father, what exactly were the relations between the persons of the Trinity? Certain leading intellectual figures in Constantinople—including a candidate for the patriarchate of Antioch and two teachers in the Patriarchal School—came to the conclusion that the Eucharistic sacrifice was offered to the Father alone, and that it was only a kind of reflection or reminder of the real sacrifice through which the salvation of mankind was attained. The traditional viewpoint was defended by Nicholas of Methone, the author of the refutation of Proklos, who argued that the new doctrine depended on a logical confusion. His arguments carried the day, and the innovators were declared to be heretics. A little later in 1166, a similar dispute arose over the interpretation of the Gospel phrase, "My father is greater than I" (John 14:28), which raised once again the philosophical problem of the Trinity. Once again there was a *cause célèbre*, and several leading intellectuals were found guilty of heresy and removed from their official positions. The dispute between the eastern and western Churches also had a philosophical side to it, as one of the points of disagreement was the relation of the Holy Spirit to the other persons of the Trinity. Many of the twelfth-century anti-Latin polemicists concentrated on logical analysis of this problem. Throughout the period there was, side by side with the more traditional Byzantine type of theological argument by the citation of authorities, a new approach in which theological problems were treated as essentially philosophical in their nature. The men who developed this new approach were often philosophers in their own right as well as theologians. They aroused fierce opposition and sometimes direct persecution by their more traditional colleagues. But in their turn they forced their opponents to meet them on their own ground of logical argument.

It is impossible not to be struck by the many resemblances with what was going on at the same time in the west, where a new, philosophical approach to theological problems often led to condemnation by the ecclesiastical authorities. The parallels are real enough. What is not clear is how far, if at all, they were the result of direct influences of the one society upon the other. There was certainly intense mutual hostility and mistrust. Yet at the same time there was far more contact between easterners and westerners than there had been before, and the contact reached even to the highest circles in Byzantine society. It is only from a chance phrase in a funeral oration that we learn that the brother of Nicephorus Basilakes, a man of letters, teacher in the Patriarchal School, and one of those condemned for his heretical views on the sacrifice of the Eucharist, was an expert on western affairs and a fluent Latin speaker often employed on confidential missions to the pope: in the words of the orator, he was "a Hellene among the Romans and a Roman among the Hellenes."

One of the techniques which the Macedonian age had learned from its renewed study of classical authors was that of writing history in which the characters of men and the causes of events were analysed. Michael Psellos in his *Chronography* or history of his own times added a personal tone to the writing of history. Not only does he himself appear as an actor in the events which he narrates, but his personal judgments, his asides, his comments constantly intervene between the reader and the narrative. The result was a kind of history in which the literary persona of the historian is always to the fore, and in which a variety of intellectual or emotional stances to the events narrated can be taken up. Ancient Greek historians such as Polybius had done something similar, but not in such a thoroughgoing way as Psellos. His example was followed to some extent by those who wrote the history of their own times in the twelfth century, though none of them had so striking an authorial persona.

Anna Comnena, the eldest daughter of Alexios I, composed, after her father's death and her own fall from influence, a long history of Alexios's reign. It is a remarkable work. Anna was intensely and self-consciously proud of her erudition, which she never missed an opportunity to display. At the same time she was a shrewd observer with an eye for telling detail. She is often better in her descriptive than in her narrative passages. She was a woman of strong passions, who took no trouble to conceal either her admiration or her hatred. Her hero is her father, and in some ways her work is as much a panegyric as a history. Her *bête noire* is Bohemond the Norman. Yet behind her scathing attacks upon him one can detect a certain admiration for the bold and unscrupulous westerner. Anna was a snob, and she spent far too much energy trying to write thoroughly classicizing Greek. But with all its faults, her history displays sharp intelligence, passion, and immediacy of response, which make it one of the great works of medieval literature.

Her husband, Nicephorus Bryennius, narrated the story of Alexios's rise to power. Careful, competent, balanced, a valuable historical source, his rather flat history cannot be compared with the sparkling narrative of his wife. John Kinnamos, a high government offficial with access to state secrets, wrote a history of the reigns of John II and Manuel I, of which only an epitome survives. His work is objective and reliable, particularly on military matters, which he understood well. He—or his epitomator—omits much of importance. But he does attempt seriously to establish the motivation of actors in the events he narrates.

The last great historian of the period, Niketas Choniates, actually wrote his history in the first decades of the thirteenth century. His theme is the glorious reign of Manuel I and the disastrous rule of his successors, culminating in the capture of Constantinople by the crusaders in 1204. Niketas writes in an extraordinary style, full of strange and rare classical words and phrases. These are often used to suggest parallelism with and difference from situations and personages of classical antiquity, in a kind of historical counterpoint. Niketas has a compelling subject, the catastrophic change from imperial grandeur to squalid impotence. He sees the cause of the decline in the personal weakness and corruption of the rulers and their entourage. But sometimes he seems to be reaching after more profound explanations which he has not the conceptual equipment to formulate. He is unusually fair-minded, and ready to understand the motives and actions of Seljuq Turks and Latin crusaders with the same empathy as those of his fellow countrymen. In spite of some weakness in his structure and an exaggerated tendency to digression, which together make his chronology unclear, Niketas is perhaps the greatest of all the Byzantine historians.

Yet if one were to ask what genre dominated Byzantine literature in the period, the answer would be rhetoric, not history. The public speech, copied and despatched to friends and contacts throughout the empire, played a role not unlike that of journalism today. Every anniversary, every trivial event, gave rise to firework displays of oratory. There were schools and fashions in eloquence. Nicephorus Basilakes was the leader of one such school, idolized and imitated by his pupils and followers. Only a tiny fraction of the oratory of the age of the Comneni has survived, but even that fraction is a very considerable body of texts. They were essentially occasional pieces, hastily composed. Much was mere blind following of the rules of the textbooks of rhetoric. The speakers themselves often refer to the rules of the art and draw attention to the skill with which they follow them. The almost hysterically panegyric tone of most of these orations grates on the modern ear. Yet it would be unwise to dismiss these orators—to whose numbers most of the men of letters of the period belong—as mere windbags. They were expert craftsmen, combining lucid narrative with allusive indirectness; their skill was critically assessed and enjoyed by their hearers and readers. They often gave expression to the immediate reaction of society to events, and sometimes to the tensions and differences between groups. Never before had so much communication occurred about matters of public interest and concern. There is evidence that these ephemeral speeches were among the sources used by the historians of the period. The orators were themselves the prisoners of the literary tradition in which they worked, with its rejection of the concrete and particular in favor of the abstract and general, and its obsessional pursuit of linguistic purism. That many of them succeeded in being both informative and moving, as well as provoking admiration by their cleverness, is a tribute to the power of their imagination and their command of a complex and sophisticated medium of expression.

A great deal of occasional poetry was composed, almost all permeated by rhetoric. There was only one poet who occasionally displayed a vein of inspiration, Theodore Prodromos. He was probably for a time a teacher of rhetoric in the Patriarchal School, but his talent for facile versification led to his receiving many commissions for poems from influential patrons, including the emperors John II and Manuel I. Poetry poured from his pen, and no complete list of his authentic works has yet been established. At one extreme are his cycles of very short poems on church festivals, saints, and the like. At the other come his long "historical" poems, addresses to or epitaphs on personages of the time. And there is much that comes between. These poems are all written in classical quantitative meters, or in the Byzantine twelve-syllable line which is a degraded version of the classical iambic trimeter. Another extensive group of poems, written in the fifteen-syllable Byzantine accentual verse, was intended to be chanted or declaimed at court ceremonials, often by the *demes*, pale, ritualized epigones of the circus factions of late antiquity, the Greens and the Blues. He also wrote a long verse romance, of which more anon, a dramatic poem with satirical overtones on *The War of the Cats and Mice*, a long poem on astrology dedicated to a niece of John II, as well as prose pastiches of the dialogues of Lucian, grammatical works, a long commentary on the liturgical hymns of John of Damascus and his brother Cosmas of Maiuma, and a number of letters and speeches. Several points of interest emerge from this catalogue. The first is the virtual takeover of poetry by rhetoric and the absence of any sense of the difference between poetry and prose. This was not, either in Byzantium or in the west, an age of inspired poets. Prodromos was elegant, clever, sometimes ironically detached, but there is no surge and thunder, no intensity of feeling, no depth of understanding. The second point is that Prodromos, like several of his contemporaries, was a professional writer, and not an official or clergyman or teacher who happened to write. The growth of the profession of letters before the invention of printing depended rather on the presence of patrons than on a large reading public. Yet there is evidence for a widespread interest in literature, even if it was confined to those whose education enabled them to appreciate the archaizing literary language.

There is a small collection of poems written in a rather uneven approximation to spoken Greek. They are attributed to a certain Ptochoprodromos (=Poor Prodromos), and whether they are the work of Theodore Prodromos or not we cannot say. They are short, partly dramatic, genre pieces—the henpecked husband of a rich wife, the monk with a grudge against his superiors, the man of education who sees the ignorant enjoying a richer life than he does, and so on. They were probably written for the amusement of court circles under Manuel I, and are something of a technical *tour de force*, since there were no rules for writing the spoken language. But they are in no sense a breakthrough into literature by the language of the people. They probably owe something to such Hellenistic genre studies as Theocritus's poem of the two ladies visiting the festival of Adonis.

One of the most interesting developments in the literature of the period is the reintroduction of pure fiction, both in verse and in prose. Ancient literary theory and practice had had little place for fiction, though some of the post-classical poetic treatments of myth came close to it: and there were Attic tragedies with entirely fictitious themes, though none has survived. The only surviving classical Greek works in which characters and plot are entirely invented are those of the Greek novelists Chariton, Xenophon of Ephesus, Heliodorus, Longus, and Achilles Tatius. All of these deal with the adventures of a pair of lovers, usually separated by a stroke of ill-fortune. Their authors avoid the miraculous or supernatural, but have no scruples about the highly improbable. In the middle of the twelfth century a number of imitations of these appeared. They all have as their central theme the adventures and final reunion of a pair of lovers, and they are set in a rather timeless classical landscape. They are in no way slavish imitations of the classical novels. Some of them are in verse, though the Greek novelists all wrote in prose. Though the characters are rather wooden, and their utterances highly rhetorical, the authors show great fertility of invention and some degree of psychological insight. Theodore Prodromos wrote one such romance in verse. His pupil and friend Niketas Eugenianos, a teacher of rhetoric, and his contemporary Constantine Manasses, who also composed a chronicle of world history in verse, also wrote verse romances. The otherwise unknown Eumathios Makrembolites wrote a similar romance in prose, which gains additional realism from being narrated in the first person. These middle Byzantine romances have long been brushed aside as artificial and boring by historians of literature, who often have not read them. Today there is a renewed interest in them, and in the eagerness with which their authors explored the techniques of fictitious narrative. The romances, both in prose and in verse, appear to have been composed to amuse and delight the refined upper strata of Byzantine society, a new task for serious literature to face.

The art of letter-writing had always been highly prized by the Byzantines. For them a letter was not merely the medium of a message. Indeed the message itself was often left to be delivered verbally by the bearer of the letter. A letter was expected to be the expression of the deepest feelings of the writer and also to give exquisite aesthetic pleasure. It was felt to provide a closer link between writer and addressee than was possible in a personal encounter, where there would be no room for the careful choice of phrase and the critical self-appraisal of the writer. As Michael Psellos observes,

> When we are present we engage in personal conversation, when we are absent we converse in letters. Speech and letter correspond to union and separation, of which the former is the better. Yet I devote myself more to the letter; it provides the best picture of a friend and shows the state of his soul. For ordinary speech is guided by the incidental and does not give a true representation of the speaker. But the mode of expression of a letter displays outwardly the inward structure of the writer. Where in everyday conversation do we find an elegantly constructed sentence or the expression of well-ordered harmony? . . . Letters penetrate deeper into the soul, than if the writer were to bring the news himself.[12]

Even more than in the eleventh century, the letter was cultivated as an art form in the age of the Comneni. Many collections of letters were published either by the writers themselves or by their friends after their death. Among the most interesting are those of Theophylact, archbishop of Ohrid (d. ca. 1126), Michael Italikos, the teacher of Theodore Prodromos, Prodromos himself, Nicephorus Basilakes, John Tzetzes, Theodore Balsamon, the canon lawyer, Eustathios, metropolitan of Thessalonica, George Tornikes, teacher in the Patriarchal School and metropolitan of Ephesus, Euthymios Malakes, bishop of Neopatras, Michael Choniates, metropolitan of Athens, and his brother Niketas Choniates, the historian. They vary from pieces of pure stylistic display to serious discussions of theological problems, from conventional expressions of friendship to detailed accounts of the activities of the writer and his friends.

The literary genres which are not practiced can be as indicative of the spirit of the age as those which are. Notable forms of literature still being composed in the Macedonian age and after, but virtually dead in the twelfth century, are liturgical poetry and the lives of saints. There was, of course, a technical reason for this. The liturgies of the Church became relatively fixed in the eleventh century, and there were no vacant "slots" to be filled by new hymns or new lives. But this seems an insufficient explanation for the decline and disappearance of two literary forms which for centuries had played a major role in Byzantine culture. It is likely that the rationalism and the aesthetic discrimination of the age of the Comneni found these often long-winded and badly structured works unsatisfying.

In an age concerned with the preservation and imitation of a classical tradition it is not always easy to draw a line between literature and scholarship. Many of the men of letters of the twelfth century devoted some of their energy to antiquarian studies of one kind and another.

There are, however, many twelfth-century writers whose main activity was the pursuit of scholarship. Gregorios Pardos, metropolitan of Corinth about the middle of the century, devoted himself to the detailed study of the Greek language in its classical forms. A long treatise on grammar and a handbook of the literary dialects of classical Greece were his principal works. Both were marked by great diligence and by a lack of adequate grammatical concepts for which he is scarcely to be blamed, since it was traditional. Try as he did to classify syntactical patterns and their functions, he rarely got beyond analytical study of individual words. John Zonaras, a high court official in the early twelfth century, wrote a universal history, valuable for the information which it contains from sources now lost, a long treatise on canon law, and commentaries on the liturgical hymns of the Church. The immense lexicon which goes under his name—it contains about 19,000 entries—was probably compiled shortly after the sacking of Constantinople by the crusaders in 1204.

The career in the public service of John Tzetzes (c. 1110–80) was brought to a premature end by an error of judgment involving the wife of a provincial governor. For most of his life he gained his livelihood by teaching and writing in Constantinople, often producing works commissioned by patrons. His range was immense, and much of his work was hastily composed without adequate access to books. He had a phenomenal memory, of which he was inordinately proud, but it led him astray from time to time. His philological commentaries on works of classical Greek poetry from Homer to Oppian depend, like all Byzantine commentaries, on compilation from the fragments of Alexandrian scholarship. But he shows much independence of judgment and is prepared to reject traditional interpretations when he thinks they are wrong. He clearly feels himself in some respects the equal of the ancients. More original are the works of scholarship in verse which he composed to the order of ladies of the imperial court who sought an easy introduction to classical literature. The most important of these are the long, allegorical commentaries on the *Iliad* and the *Odyssey*. They are composed in the fifteen-syllable "political" verse for ease of memorization and were partly written at the request of Manuel I's consort, Bertha of Sulzbach. They do not seem to have furthered the lady's interest in Homer, as Tzetzes complains that after receiving the first instalment she did not pay him for the rest. Another poem in "political" verse, the *Theogony*, was a kind of encyclopaedia of Greek mythology. Long hexameter poems recounting the tale of the Trojan War, its antecedents, and its consequences were doubtless also written as an easy introduction for laymen. These works of popularization are an interesting pointer to the interest in Hellenic tradition among readers and hearers who had not pursued the classical studies of grammar and rhetoric. Tzetzes compiled a collection of his letters, as did many of his contemporaries. He then went on, however, and equipped it with a gigantic commentary in nearly 13,000 lines of "political" verse, which is a veritable encyclopaedia of miscellaneous knowledge. Later he went on to add the elements of a prose commentary on his commentary. The whole work conveys an impression of scholarship without an object, of a powerful engine driving nothing.

Tzetzes was in some ways a misfit and a failure in his own society. Yet his devotion of immense energy and erudition to a trivial end is a feature found elsewhere in the literature of the twelfth century, and points to a breakdown in the structure of Byzantine society and Byzantine life, a growing discrepancy between ends and means.

A near contemporary of Tzetzes was Eustathios, metropolitan of Thessalonica, who was both a more profound scholar and a more attractive personality. He taught literature and rhetoric at the Patriarchal School for many years, before being appointed about 1175 to the see of Thessalonica. There he displayed a talent for organization and for distinguishing the important from the trifling which scholars do not always possess, as well as a zeal for reform of abuses among the clergy. He was present when the Normans sacked Thessalonica in 1185, and within a few months wrote a graphic and moving account of the fate of the city. He died about 1195.

Eustathios's scholarly works belong to his period as a teacher, and were written at the request of friends rather than the order of patrons. There survive extremely long commentaries on the *Iliad* and *Odyssey*, on the geographical poem of Dionysius Periegetes—which was used as a schoolbook—and on the Pentecost hymn of John of Damascus, as well as the Introduction to a commentary on Pindar; his commentary on Aristophanes is lost. Eustathios's commentaries bear many traces of oral delivery, and must be related to the lectures he delivered to his students. However he makes it clear that they were also addressed to a wider public and could be read for their own sake, without reference to the text of Homer. They are marked by great accuracy of detail, fair-minded exposition of conflicting views, immense erudition, and a certain tendency to digression, as if his mind worked by association of ideas. Unlike many scholars of the age, who remained encapsulated within the world of classical learning and mentioned the common people and their life with expressions of contempt, if at all, Eustathios was a lively observer of the world about him. His commentaries are full of incidental observations on folklore, crafts, proverbs, popular superstitions, and the everyday spoken language of the people, which he often uses to illuminate the passage upon which he is commenting. For Eustathios literature is a very important part of life and not a means of escape from life.

In addition to his works of scholarship and his account of the capture of Thessalonica, we have a number of speeches which he delivered as archbishop, homilies on church festivals, and a collection of letters. All his work is marked by learning, fairness, humanity, and an abounding curiosity. For a teacher of rhetoric his style is often involved and wooden. Yet he remains one of the most attractive of Byzantine intellectuals of any age. He was recognized as a saint—the Orthodox Church has no formal procedure of canonization—and is depicted with a halo and the legend "St. Eustathios of Thessalonica" in a fresco in the early fourteenth-century church at Gračanica in Serbia.

These are only a few of the principal writers in an age of great literary activity. They illustrate the variety of the intellectual climate, the conflicts between rationalism and dogma, between tradition and originality, between high expectations and the often disappointing reality of an age of transition.

The Comnenian emperors were themselves lavish patrons of the arts. Manuel I built "immensely long colonnaded halls" both in the Great Palace between the Hippodrome and the Sea of Marmara and in the new Blachernae Palace on the Golden Horn. In the words of a historian, its walls, "resplendent with gold mosaics, portray in diverse colors and by means of marvellous handicraft the brave deeds he accomplished against the barbarians and the other benefits he conferred upon the Romans."[13] Andronikos I repaired the church of the Forty Martyrs and set up in the square in front of the church a mosaic in which he himself was represented in the dress of a peasant and with a reaping hook in his hand. A cousin of Manuel I built the exquisite little church of St. Panteleimon at Nerezi near Skopje and had it adorned with frescos by artists from the capital in 1167. Isaac Angelos tried to make up for his ineffectiveness as a ruler by the magnificence of his buildings, and even Alexios III was a generous, if erratic, patron.

Little of this metropolitan art of the period survives. The destruction in the capital in 1204 and 1453 and rebuilding during the Ottoman period resulted in the disappearance of most of the buildings and monuments mentioned by historians. However the new world situation, in which the Byzantine Empire stood on an equal footing with a number of other European states, meant that Byzantine artists and their work were in demand far beyond the frontiers of the empire. For however unstable the political and military strength of the empire might be, in matters of art and civilization its prestige remained unchallenged. Much of this "export art" survives. It is not always easy to distinguish between the work of Byzantine artists abroad and that of their local pupils. But in some cases the superb quality and technical skill of the work leaves no doubt that it was executed by Constantinopolitan artists of the first order, probably sent abroad under imperial patronage. The mosaics of Hagia Sophia in Kiev, executed between 1037 and 1061, belong to the previous period. The painted portraits of Russian rulers and their families which accompany them are lighter and more airy in style and may well be the work of local artists. The frescos of the church of St. Michael in Kiev were painted in 1108, probably by artists sent by Alexios I to the Russian prince. Norman Sicily, in spite of the aggressive designs of its rulers, had artists from Constantinople decorate some of its new buildings, which were to symbolize the power and authority of its new Christian rulers. The mosaics in the Cathedral of Cefalù and in the Cappella Palatina in Palermo are certainly the work of first-class artists from Constantinople. The same is probably true of some of the mosaics in the Martorana in Palermo. All these date from 1143–54. It is not easy to be certain about the mosaic decoration of the church at Monreale, near Palermo (c. 1180), and many scholars believe it to be the work of local artists who had learned their craft from Byzantine masters. Some of the apparently metropolitan art in the Byzantine provinces is similarly the work of local artists who had learnt from metropolitan masters. Thus the frescos in the tiny church of St. George at Kurbinovo, in Yugoslavia, though clearly influenced by those of Nerezi, seem to be the work of several Macedonian artists, whose hand can also be traced at nearby Kastoria in Greece. The superb frescos in the little churches of Asinou and Lagoudera in Cyprus, both dedicated by Byzantine

governors in the late twelfth century, may combine the work of artists
brought from the metropolis with that of local painters.

Portable works of art have survived better than monumental art,
and it is upon a study of manuscript illustrations, icons, carved ivories,
and the like that an analysis of the styles of twelfth-century Byzantine
art must be based. For in the visual arts, as in literature, it was an
age of conflict and experiment. The lessons which the artists of the
Macedonian period had learnt from studying and copying classical
models were now the common property of all. But they were used in
different ways. Imperial portraits always tended to be conservative.
Their function was not so much representation of an individual as
symbolization of an institution. In the mosaic panel of John II and
Irene in the gallery of Hagia Sophia, the imperial pair are still depicted in stiff frontality, with impossibly small hands and feet, and all
the artist's care is devoted to their jewel-encrusted and resplendent
clothing. Yet even here the faces have a certain softness and plasticity
that is new. In view of the strongly conservative tradition of imperial
portraiture, the portrait of Andronikos I in peasant garb must have
been sensational in its impact. There are many other examples of
the conservative current in twelfth-century art, such as the miniature
mosaic of Christ Pantocrator, now in the Museo Nazionale, Florence,
which recalls the mosaics in the domes of Daphni and Hosios Lukas
at the beginning of the eleventh century, or the miniature of Christ
and the Apostles in a manuscript of the Acts of the Apostles executed
in the reign of Alexios Comnenus.[14]

Many works of the period show an elegant, dry, refined style, with
rather elongated human figures and an almost deliberate avoidance
of the grandeur of the more conservative tradition. An exquisite example is the ivory relief of John the Baptist and saints in the Victoria
and Albert Museum in London. The reliefs on an ivory casket in the
Museo Nazionale, Florence, display the same features. This elegant,
slightly detached style is also to be found in the miniature of Christ
crowning John II and his eldest son Alexios in a Vatican Gospel book
of about 1122.[15]

A more important development was that of a highly emotional

style, which sought to convey not so much the power of religious figures as their more tender human feelings. The passion cycle frescos at Nerezi (1164), particularly the Deposition and the Lamentation, are splendid examples of this new tendency, which is also represented, though less strikingly, at Kurbinovo (1191) and at Asinou and La-goudera in Cyprus. In these paintings figures which had earlier been represented as passive bystanders now enter into the emotional field of the events. In another medium, the icon of the Virgin of Vladimir, executed in Constantinople about 1130 for a Russian patron and now in the Tretyakov Gallery in Moscow, displays with superb skill the same interest in human feelings. The Child's face is pressed against his mother's cheek and his tiny hands try to encircle her neck, while she gazes at him with tenderness and sadness. Here we have not only a new style but a new iconography too. The traditional Byzantine representation of the Virgin was as the Hodegetria—She Who Shows the Way—in which the Virgin points to the Child seated on her lap, but neither looks at the other. They are there to illustrate dogma, not feeling. Many manuscript illustrations also display the "tender" or emotional style, for example the miniature of St. Thecla in a volume of saints' lives in the British Museum[16] or the Miracle at Chonae in the same manuscript,[17] the portrait of St. Luke and Theophilus—the latter incongruously wearing the dress of a Byzantine emperor—in a New Testament in the Bodleian Library, Oxford.[18] The ivory relief of Gospel scenes in the Victoria and Albert Museum, London, has this same emotional involvement of characters in events, which often involves an interest in and an analysis of movement, which is something new in Byzantine art.

Side by side with the high art which depended on the patronage of the rich and powerful there was a more popular art. Underglaze painted pottery was in common use, with religious scenes, motifs of legend, fantastic animals and birds. It has been little studied, and it may turn out that it was more open to both oriental and western influences than was the high art. Painted ceramic plaques were much used in decoration. The powerful caricature-like clay head of a man wearing a hat, found by American excavators in Corinth, shows how

The Virgin of Vladimir was painted in Constantinople and brought to Russia in the mid-twelfth century where it greatly influenced Russian icon painters. Only the faces in the icon are original, dating from c. 1125; the rest was overpainted at a later date. *Courtesy of Tretyakov Gallery, Moscow.*

many aspects of twelfth-century Byzantine art are inaccessible to us because of the perishable material used. The period was one not only of the perfection of old traditions but also of wide-ranging innovation and experiment. It would be foolish to seek too close a correspondence between the visual arts and literature. Their role in society was too different. But they did not pursue wholly contrary courses.

Both in literature and thought and in the visual arts Byzantine culture still held a predominant position in Europe. The Byzantines provided models for other peoples, but borrowed little from them. It was in the twelfth century that western scholars, who often came to Constantinople in connection with the unending theological discussions between the eastern and western churches, began to realize that their knowledge of the Greek language and their possession of classical texts gave the Byzantines access to a rich intellectual tradition of which the west knew only scattered fragments. James of Venice in the early twelfth century translated directly from Greek the whole of Aristotle's logical works, hitherto known in the west only in the ancient version of Boethius or in retranslations from Arabic versions. Later in the century Burgundio of Pisa translated, in a rather wooden, word-for-word way, John of Damascus's theological writings, many of the homilies of John Chrysostom, the curious work of Nemesios of Emesa on the *Nature of Man*, which mingles Christian dogma, Neoplatonist philosophy, and Greek medicine, and, last but not least, some of the medical works of Hippocrates and Galen. Thus the first steps were taken to close the intellectual gap that had grown up between eastern and western Europe in the early Middle Ages.

The visual arts are more easily exported than literature or philosophy, since they are not language bound. Portable Byzantine works of art, such as icons, ivories, figured textiles, and illuminated manuscripts, were objects of great prestige in the west. The sack of Constantinople in 1204 brought many more Byzantine art works to Europe. To trace detailed chains of influence is beyond the scope of this book, but this growing export of Byzantine art of all kinds contributed to the growth of a rather stiff, hieratic, style in Italian art, which Vasari in his *Lives of the Painters* stigmatized as "*maniera greca.*"

Politically disoriented and unable to defend itself militarily, Byzantium was nevertheless a treasure house of culture from which other societies were eager to borrow, and in so doing they often laid the foundations of a rich independent development of their own. The clearest example of this lies not in western Europe but in Russia. But in the west, too, in spite of much popular anti-Byzantine feeling engendered by the crusades, men were beginning to learn from the great city on the Bosphorus and its people.

5

DEFEAT AND DISINTEGRATION 1204–1453

Painted plate with a Byzantine ship dating from the thirteenth century. *Courtesy of American School of Classical Studies Athens, Corinth Excavations. I. Ioannidou, L. Bartziotou.*

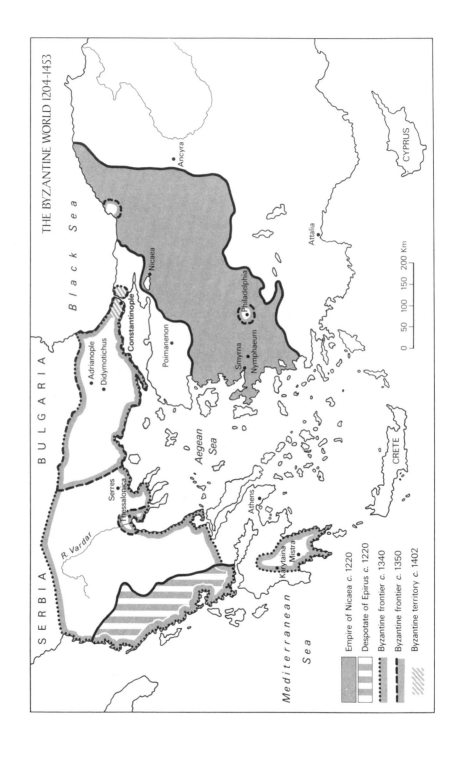

THE BYZANTINE WORLD 1204-1453

Black Sea

CYPRUS

• Ancyra

• Nicaea

Constantinople

Adrianople
• Didymotichus

Poimanenon

Philadelphia

Smyrna
Nymphaeum

Attalia

0   50   100   150   200 Km

SERBIA

BULGARIA

Serres
Thessalonica

R. Vardar

Aegean Sea

Athens

Karytaina
Mistra

Mediterranean Sea

CRETE

Empire of Nicaea c. 1220
Despotate of Epirus c. 1220
Byzantine frontier c. 1340
Byzantine frontier c. 1350
Byzantine territory c. 1402

The western conquerors of Constantinople proceeded to divide the former territories of the empire between themselves with mathematical precision. One quarter was allocated to the emperor; three-eighths went to Venice as a reward for providing transport, supplies, and naval support; three-eighths was to be divided among the Latin knights as fiefs. Constantinople itself was partitioned equally between the emperor and the Venetians. The reality, however, was somewhat different. The Latins were not in control of the whole of the territory to which they laid claim. There were pockets of resistance headed by former Byzantine officials or local dignitaries in many regions of the European provinces. Some of these were speedily conquered or came to terms with the Latins, while others never submitted to Latin rule. More important, the Latins controlled only a small strip of Asia Minor bordering on the Bosphorus and the Dardanelles. The rest of this vast territory was beyond their powers to occupy.

The immediate outcome of the conquest was that Thrace and the northwest tip of Asia Minor fell to the Emperor Baldwin; Boniface of Montferrat established a kingdom in Macedonia and Thessaly with Thessalonica as its capital; central Greece was divided among a number of petty states, of which the lordship—later the duchy—of Athens was by far the most important; the Peloponnese became the principality of the Morea, under the rule of Geoffrey de Villehardouin; while Crete, Euboea, the Ionian Islands and many of the Aegean islands, as well as a number of ports, became Venetian colonies. Michael Angelos, a cousin of Isaac II, established his authority in Epirus. In the far northeast of Asia Minor two grandsons of Andronikos I, Alexios and David Comnenus, who had been in rebellion against the authority of Constantinople before 1204, ruled over the territory between the Black Sea and the Pontic Alps, with the powerful support of Queen Thamar of Georgia; their capital was at Trebizond. Finally, Theodore Laskaris, a son-in-law of Alexios III, gained control of a large area of western Asia Minor and set up his headquarters in Nicaea. Thus there existed three embryo Greek successor states to the dismembered Byzantine Empire. That of Trebizond was too remote and peripheral to be of much account. Those of Epirus and Nicaea were a real threat to the stability and permanence of the Latin Empire.

Theodore Laskaris had the greatest difficulty in consolidating his power in Asia Minor, in the face of Latin military pressure, the resistance of local warlords and grandees who were not eager to see central authority reestablished, and the hostility of the Seljuq sultan of Iconium. The rulers of Epirus had similarly to face the Latin states of northern Greece, the sea power of Venice, and the expansionist ambitions of the Serbs. However the situation was dramatically transformed when a group of landowners in Thrace, fearful—as well they might be—that their estates would be confiscated, appealed for help to King Kalojan of Bulgaria. Eager to fish in troubled waters, Kalojan led his army into Thrace. On 4 April 1205 he decisively defeated the Latin forces at Adrianople and took the Emperor Baldwin prisoner. The weakness and disunity of the Latin Empire was clear for all to see. The Greek successor states in Europe and Asia Minor were granted respite from Latin military pressure. In Asia Theodore Laskaris rapidly built up a replica of the Byzantine administrative structure. When in 1208 he succeeded in getting his candidate, Michael Autoreianos, recognized as patriarch by the Church and was solemnly crowned by him in Nicaea, he not only transformed himself from a successful warlord to a legitimate sovereign; he also staked his claim to all territory recovered from the Latins and eventually to Constantinople itself. Though the Byzantine state had been shattered and disrupted, the Byzantine church was intact and its authority extended to all the Orthodox, including those living under Latin rule. The Church thus provided an element of continuity and unity which was all the more important now that the state no longer existed, and the Church could recognize only one empire and one emperor, who was no mere temporal ruler, but God's instrument. Thus the coronation of Theodore Laskaris by the new patriarch made Nicaea the political and ecclesiastical center of the Orthodox world, a kind of Constantinople-in-exile.

The Latins responded to the new situation by making a secret treaty with the Turkish sultan. There was much fighting in border areas of Asia Minor. But in 1211 Theodore Laskaris defeated the Turks in a battle in which the Sultan Kai-Chosrow I was killed. In 1214 the Latins signed a treaty at Nymphaeum with Theodore which regulated the boundary between their relative domains and by implication abandoned the Latin claim to sovereignty over all former Byzantine territory. The situation of the Nicaean Empire, as historians have come to call it, was now relatively secure and stable. The realistic Venetians recognized its new status by signing a treaty with Theodore in 1219 by which they obtained the same right to trade free of duty which they had formerly enjoyed in the Byzantine Empire.

In Europe Theodore Angelos and his son Michael profited by Latin weakness to expand and consolidate their power. About 1215 Theodore defeated a Latin force and took prisoner the new Latin emperor, Peter de Courtenay. A few years later he was able to give siege to Thessalonica, which he captured in 1224. Thus within twenty years of the Fourth Crusade two Greek states had established themselves on the territory of the former empire, and the Latin Empire was on the verge of collapse—though its theoretical vassals in central Greece and the Peloponnese and its Venetian allies still enjoyed their power undisturbed. Conflict between the two Greek states for the Byzantine heritage was inevitable. The next few years saw complicated and changing alliances between each of them and Bulgaria. For the Bulgarians, too, were ambitious to become the heirs of Byzantium and to realize Tsar Symeon's dream of a Bulgaro-Greek Orthodox Empire.

In 1225 John III Vatatzes, who had succeeded to Theodore Laskaris, won a decisive victory over the Latin forces at Poimanenon, south of Cyzicus. The Latins were forced to cede all their territory in Asia Minor except for a small area facing Constantinople, while Vatatzes' troops crossed into Europe and seized Adrianople. The Nicaeans now had footing on both sides of the Dardanelles. Five years later the Epirot army was defeated by John II Asen of Bulgaria at Klokotnica, near Philippopolis. Theodore Angelus was taken prisoner and blinded, and much Epirot territory was taken over by Bulgaria. But the

real victor was John Vatatzes of Nicaea, who now no longer had to
fear his western rival. For a time Nicaeans and Bulgarians made common cause against the Latins in Thrace, and in 1236 began a joint
siege of Constantinople. But their conflicting interests soon opened a
breach between them which could easily have led to open hostility. In
the following year, however, a series of domestic disasters and the
ensuing political troubles obliged the Bulgarian king to return to his
capital and abandon the struggle for Constantinople.

Unable, or unwilling, to undertake a siege of Constantinople on
his own, John Vatatzes concentrated his efforts against his Epirot
rival. In 1242 he launched a campaign to take Thessalonica, but had
to break it off because of dramatic events in another quarter. In the
spring of that year the Mongols, sweeping westward from their distant homeland, invaded Asia Minor. There was a brief alliance between the Nicaean Empire and the sultanate of Iconium, which
joined forces to resist the newcomers. But events moved so fast that
before the year was out the Turks had been defeated and reduced to
tributary status, the Mongols had moved on to attack Baghdad, and
the Nicaean Empire, no longer threatened from the east, was able
to concentrate on Europe. John Vatatzes was not slow to seize the
opportunity offered him. In 1246 he won an overwhelming victory
over the combined Epirot and Bulgarian forces, extended his domains
in Europe as far as the Maritsa and the Vardar, and entered Thessalonica without opposition, to be welcomed by a powerful party in the
city. A year or two later a second victory over the Epirots enabled him
to push his frontier further westwards.

The Nicaeans were now ready to oust the Latins from Constantinople and restore the Byzantine Empire. But there were problems.
The fortifications of the city were a notoriously difficult obstacle. The
Venetians were able to supply the city by sea without hindrance if they
wished. There was a danger that the destruction of the Latin Empire
might provoke a massive, crusade-like reaction from the western
powers. John sought friends in the west, and soon an alliance was
signed with the German emperor, Frederick II, whose control of Sicily gave him a major part in Mediterranean affairs. Relations were

cordial, but no help was forthcoming for the Nicaeans. John also began negotiations with the pope for Church unity, calculating that an ending of the schism between eastern and western churches would make it impossible to mount a crusade against him. But neither side pursued the negotiations with urgency. The pope did not wish to offend the Latin rulers of Greece, and Vatatzes was content to await his opportunity.

That opportunity never came. John died in 1254, respected by his subjects and his enemies alike, and was later recognized as a saint by the Orthodox church. It was above all during his reign that the Nicaean Empire became an economically prosperous state. Freed of the need to maintain Constantinople and its mass of unproductive courtiers and officials, the population of western Asia Minor was able to improve agricultural land and develop trade and industry. Once again an army of peasant-soldiers was settled in the border regions with the Turkish sultanate, an army whose members both ensured the defense of the country and brought new land into cultivation. The court lived relatively modestly and exploited imperial estates efficiently. John Vatatzes once gave his consort a golden crown paid for by the eggs from an imperial poultry farm. Though striving to recreate the Byzantine Empire in miniature, John and his ministers were in fact laying the foundations for a very different kind of state and a different society.

His successor, Theodore II Laskaris, was a scholar, an authoritarian, a believer in centralized power and an enemy of the powerful territorial aristocracy, and a bitter opponent of Church union. He lacked the flexibility and patience of his father. In his brief reign of four years he had no opportunity to force a major confrontation with the Latin Empire. When he died in 1258, his son and successor, John IV Laskaris, was seven years old. In a series of turbulent events Michael Palaeologus, a member of a landed family which had attained prominence under the Comneni, became regent and before the year was out had made himself co-emperor with John IV as Michael VIII. He was at once faced with a difficult situation. Frederick II had died, and his son and successor Manfred had resumed the anti-Byzantine policy of earlier rulers of Sicily. His troops occupied Corfu, Dyrrhachium, and other positions on the east shore of the Adriatic. Soon he had formed an alliance with Epirus and the Villehardouin principality of Achaea, the aim of which was to expel the Nicaeans from Europe and to reinforce the Latin Empire. Serbia, though not formally a member of the coalition, joined in the attack and seized several cities in Macedonia.

Michael VIII responded with energy and decisiveness. In 1259 his army met the forces of the coalition in the plain of Pelagonia, near present-day Bitola, and crushingly defeated them. The flower of Latin chivalry was killed or captured. The prisoners included the prince of Achaea and many other Latin rulers. The Serbs hurriedly evacuated the towns they had occupied. The Nicaean Empire was now the major power in the eastern Mediterranean, and the way lay open to Constantinople. To counter Venetian sea power, Michael signed a treaty with the Genoese, guaranteeing them duty-free trade, even within the Black Sea. The concession was needless. On 5 July 1261 a small Nicaean force which was watching the Bulgarians in Thrace noticed that the Venetian fleet was temporarily absent; it made a dash for Constantinople and took the city almost without opposition. Three weeks later, on 15 August, Michael VIII was crowned for a second time, with all the splendour of imperial ceremonial, in the church of Hagia Sophia. At the same time his three-year-old son Andronikos was proclaimed co-emperor and a few months later the hapless John IV, who had been kept in prison, was blinded.

The Latin interlude was now ended, and the Byzantine Empire restored after fifty-seven years. But it bore little resemblance to the empire in the heyday of the Comneni, which extended from the Adriatic to the Caucasus and from the Danube to the Orontes. Much of peninsular Greece was still in Frankish hands. Crete, the Ionian Islands, and much of the Aegean belonged to the Venetians. A French dynasty reigned in Cyprus. The northern half of the Balkans was divided between Serbia and Bulgaria, both of which were eager to expand their territory southwards. Epirus was still an independent state, whose rulers were animated by implacable hatred for their successful rivals in Constantinople. The Venetians and the Genoese

The Emperor Michael VIII Paleologus, who regained Constantinople and the Latin
Empire for the Byzantines. Portrait from a fifteenth-century manuscript in the monastery of St. Catherine on Mount Sinai. *Courtesy of Library of Congress.*

dominated Byzantine waters right up to the sea walls of the capital. Much of the Thracian hinterland of Constantinople had been desolated by incessant warfare. Most of the accumulated wealth of the state had been plundered by the Latin conquerors. Fragmented and impoverished as it was, the restored empire of Michael VIII had to face major problems in its foreign relations.

The first was that of countering western plans of reconquest, which became particularly menacing when in 1266 the Hohenstaufen manfred was overthrown and replaced as ruler of southern Italy and Sicily by Charles of Anjou, brother of Louis IX of France, who enjoyed full papal support. In resisting this threat Michael was drawn into playing a major role in Mediterranean politics. The second problem was that of stabilizing Byzantine power in Europe, which meant ousting the Greek rulers of Epirus and stopping the drive southwards of Serbia and Bulgaria. This was primarily a military problem, but it had its diplomatic aspect too, since it was imperative to thwart an effective alliance between the Slav states and Charles of Anjou. The third problem was the maintenance of control of western Asia Minor, the heartland of the Nicaean Empire. Here the Mongol invasion had set in motion a westward migration of seminomad Turcomans. Driven from their traditional pastures, they lived largely by plunder. Their uncoordinated but relentless pressure made them far harder to deal with than the sluggish Seljuq sultanate had been.

Michael VIII succeeded, up to a point, in meeting the first two challenges, but only by abandoning any serious attempt to meet the third. The short-term success of his policy masked a long-term failure which was in the end to prove fatal to the empire. Michael profited by his victory over the Latins at Pelagonia to obtain the cession of three key fortresses in the Frankish principality of Achaea, which served as the base for a gradual Byzantine reconquest of the Peloponnese. Many military units were transferred there from the frontier zone of Asia Minor. In 1264 he defeated the Epirot ruler, Michael II Angelos, who then recognized Byzantine suzerainty. But the advent of Charles of Anjou halted Byzantine expansion in Europe. Angevin troops were despatched to Epirus and the Peloponnese, of which

Charles had become overlord. The pope began to press Michael to bring about Church union, without which, he declared, he would feel unable to restrain Charles of Anjou. A defensive alliance with Serbia and Bulgaria against western aggression and Church union, which would have offered the empire some security, was ruled out by Michael's declared intentions to restore the empire to its twelfth-century frontiers. For a time Byzantine diplomacy in France postponed the danger by persuading Louis IX to make his ambitious brother take part in his ill-fated expedition against Tunis, where the pious Louis met his death in 1270. But it seemed to Michael in the end that the only way to counter the Angevin project of conquering Constantinople and reestablishing the Latin Empire was to yield to the pope's demands, although he knew that any move to unite the eastern and western churches would meet with bitter and lasting hostility among the clergy and people of Byzantium. In 1274 George Acropolites, Michael VIII's chief minister, attended a Church council at Lyons and undertook in his master's name to accept the Roman faith and recognize papal supremacy.

In return Pope Gregory X obtained from Charles of Anjou a promise to abandon his plans to conquer Byzantium. Minor territorial gains were made in the Peloponnese. But opposition to Michael's Church union grew more intense among his own subjects. Patriarch Joseph had to be forcibly removed, and replaced by the compliant John Bekkos. Demonstrations and riots became frequent in the streets of Constantinople, and Michael responded by arresting and persecuting the opponents of union. A dangerous rift opened between government and people, and adversaries of Michael's policy fled to Bulgaria and Epirus, which became strongholds of anti-unionism. Michael could for a time console himself with the reflection that his unpopular policy had bought security for the empire. But in 1281 the French pope, Martin IV, who was a tool of Charles of Anjou, released him from his undertaking given at Lyons. At once Charles revived his plan of reconquest, and formed an alliance with Venice and the exiled Latin emperor, Baldwin II. Michael's policy of Church union as the price of peace was in total collapse and by the next spring the situation was even worse. Serbia was acting in concert with the western coalition and had taken the city of Skopje. Bulgaria was ruled by the fiercely anti-Byzantine George I Terter, who was ready to cooperate with any enemy of Constantinople. It seemed as though the empire was about to face a repetition—on an even grander scale—of the catastrophe of 1204.

But Byzantine diplomatic connections—and Byzantine gold—reached far. French rule was bitterly resented by the Sicilians. Byzantine agents fanned their resentment, and soon a vast conspiracy was mounted in Sicily and won massive popular support. At the same time King Peter of Aragon was persuaded to lend his aid to the anti-French movement by the prospect of becoming ruler of Sicily. On 31 March 1282 there was a mass uprising in Sicily and a massacre of the French garrisons, the so-called Sicilian Vespers. Though fuelled by Sicilian hatred, the uprising owed much to Byzantine aid and encouragement. The surviving French hastily withdrew from Sicily, and a few weeks later Peter of Aragon was crowned in Palermo as king of Sicily. Charles of Anjou's plan to restore the Latin Empire was now finally frustrated. Michael VIII had saved Byzantium, but he died in December 1282 amid the hatred and contempt of his subjects, who abhorred Church union on any terms and denied their emperor a Christian burial. While he was pursuing his laborious diplomatic intrigues in the west, the bands of Turkish *ghazis* were penetrating ever more deeply into Byzantine territory in Asia Minor, which had been largely stripped of its defenders.

Michael VIII was succeeded by his son Andronikos II. The long reign of Andronikos was marked by a sorry succession of disasters and humiliations, of which only the most important will be mentioned. The empire was being forced to adapt itself to its new role as a small and weak Greek state, and to abandon reluctantly the great-power attitudes which Michael VIII had still been able to adopt. Such a period of diminishing opportunities and reduced initiative is usually an unhappy one, and the age of Andronikos II is no exception to the rule. Yet it witnessed a lively development in literature, art, and thought, in which some have seen a kind of pre-Renaissance. Other societies and other periods have sometimes displayed the same combination of political and economic decline and cultural revival. Andronikos began by reversing many of his father's policies. There was no longer any need to buy security in the west at the price of Church union, and Andronikos was himself a devout adherent of Orthodoxy. He at once abrogated the hated union with Rome. Patriarch John Bekkos was deposed and exiled, his aged predecessor Joseph was restored to office, and those imprisoned for opposing the union were released. But Byzantine society did not thereby become united in thought and feeling. A group in the Church, the Arsenites, who had condemned Michael VIII as a usurper and a murderer, continued to refuse to recognize his son as a legitimate sovereign. For a time they grew in numbers and influence, perhaps because they offered an institutionalized and intellectually respectable expression for the feelings of the disgruntled and discontented, of whom there were many.

Michael VIII had overstrained the financial resources of the empire and exhausted its reserves. Andronikos began his reign by cutting down the size of the army, virtually abolishing the navy—he counted for defense on the Genoese, whose city and port of Galata faced Constantinople across the Golden Horn—and increasing direct taxation in money and in kind. The virtual disappearance of free peasants, as large ecclesiastical and secular estates came to dominate the countryside, meant that the burden of the new taxes was mainly borne by a downtrodden and dependent peasantry, many of whom gave up the unequal struggle and moved to the city, where they swelled the numbers of the homeless and destitute.

In foreign affairs, Andronikos put his trust in diplomacy rather than force, and maintained peace with Epirus and with Serbia—in the latter case by arranging an outrageous marriage between his five-year-old daughter and the middle-aged King Milutin and granting to the Serbs as dowry the Byzantine provinces which they had already conquered. In the Peloponnese he succeeded in further extending the Byzantine domain at the expense of the Latin principality of Achaea at the cost of mere local skirmishes. Only in Asia Minor did he fight regular campaigns, and with uniform lack of success. By 1300 almost the whole of Byzantine Asia Minor had been lost to the Turkish *gha-zis*. Among these was a leader called Osman, who won a local victory in Bithynia in 1302 and laid the foundations of what was soon to become a great empire. To men of the time, however, the exploits of the emir of Aydin, who took Ephesus and Smyrna in 1304, and the emir of Menteshe, who took to the sea and captured Rhodes about the same time, appeared to pose a more immediate threat.

Andronikos's reaction to these misfortunes was to take into his service a company of Catalan mercenary soldiers, some 6,500 strong, who had been defending Sicily for the king of Aragon. The undisciplined Catalans proved beyond the control of the Byzantine authorities, and after a few minor successes in Asia Minor they mutinied and began to plunder and devastate Thrace. For years they rampaged through northern Greece, leaving a desert behind them, until in 1311 they destroyed the army of the Latin dukes of Athens and took over the duchy as feudatories of the king of Aragon. Their depredations and the terror they inspired caused even more peasants to take refuge in the city and swell its unproductive proletariat. Andronikos in vain sought military aid from the Genoese, the Mongols, and others against the Turkish advance in northwest Asia Minor. His dependence upon the Genoese led to the involvement of the empire in a long naval war between Genoa and Venice—itself the result of the final collapse of the crusader states in Syria with which Venice had enjoyed a lucrative trade. In the end the helpless emperor found himself forced to pay an indemnity to both belligerents after they had settled their dispute.

Discontent with Andronikos's rule grew as the years passed. His son and designated successor, Michael IX, died in 1320. His grandson Andronikos enjoyed the friendship and support of many of the great landowners, whose interests often conflicted with those of the state. He was a less than satisfactory youth. When one of his rash exploits led to the death of his brother, the old emperor disinherited him. In 1321 the younger Andronikos put himself at the head of a revolt in Thrace, and began the series of civil wars of the fourteenth century, which were to contribute as much as foreign pressure to the decline and collapse of the empire. He was supported by many magnates who chafed at the vestiges of central control still exercised by Constantinople. After a few years of fighting, a compromise was reached, and the younger Andronikos was proclaimed co-emperor as Andronikos III. In 1328 he forced his disillusioned and despairing grandfather to abdicate and enter a monastery. During the years of the civil war the Osmanli (or Ottoman) Turks pressed forward in the regions of Asia Minor nearest to the capital, and in 1326 they took Prusa (Bursa) and set up their capital there, only 100 kilometers from Constantinople.

The closest associate of the new emperor, and in a sense the power behind the throne, was the able, energetic, and immensely wealthy landowner John Cantacuzenus. In 1329 Cantacuzenus took an army to Asia Minor in the hope of evicting the Turks from the newly won territory. He was roundly defeated at Nicomedia and fled headlong to the safety of the Bosphorus. After that the government appears to have decided to write off Asia Minor and to concentrate on the reorganization and defense of the European possessions of the empire. The cynical will note that Cantacuzenus's vast estates lay mainly in Thrace. The Turks made the most of their opportunity. In 1331 they took Nicaea, in 1337 Nicomedia, leaving nothing to the Byzantines but a tiny strip of land facing Constantinople and the inland city of Philadelpheia (Alaşehir), 100 miles east of Smyrna, which remained in Byzantine hands until 1390. The new European policy met with considerable success at first. Much of the Peloponnese was regained from the Latins, and Mistra, the capital of Byzantine Greece, grew to be a notable city, adorned with palaces, churches, and monasteries. In northern Greece, Thessaly was occupied in 1333, and the whole of the despotate of Epirus in 1340. But the new policy brought the empire into conflict with the two Christian Slav states of the Balkans—Bulgaria, whose power was already beginning to decline, and Serbia, which was still in the phase of expansion and consolidation.

The social division within the empire between the great landowners and wealthy ecclesiastical institutions and the impoverished peasantry grew ever deeper. It was a division which existed in the cities as well as in the countryside, for much of the power and wealth of the cities was in the hands of the same great families that dominated the countryside; the artisans and merchants of the cities, to say nothing of the penniless refugees who crowded within their walls, were objectively on the same side of the social and economic cleavage as the peasants. It was an explosive situation. Andronikos III tried to reestablish the impartiality of the state by a reform of the judiciary, which took judicial powers from local officials and entrusted them to high officers of state directly appointed by the emperor. Needless to say, the new judges soon proved as corruptible as the old.

In 1341 Andronikos III died, leaving a six-year-old son, John V, under the regency of the dowager empress, Anne of Savoy. Before the year was out John Cantacuzenus, who had hoped to be regent and effective ruler of the empire, was proclaimed emperor in Thrace, and another round of devastating civil war began, which went on uninterrupted until 1347. Contemporary writers noted that everywhere the rich and powerful supported Cantacuzenus, while the common people took the side of John V and the empress regent. Like other struggles for the throne, the war was partly a conflict between factions of the ruling class. But such was the social tension in the shrunken and humiliated empire of the mid-fourteenth century that it also became the vehicle for the clash of interests between rich and poor, landowners and peasants. In a number of cities in Thrace and Macedonia the power of the local aristocracy was challenged by the merchants and artisans in the name of loyalty to the legitimate emperor. The assemblies of the citizens, which had hitherto generally given passive approval to the proposals of the local magnates, were the scenes of angry debate and tense confrontation. Sometimes the grandees were forced to flee for a time to the safety of Cantacuzenus's camp.

In Thessalonica, the second city of the empire, a revolt broke out in 1342 when the aristocracy proposed to hand over the city to Cantacuzenus. It was headed by a group calling themselves Zealots, who seem to have had particular support from the guild of sailors, and to have had adherents among the upper classes as well. The Zealots, who were probably a kind of secret society rather than a political party in the modern sense, governed Thessalonica until 1350, ostensibly in the name of John Palaeologus, in fact almost as an independent republic. There were purges of the adherents of Cantacuzenus, confiscations of their property, and some redistribution of wealth. Whether the Zealots actually had a program of social reform is hard to decide. Throughout the period of their rule the city was more or less under siege, and siege conditions make for rough and ready egalitarianism. All the available information on the Zealots comes from their enemies. Educated writers naturally saw the Zealots and their works in terms of the political thought of the ancient world, since it provided the only political concepts with which they were familiar, so we hear a great deal about slaves taking the place of their masters, cancellation of debts, redistribution of property and the like, all expressed in terms of remarkable vagueness.

It is diffficult to believe that the events in Thessalonica, a great port with many western connections, had nothing to do with those in Genoa a little earlier, where the common people, led by Simone Boccanegra, overthrew the feudal aristocracy and set up a commune. But the parallel must not be pressed too closely since there was little or nothing in a Byzantine city to correspond to the powerful mercantile and financial bourgeoisie of the Italian trading cities. In Byzantium all long-distance trade and much local trade was by now in the hands of foreigners, who often lived under their own laws in a kind of extraterritoriality, and whose ships exported the agricultural produce of the great estates, lay and monastic. Maybe the Zealots were imitating western models without clearly realizing the difference between Genoese society and their own. More probably they were merely reacting to a series of emergencies and trying to retain some freedom of action for the citizens while the great magnates fought one another to a standstill. At any rate they demonstrated that a Byzantine city could exist for nearly eight years without its aristocracy and their followers.

Besides the factional and social divisions, there was a further dimension to the civil war of 1341. The Orthodox church had a long tradition of mysticism, in which the believer sought through meditation a momentary glimpse of the uncreated divine light and a momentary enjoyment of that union with God which, in the view of Orthodox theologians, it was open to every Christian to attain. In the early decades of the fourteenth century groups of monks, particularly on Mount Athos, added to the traditional intellectual discipline of meditation physical practices which were probably of Indian origin. These included adoption of a special posture, control of breathing, endless repetition of a short formula of prayer, and the like. The new technique of meditation was greeted with ridicule by many theologians. An Italian Greek, Barlaam of Calabria, was among the leading opponents of the new practice, to which its adherents gave the name of Hesychasm. The defense of Hesychasm was taken up by Gregory Palamas, a monk of noble family, who provided the doctrinal justification for the new practice of meditation. By 1340 the issue was one which divided the Church. At two councils held in 1341, Barlaam and his followers were condemned and Palamas vindicated. John Cantacuzenus, who presided at the second council, was a wholehearted supporter of Hesychasm. In this way the theological dispute became involved with the political conflict. Not all of Cantacuzenus's supporters were Hesychasts, nor did all Hesychasts support Cantacuzenus. But he derived great authority from the Hesychast connection, and by a natural process of polarization, those who rejected the theology of Palamas tended to give political support to John Palaeologus and the empress regent. It is difficult not to see in the Hesychast movement, with its concentration on individual perfection, its markedly anti-intellectual tone, and its abjuration of political responsibility, a despairing response to the apparently insoluble problems of a decaying empire, in which the gap between traditional ideology and reality grew ever wider.

Byzantium's crisis was its enemies' opportunity. During the struggle for power between John Cantacuzenus and John Palaeologus, King Stephen Dušan of Serbia gave his support now to one side, now to the other, in accordance with his own expansionist policy. He made notable territorial gains in Macedonia and in 1345 captured the important town of Serres, northeast of Thessalonica. In 1346 he had himself crowned emperor of the Serbs and Greeks. He thus became

Icon of the Archangel Michael, dating from the first half of the fourteenth century. Michael holds the scales of judgment in his hand, while a little black devil tries to weigh down one side to capture the soul of its occupant for torment. *Courtesy of Museo Civico, Pisa (Hirmer Fotoarchiv).*

for a time a third claimant to the throne in Constantinople, and raised again the question of a Greco-Slav Orthodox Empire, a question first posed by Tsar Symeon of Bulgaria 400 years earlier. The Turks also profited by the disarray of the empire. John Cantacuzenus called on the aid of Turkish troops furnished by Emir Umur of Aydin in his struggle to get control of Thrace. Once in Europe, the Turkish auxiliaries were loath to leave.

In 1347 Cantacuzenus entered Constantinople with virtually no resistance, and was crowned for a second time as co-emperor with John V. Sporadic fighting still continued in the provinces, and Thessalonica remained in the hands of the Zealots for a further two years. Cantacuzenus, now master of what remained of the empire, set out to reassert Byzantine authority and influence. But the civil war had left deep wounds in Byzantine society, quite apart from the devastation it had caused. The military and political resources available to the new emperor were inadequate for his purpose.

In the year 1347 another visitor came to Constantinople, unbidden. A Genoese vessel from the port of Caffa in the Crimea carried passengers—or rats—infected with bubonic plague. The disease spread rapidly in the capital and the other cities, and was soon conveyed to the ports of Italy, whence it swept through most of Europe. This visitation, known as the Black Death, was by far the most severe of the several plague epidemics of the Middle Ages. In England it has been calculated that it killed about a third of the population. Byzantine records do not permit such a precise calculation, but the physical and moral effects of the plague were devastating, and the cities of the empire were more vulnerable to the disease than the more agrarian societies of its enemies.

In 1348 the Serbs were able to occupy Epirus and Thessaly almost without opposition. There King Stephen Dušan established a Greek-speaking chancellery to emphasize his claim to be emperor of the Serbs and Greeks. In 1350 war broke out once again between Venice and Genoa, and once again the empire became embroiled. In 1352 the few ships which were all that remained of the Byzantine navy took part on the Venetian side in an indecisive battle in the Bosphorus.

When the Venetians gave up the struggle and sailed off to Crete, the Byzantines were left to face humiliating Genoese demands for an indemnity. In the same year the Turks, who had been taking part as mercenaries in the continuing skirmishes of the civil war, seized a fort near Gallipoli, and two years later occupied the city of Gallipoli itself. Overwhelmed by failure and faced with growing opposition from his former supporters, John Cantacuzenus abdicated and retired to a monastery, from which he kept a watchful and censorious eye on his successors till his death thirty years later. In 1355 Stephen Dušan died, and his dream of a great Greco-Serbian Empire died with him, as his dominion broke up into a number of quarrelsome mini-states.

The abdication of John Cantacuzenus marks the end of an epoch— some would say an epoch of missed opportunities. From now on the empire had only one enemy, the Ottoman Turks. Unable to put in the field an army that could face that of their foes, successive Byzantine governments were driven more and more desperately to seek foreign aid, whatever the price might be. And as the Orthodox Slav states of the Balkans were one by one conquered and swallowed up by the expanding Ottoman Empire there was only one possible source of aid left—the Latin west, which the Byzantines had since the twelfth century mistrusted and feared, which had shattered the empire and colonized its territory, which had tried to impose on the empire a religion condemned by its theologians and spurned and hated by the mass of the people. The choices which now had to be made were traumatic.

John V pinned his hopes on Genoese support in particular, hoping that the Genoese would fight to defend their monopoly of the Black Sea trade. He was disappointed. In 1359 Turkish bands from Gallipoli encamped before the walls of Constantinople. In 1363 they took Philippopolis, cutting off Constantinople from Serbia and the west. In 1369 their army captured Adrianople, the key to Thrace. In the meantime John V had been negotiating with Pope Urban V for a crusade to stop the Moslem advance, and in 1366 he had gone to Hungary to plead for help. The response of the west was encouraging, but inadequate. A mixed force under Prince Amadeo of Savoy was despatched down the Danube with the pope's blessing. It succeeded in expelling the Turks from Gallipoli for a time, but was not strong enough to undertake further operations. In 1369 the emperor went to Rome and was personally converted to the Latin faith, a step which alienated him from his subjects without winning any concessions from the pope. In 1371 the Serbian army was destroyed in a battle on the River Maritsa, and Serbia, Macedonia, and northern Greece were laid open to Turkish invasion. The armies of the Serbian princes were required to fight alongside their Turkish conquerors.

Turkish power made itself felt in the internal politics of the empire as well as on the field of battle. John V had to acknowledge by treaty his status as a vassal of the sultan. When his younger son Andronikos revolted and made common cause with a rebellious son of Sultan Murad, John V was ordered to imprison and blind him. He was not actually blinded, but he was held in captivity for some years. In 1376 he escaped to Galata and with Turkish and Genoese help seized Constantinople and arrested his father and his elder brother, the co-emperor Manuel. For a time there were four emperors in the city maneuvering against one another, all in some degree the tools of Turkish or Italian policy. In 1379 John and Manuel escaped, fled to the Turkish court, and were restored to the capital by the Turkish army and the Venetian fleet. Thus while maintaining a semblance—and for brief moments the reality—of independence, the mosaic of islands and towns which was all that was left of the empire was reduced more and more to a state of subservience.

Meanwhile the Turkish advance was pursued relentlessly. In 1377 they established their capital at Adrianople. In 1385 Sofia fell, in 1366 Niš, in 1387 it was the turn of Thessalonica, which surrendered to the Turkish army to avoid being pillaged. In 1389 came the crushing defeat of the Serbs at Kosovo, which put an end to all hope of successful resistance by the Slav states of the Balkans. In 1393 what remained of Bulgaria was conquered and annexed after a revolt. From being a Turkish vassal state it became a province of the Turkish Empire.

By now there were new rulers in Constantinople and Adrianople. Manuel II, the son of John V, was crowned in 1392. Bajezid I (nicknamed Yildirim, "the Thunderbolt") succeeded his father Murad as sultan in 1389. He was determined to put an end to the anomaly of a quasi-independent Orthodox empire in the middle of Turkish territory, and the opportunity which it might offer for intervention by the western powers. By 1394 the Turkish army began the blockade of Constantinople. It was not complete, since Venetian and Genoese ships could still occasionally sail into the Golden Horn. But there was no doubt in anyone's mind that the sultan intended to capture the city and incidentally to win the reward promised by Islamic tradition since the days of the Prophet to whoever should conquer Rûm. Famine soon made itself felt in the city. Bewildered and without direction, the citizens were divided among themselves. Some were for capitulation to avoid the horrors of a sack. Had not Thessalonica surrendered? Were not many thousands, perhaps millions, of Orthodox Greeks already living under Turkish suzerainty and adapting themselves as best they could to the new turn of events? Others pinned their hopes to a decisive intervention by the west, and were ready, or even eager, to pay the price of Church union. Others lost themselves in millennary speculations on the date of Christ's Second Coming, when He would gather together the faithful in glory. It was widely believed to be near at hand, and a favorite date was 1492, the seven-thousandth year since the creation of the world, according to Byzantine reckoning.

In the west there was a new readiness to intervene. What worried western rulers was not the fate of the Byzantine Empire, whose citizens were merely schismatic Greeks. They were anxious rather about the advance of the Turks into central Europe and the security of their own domains. The most immediately threatened were the Hungarians. The king of Hungary appealed to his fellow monarchs and to the pope in Avignon to launch a crusade. The appeal was favorably received, and soon a major force of about 100,000 men was gathered together. About half were supplied by Hungary, and the rest by France, England, Spain, Poland, Bohemia, and other states. In summer 1396 the crusaders marched off down the Danube, determined to roll back the tide of Islam. They were outmaneuvered by the Turks, and on 5 September their huge and cumbersome army was surrounded at Nikopolis in northern Bulgaria and most of its members put to the sword. Bajezid maintained his blockade of Constantinople, and in 1397 launched a major punitive expedition against the Byzantine possessions in the Peloponnese.

The French, who had become the feudal superiors of Genoa and hence of the Genoese colonies in the eastern Mediterranean and the Black Sea, were still anxious to make a show of force against the Turks. In 1399 a French force of 1,200 men under Marshal Boucicaut succeeded in breaking through the blockade and entering Constantinople. The gallant marshal's exploit fired the enthusiasm of the pro-Latin party within the city, but did nothing to change its desperate situation. It did, however, arouse hopes in governing circles of some more solid western support. Manuel II accordingly set out on a prolonged journey around western states in pursuit of military aid. He reached Paris in 1400 by way of Venice and the north Italian cities. King Charles VI received him with honor and undertook to send another force under Boucicaut. By the end of the year he was in London, where he was received with equal honor but no specific promises of help. Gradually he came to realize that the promises of western sovereigns were vague and illusory, and that no significant help could be expected from the Latin world.

Help did come, but from an unforeseen quarter. The Mongol leader Timur Lenk, or Tamerlane as he was known in the west, had by ruthless conquest built up an empire which stretched from Delhi almost to the gates of Moscow. The Caucasus, Syria, Iraq, and Egypt were subject to his rule. The growth and consolidation of Ottoman Turkish power in Asia Minor and Europe were in his eyes a threat, a center round which his own disaffected subjects might rally. He sought and easily found a *casus belli*. In 1402 he led his army into Asia Minor, outmaneuvered the Turkish host and suddenly appeared in its rear, then forced it to stand and fight before the walls of Ankara. The Turks were routed, their army destroyed, and Sultan Bajezid taken prisoner. As the Mongol columns swept through Asia Minor to the sea, burning, pillaging, and massacring as they went, the Turkish blockade of Constantinople melted away. Joyfully the Byzantines sent envoys with rich gifts to their unexpected savior.

The nascent Ottoman state was in fact gravely shaken, and Byzantium was granted a long respite in which to work out its salvation. At first things went well. Emperor Manuel hastened back from the west. A treaty was signed between the Byzantines, the Turks, Genoa, and Venice which restored to the empire Thessalonica and much other territory. The payment of tribute to the Turks was ended, and they even recognized in a vague way the overlordship of the emperor. Manuel was for a time able to interfere in Ottoman internal politics, playing off the sons of Bajezid one against the other. By 1413 the Byzantines succeeded, with Serbian help, in installing on the Turkish throne Mehmed I, who confirmed the treaty of 1403. But nothing was done to prepare for the day when the Ottoman state would recover its strength. No new relation with the western powers was worked out. No league of Orthodox states was built up in the Balkans.

The death of Mehmed I in 1421 marked the end of the period of Turkish weakness. His son and successor, Murad II, ended the policy of détente and passed over to the offensive in Europe. The year 1422 saw an assault in strength on Constantinople and Turkish advances in Albania, Epirus, and central Greece. Even the Peloponnese, now almost entirely in Byzantine hands, was not spared. In 1424 the now aged Manuel was obliged to make a new settlement in which he undertook once again to pay tribute and recognized the Turkish conquests of the preceding years. The opportunity, if there ever was one, had been lost. When Manuel died in 1425, the empire was in a more desperate situation than when he ascended the throne thirty-four years earlier. The choice was now clear: absorption into the Ottoman Empire or salvation by the Latin west. There was no middle course, however much Byzantine rulers and statesmen might delude themselves that there was one. Overtures and appeals to the western powers grew more frequent and more anxious. Already in 1423 Manuel's son Andronikos had ceded Thessalonica, of which he was governor, to the Venetians, in the hope that their trading interest would induce

The Emperor John VIII, who made desperate attempts to unite the eastern and western Churches in order to resist the Ottoman threat. Portrait from a fifteenth-century manuscript in the monastery of St. Catherine on Mount Sinai. *Courtesy of Library of Congress.*

them to defend it. Defend it they did, but inadequately. In 1430 the city was captured, for the second time, by Sultan Murad, to remain a Turkish possession until 1912. John VIII, Manuel's successor, made vain visits to Hungary and to Italy. But the western powers, uneasy though they were about the Turkish advance in Europe, were not willing to risk a confrontation in order to save the crumbling remains of the Byzantine Empire. The dispute between the eastern and western churches prevented any feeling of Christian solidarity between the Catholic west and the Orthodox east.

In the 1430s the western Church was itself divided between the adherents of papal supremacy and those who believed that the true spiritual authority of the Church could be exercised only through a council of its bishops. Such a council had actually begun to meet, without papal approval, in Basle. Perhaps Church union could be attained without the hateful corollary of papal supremacy. John VIII, who had made proposals for unity in 1432 to Pope Eugenius IV, turned in the following year to the Conciliarists assembled at Basle. They found the Byzantine approach interesting. The papal curia was uneasy about the course which events were taking, and proceeded to outflank the Conciliarists by calling a council of its own, to which the emperor and the representatives of the Byzantine church were invited. Preparations went ahead rapidly, and in 1438 John VIII and Patriarch Joseph II, together with representatives of the other eastern patriarchates and an impressive group of Byzantine scholars and theologians, set sail for Italy in the papal fleet.

The council began its work in Ferrara, and in 1439 moved to Florence. All the long-standing differences between the two churches were debated earnestly and at length. The Byzantine representatives made concessions on many of the points in dispute, such as the use of unleavened bread in the Eucharist and the celibacy of the clergy. On the central theological question of whether the Holy Spirit proceeded from the Father alone or from the Father and the Son a compromise formula was found. The Holy Spirit was declared to proceed from the Father through the Son. On 6 July the reunion of the eastern and western Churches after a schism of nearly three centuries was proclaimed and celebrated with both Greek and Latin liturgy. Of all the Byzantine representatives only one refused to sign the proclamation of union. Events showed that others had serious reservations. But the situation was desperate, and the Orthodox church had always recognized the distinction between what is ideal and what is practicable. The emperor and his entourage returned to Constantinople to be greeted with bitter hostility by most of his subjects and with sullen suspicion by the Turks.

In 1443 the crusade promised by the pope as the price of unity began its slow and cumbrous preparations. The moment was opportune. Sultan Murad had been called away to deal with his rebellious Turcoman subjects in Asia Minor. In Albania George Castrioti, otherwise Scanderbeg, was conducting a successful revolt against his Turkish masters. In Serbia and Bulgaria things were stirring, as men waited to see what would happen. The crusading force assembled in Hungary, marched down the Danube and up the Morava, took Niš and Sofia, and went on towards the Black Sea. Murad hastened back from Asia and prepared to meet the crusaders. Confronted by the formidable Ottoman army, the leaders of the crusade lost their nerve and signed a truce with the sultan which was to last ten years. In late autumn hostilities began again, allegedly because of an infraction of the truce by the crusaders. Murad fell upon their army near Varna on 10 November 1444 and routed it. The survivors of the crusade made what haste they could for the safety of Hungary. The Turks were more alarmed by the stirrings of the revolt in Serbia and Albania than by anything that might happen at Constantinople. For a time the city was left untouched, while punitive operations were carried out in the west.

In 1448 John VIII died, and was succeeded by his brother, Constantine XI Dragases, who had for some years been governor of the Peloponnese. It was at Mistra that he was crowned emperor. There was no patriarch in Constantinople to crown him, because of the unshakeable opposition of the mass of the clergy to union with the Church of Rome. In 1451 Sultan Murad II died, and was succeeded by his son, Mehmed II, a young man of wide culture—he spoke half a dozen languages, including Greek—quick intelligence, and bound-less ambition. Mehmed decided to settle the problem of Constantino-ple once and for all. In the winter of the same year he ordered the encirclement of the city to begin. A great castle, Roumeli-Hissar or the Fortress of Europe, was rapidly built on the European shore of the Bosphorus, within sight of Constantinople and facing the castle of the Anadolu-Hissar built by Bajezid half a century earlier. It was completed in 1452, just as a papal delegation arrived in the city, headed by Isidore, formerly archbishop of Kiev and now a cardinal of the Roman church. The envoys brought with them 200 archers to take part in the defense of the capital. But their presence raised anti-Catholic and anti-western feeling to an even higher pitch than before. When the cardinal celebrated the liturgy in Hagia Sophia in accor-dance with the Roman rite and in the presence of the emperor, many citizens, clergy and lay alike, felt that both Church and state had been humiliated as never before, and that the wrath of God would surely descend upon the city. George Scholarios, one of the delegates who had signed the act of union in Florence, pinned a manifesto to the door of Hagia Sophia declaring that he would rather die than abandon the Orthodox faith. His change of position was symptomatic of the despair of many Byzantines, now that union with the Latins had brought no defense against the Turks. Of western sovereigns, only King Alfonso of Aragon was interested in war with the Turks, and his ambition was to restore the Latin Empire, not to save the Byzantine Empire. In the end he did nothing.

In spring 1453 Sultan Mehmed prepared the final attack on Con-stantinople. The impregnable walls built by Theodosius II a thousand years earlier were not proof against the new weapon of artillery. The Ottoman army had some fifty primitive cannons, including one mon-ster piece which required sixty oxen to haul it. The Ottoman fleet was now strong enough to cut off the city entirely by sea, except for the occasional small ship which slipped through the blockade under cover of darkness or bad weather. But the Byzantines were still able to close the Golden Horn with a boom and so prevent the Turkish ships from anchoring in sheltered water close to the weakest stretch of the sea wall. They had not more than 7,000 men to defend the walls, including many of the Venetian residents in the city and a company of 700 Genoese volunteers commanded by the experienced *condottiere* Giovanni Giustiniani. The army which faced them was at least fifteen times as numerous, and disciplined by victory.

On Easter Monday, 2 April, Mehmed pitched his camp before the walls of the city, and four days later the artillery began its bombardment. The defenders repaired by night the damage done by the cannon by day. While this inconclusive exchange went on, the sultan was preparing his coup, which only his immense superiority in manpower made possible. He constructed a roller-way up the hill from the Bosphorus, behind Galata, and down into the Golden Horn. On 22 April the Byzantine defenders saw with consternation the Turkish ships being launched down a slipway behind their own defensive boom. Had the Genoese of Galata been so minded, they could probably have sunk them. But the price would have been the pillaging and destruction of their city, so they maintained their watchful and uneasy neutrality.

Within the city the tension grew. Brawls and ugly incidents between Greeks and Latins, between Venetians and Genoese, between supporters and adversaries of Church union grew more frequent. The overstrained defenders now had to man the sea walls along the Golden Horn as well as the land walls and the Marmara walls. Untoward events took place which were seen as harbingers of disaster, as when an icon of the Virgin fell from its framework during a procession. But the will to resist was maintained. In early May the sultan offered terms of surrender, which included evacuation of the city by the Greeks. Constantine replied that he and his subjects would rather die than abandon the God-guarded city in which their ancestors had dwelt for eleven centuries. Mehmed moved up his troops for the final assault on 27 May, and on the following day his army rested. In the city, icons and relics were carried round the streets; the emperor visited the walls, urging the defenders to resist to the end; in Hagia Sophia, Greek and Latin clergy celebrated the Eucharist together, their quarrel forgotten in the hour of common danger.

Sultan Mehmed II, whose capture of the city of Constantinople in 1453 brought to
an end the Byzantine Empire. Portrait attributed to Gentile Bellini, in the National
Gallery, London. *Courtesy of National Gallery, London.*

On Tuesday, 29 May, the assault began, with wave after wave of Turkish soldiers hurling themselves against the walls. A few Turks broke in through a postern gate, and hoisted the standard of the Prophet on the ramparts. The janissaries pressed on behind them and through other gaps in the walls as they appeared, and fanned out behind the defenders. Soon there were only a few groups of Byzantine soldiers holding out at isolated points. One by one they were overcome. In one of these groups, near the St. Romanos gate, the Emperor Constantine fell in hand-to-hand fighting. His body was never found.

Those Latins who could, fled to their ships, and made headlong for Chios, Crete, or Venice. The Greeks waited. The sultan had promised his soldiers three days in which to plunder the city, in accordance with Islamic law. Flushed with victory and avid for booty, they massacred and looted unchecked. None can guess how many citizens were killed, how many priceless works of art destroyed. Many had taken refuge in Hagia Sophia, still hoping for a miracle. The Turkish troops broke in, tore the precious church furniture from the walls, rounded up the captives, and slew those who resisted. Soon the sultan himself arrived, and as an imam standing upon the high altar led the prayers, gave thanks to Allah for the fulfilment of his prophecy.

After the orgy of looting, discipline was swiftly restored. Many Turks settled in the city. Many Greeks were brought in from other towns to replace those who had been killed or had fled. The sultan had no intention of letting the great city on the Bosphorus dwindle into insignificance. He was anxious, too, to regularize the position of the Greek Orthodox community within the Ottoman Empire. What remained of the civil administrative structure of the Byzantine Empire had been swept aside. The only organ which could unite and represent the people was the Church, but the Church must have a head. In the first months after the conquest Mehmed began to look round for someone to fill the vacant office of patriarch, someone who would enjoy the confidence of the Greek Orthodox population—which by now formed a sizeable element in the Ottoman Empire—and who would be answerable to him for its loyal conduct. His choice fell upon George Scholarios, now the monk Gennadios, who after agreeing to Church union at Florence had publicly and uncompromisingly renounced it in Constantinople. He was unlikely to make fresh overtures to the pope and embroil the Turks in unwanted confrontations with the western powers. In January 1454 Scholarios was ordained patriarch in the church of the Holy Apostles. The great church of Hagia Sophia had already become a mosque.

Thus a state which had existed as the Christian Roman Empire since the days of Constantine, more than eleven centuries earlier, and whose ultimate origins went back to the seven hills by the Tiber more than 2,000 years earlier, had finally ceased to exist. Since the reign of Andronikos II it had been a quaint but prestigious fossil. And though the final blow was struck by the Ottoman Turks, it can plausibly be argued that the fatal injury was inflicted by the Latin crusaders in 1204. It was the damage, the disruption, and the humiliation which they had brought about that prevented the empire from establishing a lasting balance of power with the nascent Ottoman state, as it had in earlier centuries with Sasanian Persia, with the Moslem caliphate, and, up to a point, with the Seljuq sultanate of Iconium.

The empire was gone, but the Church lived on, not only providing spiritual authority, as it had always done, but regulating many of the secular affairs of the Greek community, and having a claim upon the loyalty of the many Orthodox Christians who were not subjects of the Ottoman Empire. The few remaining enclaves of Byzantine rule were soon mopped up. The Byzantine province of the Morea (the Peloponnese) was already an Ottoman vassal state. In 1460 Mehmed decided to absorb it into his empire. Mistra, the capital, surrendered without resistance, perhaps because of the predominant influence there of wealthy monasteries, which saw their position within Ottoman society guaranteed by the sultan's agreement with the Church. Some of the smaller towns put up fierce resistance. But they were captured one by one, until resistance to the Turks was limited to partisan warfare in the inaccessible mountain regions. The empire of Trebizond, in the far northeast of Asia Minor, was another anomaly. Its rulers never gave up the forlorn hope of forming an anti-Turkish alliance. In 1461 the sultan attacked the city with an enormous army and fleet. Success-

ful defense was impossible, and the last emperor of Trebizond surrendered his city. He was taken off to honorable captivity in Adrianople. But two years later the sultan found it expedient to put him
to death. A man who had worn the imperial purple was a dangerous
guest to harbor.

THE RESILIENCE OF CULTURE

The capture of Constantinople by the crusaders in 1204 and the
establishment of Latin rule over the ruins of the Byzantine Empire
brought with them the destruction of those institutions within which
Byzantine art, letters, and thought flourished. There was no longer
an emperor and a court to provide patronage. The Church still survived, but much of its wealth was now in western hands and its hierarchy scattered and impoverished. Many monasteries, however, continued to provide, albeit on a reduced scale, the conditions for the
execution of works of art and the copying of manuscripts. The cultivated metropolitan milieu by which and for which so much of the
literature and art of the twelfth century had been produced existed
no longer. Its members had fled as refugees to one or another of the
regions still outside Latin control, or had sunk into obscurity. Niketas
Choniates, the historian and theologian, made his way to Nicaea. His
brother Michael, the learned metropolitan of Athens, spent most of
the closing years of his life in poverty on the island of Keos, from
which on a clear day he could look across the sea to the hills of Attica;
he died ca. 1222 in the monastery of the Prodromos in Bodonitsa.
There was no longer any career in the bureaucracy of Church or state
awaiting those with a classical literary education. The imperial factor-
ies had vanished in the general débâcle, and their silk weavers, mosaicists, goldsmiths, and other craftsmen were scattered to the four
winds, unable to pass on their centuries-old skills to a following generation.

Yet there was no complete break with the past. The rulers of the
Greek successor states in Asia Minor and Epirus, just as they tried to
reconstruct the administrative system and court ceremonial of the

empire, soon began to encourage art and literature as best they could. Their vision of the society which they were trying to preserve went far beyond mere administration. It embraced the whole of the triple heritage of the Byzantines, as heirs of the Roman Empire, of Hellenic tradition, and as the New Israel, the Chosen People of the Lord.

In the Nicaean Empire schools were set up in the capital, where men who had studied, and often taught, in Constantinople before 1204 recreated and transmitted their traditional culture. The names of some of them are known. Michael Senachereim (whose commentary on Homer still survives, though unpublished) taught literature. Theodore Hexapterygos taught rhetoric. A little later Nicephorus Blemmydes, a cantankerous monk of stupendous learning, taught first in Nicaea and later in a monastery near Ephesus. His writings ranged over theology, philosophy, medicine, rhetoric, and indeed the whole Byzantine intellectual tradition. The emperors John Vatatzes and Theodore II Laskaris were patrons of literature and learning. One of the problems they had to face was a shortage of books, and Nicephorus Blemmydes was sent on a mission to the newly reconquered European provinces to seek out manuscripts for the library which Vatatzes established in his Asian capital. Several manuscripts still survive, probably copied in the Nicaean Empire, which contain collections of the poetry, letters, speeches, essays, and other occasional compositions of the age of the Comneni. Clearly there were men who strove to gather together the scattered fragments of this often precious and rhetorical literature and to preserve it as an example for their own and future generations. Theodore II Laskaris was a man of letters and a scholar, who poured out a stream of works on theology and philosophy, ceremonial orations, religious poetry, essays, and letters. By the time he succeeded his father in 1254, the days of the Latin Empire were evidently numbered. Byzantine ruling circles in Nicaea were ready not only to take over the political role their forefathers had lost in 1204 but also to maintain and foster the brittle, self-consciously élitist culture which they had so laboriously conserved.

The despotate of Epirus in northwest Greece was in every respect a less viable political unit than the Nicaean Empire. It had neither extensive territory nor the legitimacy and prestige conferred by the presence of the ecumenical patriarch. And it was more directly exposed to military threats both from Italy and from the expanding kingdom of Serbia. Less effort seems to have been made by the rulers of Epirus than by those of Nicaea to establish and maintain educational institutions, and few surviving manuscripts can be attributed to scribes working there. Yet there was no shortage of men of letters who continued in difficult conditions the literary traditions of their forefathers. John Apokaukos had been appointed metropolitan of Naupaktos before the Fourth Crusade, after a long career in the patriarchal bureaucracy in Constantinople. After 1204 he fled to Arta, the capital of Epirus, where he lived till 1233. He played an important role in the political stabilization of the new state. His poems on religious subjects, his letters, and the many official documents which he composed are written in the most archaizing classical Greek, in the use of which he had become adept in his Constantinopolitan days. George Bardanes, an Athenian and a protégé of Michael Choniates, with whom he fled to Keos in 1204, became metropolitan of Corfu in 1219. Active as a churchman and diplomat, he left a number of letters and occasional poems in the classical manner. Demetrios Chomatianos held a post in the service of the patriarchate before 1204. After the conquest of the city he fled to Ohrid in Macedonia, where he became first archivist, then archbishop. He was a learned and subtle lawyer, fully familiar with the vast legal literature of Byzantium. In addition to his numerous legal decisions, which are often of great interest to the social historian, he left a collection of religious poems. There is no evidence that any of these men engaged in systematic teaching, but their presence and influence provided a link with the world before the catastrophe of 1204.

The successor states of the thirteenth century had neither the resources nor the security to engage in monumental building. The thrifty Nicaean Empire built little, and most of what it built has since vanished. However, a few traces remain of the fresco redecoration of the church of Hagia Sophia in Nicaea, which suggest that the work was metropolitan in style, and probably executed by refugee artists from Constantinople. The tiny empire of Trebizond, enriched by the transit trade from the Far East, built more lavishly. We hear of mosaic decoration of churches, though none now survive. But the many frescos display a metropolitan and classicizing taste which is subtly different from that of the twelfth century. The painters use a much wider palette, and often prefer delicate shading to the more linear style of the age of the Comneni. They delight in a decorative and fanciful use of color for its own sake rather than in an illusionistic reproduction of the colors of the real world. The art of Epirus seems to have been less metropolitan and more provincial. Little remains of Epirot painting, but the Epirot rulers were indefatigable builders. Though their palaces have vanished, all over their former domain there survive small basilical churches, often wooden-roofed, and decorated on the exterior with ornamental brickwork, a fashion which soon spread to other regions of the Byzantine world. The metropolitan church of the Paregoritissa in Arta, built in 1282–89, is a rather unsatisfactory combination of basilica with cross-in-square, crowned by no fewer than seven small domes on drums. Its interior decoration recalls that of tenth-century churches in central Greece and elsewhere. In other words, architects and craftsmen of the first rank were not attracted to the despotate of Epirus, which was forced to resort to local work of a provincial character.

When Michael VIII was solemnly crowned in the great church of Hagia Sophia on 15 August 1261, the Latin interruption was brought to a close and the Christian Roman Empire of Constantine and Justinian was restored, as it had been before 1204. Such at least was the official position. And there was indeed continuity of government through the Nicaean Empire. Yet the Byzantine Empire in its last two centuries was in a number of important ways very different from what it had been before the disaster of the Fourth Crusade. Irreversible changes had occurred in the political, economic, and social structure of Byzantine society, which were accompanied in their turn by changes in the values recognized by its members and in the goals that they pursued.

First of all, the territory controlled by the empire was much reduced, and continued to diminish almost to vanishing point. The revenue produced from this shrunken territory, even had it been assessed and collected with the same efficiency as before, would have been insufficient to maintain the costly and unproductive life of court, church, and central administration on the same scale as in previous centuries, let alone to support an adequate military force. But revenue was not as efficiently collected as before. Grants of land in *pronoia*, which had previously been terminable and had carried an obligation to military service, became hereditary, and the duty of providing soldiers was in practice neglected. This was both a consequence of the weakness of the central government and the cause of its further weakening. Landowners, both ecclesiastical and lay, were granted the right to collect taxes from their tenants. All kinds of immunities from taxation proliferated. These tendencies had all shown themselves before 1204, but they were far more pervasive in the restored empire after 1261. This decentralization and devolution of state power was not confined to fiscal matters. In all respects the old, centralized, bureaucratic empire, in which decision making was concentrated in a few institutions in the capital, was replaced by a much looser kind of political community, in which it was more widely diffused and more uncoordinated. The geographical separation of the territories composing the empire favored the decentralization which was arising in any case as a result of the growing feudalization of Byzantine society. Detached regions like Thessalonica and above all the Peloponnesian possessions were more and more frequently put under the control of members of the imperial family, who administered them almost as independent states, raising revenue and conducting foreign relations and military operations on their own initiative. The Byzantine province of the Morea or Peloponnese was at first governed by an official appointed annually from Constantinople. Soon the period of tenure began to be lengthened. About the end of the thirteenth century, Andronikos Palaeologus Asanes, a son of the former Bulgarian King John III and a grandson of Michael VIII, was appointed governor and remained in office for a quarter of a century. In the mid-fourteenth century, John Cantacuzenus sent his brother Manuel to govern the

Morea, and thereafter the province was always ruled by a son or brother of the reigning emperor, to whom all authority was delegated. The last emperor, Constantine XI, who fell defending his city against the Turks in 1453, had been for many years ruler of the Morea before he came to Constantinople to succeed his brother in 1449.

At the same time the various privileges and rights of city communities—some of which may well have gone back to the civic government of late antiquity, although most were of much later origin—began to receive greater emphasis. This emerges in particular in the stormy civil wars of the mid-fourteenth century, where we hear again and again of assemblies of citizens, acrimonious debates, conflicts between the leading families and the body of the citizens, the role played by guilds, and so on. An extreme case is that of Thessalonica, where effective civic self-government was established under the leadership of the Zealots and maintained for nearly eight years. Much in these events recalls the development of the city commune in contemporary Italy, but there are important differences. The families which dominated the Byzantine cities were the same as those which controlled the countryside, for the Byzantine aristocrat lived as much in his town house as on his country estate. And the movement towards city self-government did not have the support of a powerful and growing commercial class as it had in Italy. Too much of Byzantine trade was in the hands of foreign merchants or territorial magnates or both.

For a time the growing impoverishment of the state was partially offset by the boom in long-distance trade resulting from the Mongol conquests. Now that the whole of Asia and eastern Europe from Korea to Poland was under Mongol rule, commercial exchanges between Europe and the Far East became easier. Much of this caravan trade passed through Tabriz to Trebizond, whence it was shipped to Constantinople and then to the Italian ports. Although this trade was almost entirely carried on by Italian merchants in Italian ships, much of it was trans-shipped in Constantinople and some of it paid Byzantine customs dues or changed hands in the markets of Constantinople. It was largely the revenue from this favorable conjuncture in world trade which enabled Michael VIII to carry out an active foreign policy embracing the whole of the Mediterranean world. The disintegration of the vast Mongol empire led to the drying up of the revenue from long-distance trade, and brought the Byzantine world face to face with the harsh reality of its situation. By the mid-fourteenth century it was observed that the crown jewels were now made of glass and that the gold and silver plate of the palace had been replaced by pottery. Posts no longer existed in the service of state or church for all those who had pursued a higher education in the capital. Overproduction of intellectuals ensued, and the poor scholar became a frequent figure in the streets of Constantinople.

The imperial family and the central government were no longer able to play their role as munificent patrons of art and literature. Some of the emperor's subjects were now richer than the emperor, insofar as riches can be measured by money. Private patronage appeared by the side of and eventually replaced imperial patronage. This development, together with the devolution of political authority to the separate parts of the fragmented empire, led to the growth of centers of literature and art outside Constantinople. For the first time since the great Arab conquests of the seventh century, Byzantine culture became polycentric. Literature and art flourished in Thessalonica and in Mistra, the new capital of the Byzantine Morea. While Constantinopolitan influence remained dominant, though not exclusive, in the field of literature, in that of the visual arts local traditions and influences began to make themselves felt. The same is true of Epirus and of such Byzantine possessions on the Black Sea coast as Mesembria (Nesebǔr).

The new situation of the empire involved a change in the relations of Church and state. The territory of the empire might be sadly reduced and fragmented. But the authority of the Church of Constantinople still covered the whole of the Orthodox world with the exceptions of Egypt and Syria on the one hand and Bulgaria on the other. The patriarch had spiritual jurisdiction not only over all the Greeks who lived under Latin or Turkish rule, but also over Serbs and Albanians and, most important of all, over Russians. The Byzantine Empire might dwindle to a kind of mini-state with no real freedom of action. But the Byzantine church still operated, within its own domain, on an international scale. The revenues of the Church were less reduced than those of the state—though this point cannot be pressed too far, since both in areas of Turkish occupation and in those under Latin rule ecclesiastical estates were often confiscated or made over to representatives of the western Church. Thus Church and state were no longer, as they had so long been, the two faces of the same coin. The fact that Michael VIII, John V, and John VIII all went over to the western Church, and the first and last of them vainly tried to take their subjects with them, strengthened the independence of the Church *vis-à-vis* the institutions of the empire. During the reign of Andronikos II the austere and ascetic Patriarch Athanasios I often rebuked the emperor sharply for alleged dereliction of duty. And when the depredations of the Catalans brought thousands of destitute peasants to the city, it was the patriarch who organized food and lodging for the refugees, while the emperor and his ministers stood by helplessly. The spread of the Hesychast movement increased the influence and prestige of the Church at the very time when emperors were becoming the humble and impotent vassals of the Ottoman power. When the end came, the patriarchate and the Church were able to survive, to adapt themselves to the conditions of Ottoman sovereignty, and to take over certain of the civil functions of the state.

The conflict between traditional concepts and present reality, which had always been present in Byzantine society, grew sharper and more difficult to conceal in the last two centuries of the empire. To maintain that the Byzantine emperor was the only truly legitimate ruler, whose authority was different in kind from that of other sovereigns, grew more and more absurd as the extent and power of the empire diminished. And the fact that there was sometimes more than one claimant to imperial authority did not make things any easier. It grew daily harder to believe that the Byzantine state had an eschatological purpose and was an essential piece of a divine plan for the salvation of mankind. In the same way, the empire was no longer richer than other states, nor better governed, nor more formidable in the field of battle. A whole structure of ideas, formed in the heyday of Byzantine power, was left without any support in reality. The one field in which Byzantine society did still enjoy superiority was one which had not always been in the foreground of Byzantine thought— namely, the direct access which it enjoyed both to classical Greek literature and thought and to those of the patristic age through its exclusive possession of the Greek language.

The Byzantines were no more ready than other peoples at other epochs to recognize that their greatness was a thing of the past. Most of the literature and thought of the age strikes a note of exaggeration and self-aggrandizement which consorts ill with the sorry state of Byzantine society. The old rhetorical comparisons were applied, with wild inappropriateness, to the new circumstances. Trivial and local victories were likened to the campaigns of Alexander. The future Emperor Constantine XI, who had gained some patches of territory from the enfeebled Latin states when he was ruler of the Morea, was called a new Agesilaus, preparing to set off from Sparta (Mistra) and to carry the war into the land of the Persians (that is, the Ottoman Turks). In 1393, when Sultan Bayezid had just swallowed up Bulgaria and was about to begin his eight-year blockade of Constantinople, Vasilij Dmitrijevich, grand duke of Moscow, informed Patriarch Anthony IV that he proposed no longer to commemorate the emperor's name in the churches of Russia, since Muscovy owed no political allegiance whatever to Byzantium. "We have a Church," he said, "but no Emperor." The patriarch at once replied that although Byzantine territory was sadly reduced and the enemy was all but at the gates, yet the emperor was still God's regent on earth, the superior of all other princes, and the head of the universal Church of all true believers. His name must therefore be retained in the prayers of the Church. The patriarch's reply underlines both the unwillingness of most traditional Byzantines to relax in the slightest degree the claim of their society to a special status, and the way in which the Church came to have a wider range of influence than the state. Byzantine scholars and statesmen were not fools, and most of them were only too well aware of the difference between the world in which they lived and that of the tenth century or even the twelfth. But the complex of traditional ideas and images which they had inherited and of whose prestige they were at all times conscious was ill fitted to express new thoughts. Occasionally doubts were uttered. Theodore Metochites, chief minister of Andronikos II and leading man of letters of his age, from time to time complained of the constraints imposed by the dead weight of tradition, and the impossibility of saying anything that had not been said before. But he found few followers.

What thinking Byzantines did was to concentrate upon the one domain in which their superiority was still, so they thought, unchallenged and unchallengeable—that of Greek language, literature, and thought. This led to a growing emphasis upon their identity as Greeks, rather than simply as Christians, and hence to a renewed preoccupation with the literary and linguistic scholarship which preserved the traditions of the Hellenic past. Strict Atticism became essential for all serious literature, and imitation of classical models became the principal aim of literature. This imitation went beyond questions of language and style—places had to be called by ancient names, even when they were not known with certainty. The town of Serres, northeast of Thessalonica, is often called Pherae because of the similarity of sound of the two names, though the real Pherae was a hundred miles to the south, in Thessaly. The peoples and countries of the late medieval world are dressed up in classical garb, often most confusingly. The Turks appear as Persians, the French are Gauls, the Serbs Triballi—an Illyrian tribe mentioned by writers of the fifth century BC—the Bulgarians often Mysians; Scythians can be Russians, Bulgarians, Cumans, Mongols, or Ottoman Turks. Even the Roman names of the months, which had been in current use in the Greek-speaking world for a thousand years, are replaced by those of the ancient Attic months, although there was no general agreement on equivalences between the two systems. Much of this literature must have been fully comprehensible only to a tiny minority. It was élitist literature, composed in a very diffficult form for a limited readership. But it was no more élitist than most of the literature of the Italian Renaissance, which it resembles in many respects, including that of having been written by sharp-witted and well-informed men.

Theodore Metochites, Andronikos II's chief minister, offers the church of Kariye
Camii to Christ. Metochites was the donor of the mosaics in the church, but soon
after they were completed he fell from favor. In this mosaic portrait from the church,
he is clothed in the rich costume appropriate for the chief minister of the emperor.
Courtesy of Josephine Powell, Rome.

As later in Renaissance Italy, and perhaps even in a higher degree than in Italy, literature and scholarship became an occupation of statesmen, to which they frequently attached greater importance than they did to their more public activities. Theodore Metochites, who was for many years the principal minister of Andronikos II, was renowned for the breadth of his learning. Apart from letters, poems, speeches, and a collection of literary and philosophical essays, he wrote lives of saints, commentaries on the works of Aristotle, and a handbook of astronomy. Like many late Byzantine men of letters, he was the center of a kind of literary and philosophical salon in which he played the role not only of arbiter of taste but also of teacher. His contemporary, Nicephorus Choumnos, friend and counsellor of Andronikos II and father-in-law of the emperor's younger son John, was at the center of affairs for a generation. Letters, poems, and rhetorical exercises poured from his pen, as well as nine philosophical treatises and a series of works on physical science of Aristotelian tone, which display close familiarity with the Greek tradition of mathematical and scientific thought. Two treatises on the soul were largely directed against the view of the Neoplatonist philosopher Plotinus. A series of homilies on biblical themes brought the heritage of Hellenic philosophy to the interpretation of problematic scriptural passages. Choumnos had strong views on literary matters, and advocated a strictly classical language and style based on detailed study and imitation of ancient writers. He was sharply critical of what he regarded as the loose and innovatory style of his friend Metochites. It is likely that their literary dispute concealed radical differences of view on political matters which could not easily be expressed openly. He was intensely serious about his literary work, which he regarded as far more important than his achievements as a statesman. "There is nothing in the world," he declared, "which I would prefer to literary fame." The thought would be echoed by many other public men of the age. Constantine Akropolites, grand logothete under Andronikos II, compiled an epitome of Roman and Byzantine history from Aeneas to 1323. Demetrius Kydones, chief minister under John VI and a convert to the Latin church, translated many works of Thomas Aquinas, Au-

gustine, Anselm of Canterbury, and other western theologians into
Greek, composed theological treatises attacking Hesychasm, and
published an extensive collection of speeches and letters which gave
a vivid picture of intellectual life in Constantinople in the second half
of the fourteenth century.

Emperors, too, devoted much of their energy to letters. Michael
VIII, a man of action on a grand scale, wrote a long autobiography.
His predecessor, Theodore Laskaris, was a compulsive writer. John
Cantacuzenus devoted the long years of his retirement to the composition of a history of his own times and of Hesychast theological treatises, many of which still remain unpublished. Manuel II found time
during his long struggle to preserve his dwindling and threatened
empire to compose a large body of letters, speeches, essays, and poems,
a treatise on the duties of a king, and a number of theological works.
In spite of their rigidly classicizing language, Manuel's works bear
witness to his lively intelligence and his grasp of reality as well as to
his impressive learning.

Late Byzantine writers, whether public men or cloistered scholars,
were all in some degree polymaths and made a virtue of their ability
to handle material from all domains, including even the most formi-
dably technical, such as medicine and mathematics. Nicephorus Gregoras was historian, theologian, mathematician, astronomer, musicol-
ogist, and reformer of the calendar. Barlaam of Calabria wrote not
only on theological matters but also on logic and dialectic, geometry
and the determination of eclipses. George Pachymeres, the historian
of the reign of Michael VIII, also wrote treatises on rhetoric and on
theology, an outline of the philosophy of Aristotle, and a vast compen-
dium of mathematical sciences. Theodore Meliteniotes, theologian
and ecclesiastical dignitary, composed an immense handbook of astronomy, of which only the introduction has been published. Maximos Planudes wrote textbooks of grammar and rhetoric, commentaries on classical texts, a commentary on Diophantus's work on the
theory of numbers, a handbook of astronomical computation, polemical theological treatises, and translations from Latin. This conscious
striving to embrace the whole of knowledge foreshadows in many

ways the attitude of Renaissance figures like Leon Battista Alberti and Leonardo da Vinci.

The deliberate harking back to the Greek past which was so prominent in the literature of the time was in part a phenomenon of the confrontation between the Byzantine and Latin worlds. Since 1204 the Byzantines had been humiliated, insulted, exploited, and deceived. Many of them had become the subjects of Latin overlords, in whose eyes they were schismatics or heretics. They sought consolation for their military inferiority in reflecting on their intellectual and cultural superiority, their possession of an uninterrupted tradition of literature and learning going back to classical antiquity, and their direct access to the basic texts of that tradition, which the Latins could approach only in translation, if at all. The plans of Charles of Anjou to reconquer Constantinople, which were frustrated at the last moment by the diplomacy and intrigue of Michael VIII, strengthened this mistrust of the west and this eagerness to emphasize the Byzantines' Hellenic tradition. But relations were always complex. A scholar like Maximos Planudes at the end of the thirteenth century devoted some of his abounding energy to making translations from Latin literature—Cicero, Caesar, Ovid, Augustine, and Boethius. He was not a religious or political westernizer, and was not involved in Michael VIII's ill-starred attempt to secure Church union as the price of peace. His interest in the Latin world appears to have been entirely literary and aesthetic. He had learnt Latin as a diplomat and made the surprising discovery that some Latin writers had interesting things to say and said them well. Such detached interest was rare. Most articulate Byzantines treated the Latin world with a contempt and hostility which are easy to understand. But as the advance of the Ottoman Turks in the early fourteenth century began to be a real threat to the very survival of the empire, the Byzantines found themselves faced with a dilemma. Were they to turn to the despised and hated western world for salvation, at the price of denying their own traditions? Or were they to maintain their religious and intellectual independence, at the risk of annihilation?

Spokesmen of the Church came out clearly for rejection of western entanglements. "Do not think," wrote Patriarch Athanasios I to Emperor Andronikos II, "that we shall prevail by means of armed attack, even if the whole of the western world were to join to help us, were that possible." And the stream of anti-Latin polemical literature flowed undiminished. The Hesychast movement certainly strengthened feeling against the Latins, not only by providing a further point of theological difference, but also by reinforcing the Byzantines' sense of their own superiority and privileged position in the cosmic scheme. But not all thought along these lines. Some men of affairs and scholars became convinced that the Byzantines' sense of their own importance had no foundation, and that whatever may have been the case in the past, in their own time the western world not only enjoyed military and commercial superiority but also had much to offer in the intellectual domain. "How absurd," wrote Demetrius Kydones, chief minister to John V, "that people calling themselves Christians should put their trust only in what is written in Greek and refuse to listen to anything in Latin, as if the truth were a monopoly of one language." Kydones had come to know western theology through the Dominicans of Galata, and ended by accepting the doctrine of papal supremacy and joining the Latin church. Others among his contemporaries and friends were able to take a historical rather than a theological view of the differences between the Greeks and the Latins without alienating themselves from their own community. All of these Latinizers of the later fourteenth century were sharply critical of their countrymen's intellectual pretensions. Kydones wrote in 1376 that his colleagues in Thessalonica and Constantinople despised philosophy; he dismissed much anti-Latin theological polemic as mere verbal hairsplitting. Some of the Latinizers found their careers blocked or their persons in danger from a church now dominated by Hesychasm, and took refuge in Italy. John Kyparissiotes, a pupil of Nicephorus Gregoras, fled to Cyprus then to Italy, where he expounded Orthodox theology in the western scholastic manner. Manuel Kalekas, a pupil of Demetrius Kydones, lived in Italy and the Italian-held islands of Crete and Lesbos, where he translated Boethius and Anselm of Canterbury into Greek. Andreas Chrysoberges, a member of Kydones'

Thomistic circle, taught philosophy and theology at Padua, acted as interpreter at the Council of Constance in 1414 and the Council of Florence in 1439, and ended his days as Latin archbishop of Nicosia.

These "religious refugees" were the forerunners and contemporaries of the Byzantine scholars who from the end of the fourteenth century onwards went to Italy to teach Greek to the early Italian humanists. The earliest and in some ways the most important of these was Manuel Chrysoloras, friend and collaborator of Manuel II, who went to Florence in 1397 at the invitation of Coluccio Salutati, chancellor of Florence, to take up a chair of Greek which Salutati had established. He numbered among his pupils Guarino of Verona, Leonardo Bruni, Jacopo d'Angeli da Scarparia, and Pier Paolo Vergerio. The texts which he brought with him and the method of study which he advocated determined the pattern of Greek studies in the Renaissance for half a century. He was followed by men like John Argyropoulos, Theodore Gaza of Thessalonica, Demetrius Chalkokondyles, and many others. To trace the influence of these Byzantine émigrés upon the literature and thought of the Renaissance would go far beyond the theme of this book and into a study of the formation of modern European culture. What is important is that these were all members of the Byzantine cultural "establishment" who had overcome their prejudices against the western world and were for that very reason capable of transmitting to the west the heritage which the Byzantines looked on as peculiarly their own.

Another sign of the tension within Byzantine society created by the discrepancy between traditional ideals and present reality was the appearance for the first time of a literature in vernacular Greek. This new literature was largely anonymous and is difficult to date, but the earliest examples certainly belong to the first half of the fourteenth century, if not a little earlier. Most of the vernacular works were narrative poems. Some treated of wholly fictitious subjects—for instance, the romances of *Kallimachus and Chrysorrhoe*, of *Belthandros and Chrysantza*, of *Lybistros and Rhodamne*, of *Imperios and Margarona*, of *Phlorios and Platziaflora*. Others, like the poems on Alexander and on Belisarius, had a slender link with historical reality. Several of the poems were more or less close adaptations of works of western literature. The romance of *Imperios and Margarona* was adapted indirectly from a Provençal original, that of *Phlorios and Platziaflora* from a Tuscan *canzone*; a very long poem on the Trojan War was a fairly close translation of the Old French *Roman de Troie* of Benoît de Ste. Maure. The *Chronicle of the Morea* recounts the origin and history of the Latin principality of the Morea from a very anti-Greek point of view. There is virtually no prose literature in vernacular Greek of the Byzantine period. The works mentioned are all written in fifteen-syllable accentual verse, for which there were no classical models and hence no prescriptive rules. Their language is not homogeneous. There were no standards and no rules for writing the spoken language, and all who learned to write had been at least minimally exposed to the classical grammatical tradition and the prestige of archaism. So these early vernacular texts are all to some extent macaronic; spoken forms and constructions were mingled with those of the classicizing literary tradition in an uncomfortable amalgam. There were other common features which marked these texts. They all dealt with what from the traditional point of view were "trivial" subjects. Serious literature—history, theology, rhetoric, and philosophy—was the exclusive domain of the learned language with its laboriously studied archaisms, recondite allusions, and intellectual hypertension. It was impossible to handle most of the heritage of classical thought in the new medium. Since the custodians of the classical tradition, and in particular the grammarians, passed over vernacular literature, its means of expressions never became codified. There could be no Greek Dante to treat elevated subjects in the tongue of the people and to lay the foundations of a new literary language.

It will already be clear that vernacular literature was in some ways less restricted in content than classicizing literature, and in particular that it readily took over and adapted western themes and motifs. Several of the works mentioned were direct or indirect adapations of western originals. All of them readily admitted loan words from Italian and French current in the spoken language and minor cultural loans such as the prestige attached to jousting or, among women, to

Drawing of the scholar Manuel Chrysoloras, who emigrated to Florence at the end
of the fourteenth century. He was the earliest of many Byzantine scholars who went
to Italy to teach Greek studies, thereby greatly influencing the course of the Italian
Renaissance. *Courtesy of The Louvre, Paris (Cliché des Musées Nationaux—Paris).*

wearing western clothes. It has often been suggested in the past that it was in the regions of Frankish occupation that the spoken tongue began to be used for literary purposes. There is little evidence for this view. What is probably the earliest of the vernacular verse romances, that of *Kallimachus and Chrysorrhoe*, seems to have been composed by Andronikos Comnenus Dukas, a first cousin of Andronikos II, who followed a military career in the imperial service. And several vernacular poems, such as the Belisarius poem and a curious allegorical poem on the four-footed beasts, were clearly the work of metropolitan circles. This is not to say, however, that none of the works of vernacular literature were composed in regions under Latin rule.

It has also been suggested in the past that the early vernacular literature represents a kind of counter-culture of the masses, who were beginning to develop a sense of identity and of opposition to the élite which had so long exploited them and excluded them from the prestigious traditional culture. But it now looks rather as if the earliest works of vernacular poetry emanated from circles familiar with traditional classical culture. Andronikos Comnenus Dukas wrote prose works in the learned tongue as well as the verse romance of *Kallimachus and Chrysorrhoe*. And the authors of many of the other verse romances display a familiarity with classical material which suggests that they had at least the rudiments of a classical education. In other words it is most generally held today that the vernacular literature spread from the top down rather than from the bottom up, and that it was originally the work of members of the cultural élite who sought a more flexible and expressive medium of communication which would be accessible to a wider range of readers and hearers. However, the question is still open, and we still have much to learn about the earliest Greek vernacular literature. One important point is that its existence presupposes a class of readers who possessed full functional literacy but were unable or unwilling to spend long years in the study of the literary tongue. There is plenty of evidence for the existence of such a class. Of those who spent a few years at school and learned to read and write, only a tiny proportion of the wealthy or the ambitious went on to study grammar and rhetoric. It is to such men and women that the vernacular literature was addressed. That they were deemed worthy of notice is a symptom of the breakdown of the traditional system of social values.

Scholarship and piety were two reactions to the challenge of the post-restoration Byzantine world. Both had long-standing and respectable antecedents in Byzantine culture. Each laid weight on a different aspect of that culture—its roots in Greece and in Palestine; they did not necessarily exclude one another. The Emperor Andronikos II was both a patron of letters and a man of almost morbid piety. His chief minister, Theodore Metochites, was a literary polymath who devoted much of his great wealth to the reconstruction and decoration of a monastery to which he retired in his old age. The triumph of Hesychasm changed the relationship. The Hesychast movement contained a strong current of anti-rationalism. Gregory Palamas had censured those who pursued the study of classical literature beyond what was necessary for the understanding of Christian doctrine. Rhetoric and philosophy brought a man no nearer to the vision of God. The disastrous civil war, the Black Death, and the triumph of Hesychasm combined to change the balance of values in Byzantine society. Sanctity became a more acceptable means of distinction than scholarship. It was one which was more widely accessible, too. And as a vehicle of ethnic and social identity, a somewhat overemotional Orthodoxy was far better adapted to the needs of the times than familiarity with classical literature. At the same time, however, the Hesychast movement, which rapidly spread to monasteries in Bulgaria and Serbia, contributed to the formation of a common Orthodox culture, shared by the Greeks, Slavs, and Rumanians alike. Tŭrnovo, the capital of Bulgaria, became an important center of learning and of translation from Greek to Old Slavonic. A typical representative of this common culture was Kiprian (ca. 1335–1406), a Bulgarian by birth, long a monk in Constantinople and on Mount Athos, who ended his days as metropolitan of Moscow, and contributed significantly to the transmission of Byzantine ecclesiastical culture to the nascent Muscovite state, often through translations made in Bulgaria.

From the middle of the fourteenth century there is a marked

change in the character of Byzantine literature. The long series of
historians of their own times comes to a sudden end with John Cantacuzenus and Nicephorus Gregoras. It was not until after the capture
of the city by the Turks in 1453 that the tradition was taken up again,
in very different circumstances. The lively interest in mathematics,
astronomy, music, and science so characteristic of the age of Pachymeres, Metochites, and Gregoras is strikingly reduced in the last century
of the empire. The same is true of the critical study of classical texts.
Planudes, Manuel Moschopoulos, Thomas Magister, and Demetrius
Triclinius all did work between 1270 and 1350 which has earned them
a sure place in the history of classical scholarship. Thereafter there is
silence. Well-meaning and muddled schoolmasters take the place of
original scholars. One branch of literature in which there was no falling off was that of anti-Latin polemic, though the intellectual quality
of the later treatises leaves much to be desired.

It would be unwise to exaggerate the universality of this change of
direction or loss of nerve in the mid-fourteenth century. There were
certainly scholars and men of letters in the last century of the empire
who were easily familiar with the heritage of Greek thought and
literature, but they tended to be rather isolated figures, or to be fussy
pedants rather than original scholars. Classical literature continued
to be the foundation of all education beyond the elementary level, but
it appears that rather less of it was read than in the previous century,
if one can judge from surviving school books. However one may qual-
ify it, the reality of the break in the years around 1350 is undeniable.

Fortunately, however, enough scholars continued to follow, albeit
at a distance, in the footsteps of their great predecessors to be able to
transmit to the west, when the west was ready to receive it, not merely
a body of texts but a critical and rigorous approach to them and their
contents, which can be traced back without interruption to the Museum and the Library of Alexandria. The gap of time to be bridged
was not long. Manuel Chrysoloras, the first public teacher of Greek
in Florence, could as a child have seen Nicephorus Gregoras.

If one reaction to the "lack of fit" between the traditional ideal of
Byzantine society and the reality of the late Byzantine world was to

concentrate upon a rather simplistic holiness to the neglect of reason and learning, another was to reject altogether the Christian element in Byzantine tradition. This radical step was taken in the last years of the empire by George Gemistos Plethon and some of his followers in Mistra. George Gemistos was born in Constantinople in 1353 and taught philosophy in the capital for a number of years. Always something of a showman, he took to replacing his family name of Gemistos (= full) by its classical equivalent, Plethon, which had the advantage of resembling the name of Plato (Platon in Greek). At the time of the long blockade of Constantinople by Sultan Bajezid he left the capital for Mistra, where he held high office as well as continuing his teaching for many years. He gathered round himself there a circle of pupils which included Bessarion, the future cardinal, John and Mark Eugenikos, John Argyropoulos, later a teacher of Greek in Florence, the historian Laonikos Chalkokondyles, John Moschos, who succeeded Plethon as head of his school, Michael Apostolis, who later copied manuscripts for many Italian scholars, Demetrius Raul Kabakes (Plethon's secretary), and many others. In 1438–39 he was one of the Byzantine representatives at the Council of Ferrara-Florence. He took little part in the theological discussions, but enthralled his Florentine audience by his lectures on Platonic philosophy. Renaissance Platonism owed much to the inspiration given by Plethon's teaching during his stay in Florence. Plethon died at Mistra in 1452, at the age of ninety-nine, one year before his native city fell to the guns of Mehmed II. In 1464 Sigismondo Malatesta, commander of the Venetian forces in the Peloponnese, besieged and captured Mistra. An enthusiastic Platonist, he took the remains of Plethon back with him to Rimini, where his sarcophagus still rests in the outer wall at the Tempio Malatestiano.

Like all Byzantine Platonists, Plethon was strongly influenced by the Neoplatonism of Plotinus and his successors. Yet he was no blind follower in their wake. Like his master Plato, he was both a practical teacher and a creative dreamer. His works comprise numerous speeches and occasional writings, including a treatise on political and economic reform in the Morea, a handbook of geography, a penetrating analysis of the differences between Plato and Aristotle, and a vast program for an ideal state, which he entitled *Laws* after its model, the *Laws* of Plato.

For Plethon, Hellenism was not something to be imitated in speeches and essays. It provided a model for life as well as for literature, and who was better fitted to imitate the model than those who were both the physical and the cultural descendants of the ancient Greeks? He developed this theme in a funeral oration delivered at Mistra in 1409, in which he observed that the Peloponnese had been inhabited by the same Greek stock as far back as human memory ran, and he continued to dwell on it for the rest of his life. The Peloponnese was for him what Syracuse had been for Plato, the land in which his ideal state could be translated into practice. In a series of treatises he outlined his scheme of reform. A strongly centralized monarchy— naturally under the rule of a philosopher-king—was to replace the feudal separation of his own day. Its subjects were to fall into two categories. A locally recruited standing army was to be exempted from all taxation. The tax-paying peasants were to be exempted from military service. All land was to be publicly owned, but a man was to be entitled to the use of all the land that he could cultivate, provided he paid tax upon its produce. Foreign trade, both import and export, was to be strictly controlled, and its pattern was not to be determined by foreigners, in the particular instance by Venice. The monarch was to be aided by a council of learned men, trained for the purpose and dedicated to giving a moral example to their fellow citizens. These and similar proposals were supported with a wealth of argument and example drawn from ancient Greek history. There has been much argument about the nature of Plethon's proposed reforms. Some have seen in him a kind of socialist before his time. Others dismiss him as an unpractical dreamer, yet others as an archetypal fascist. The truth is probably that his proposals, although not fully worked out and riddled with concealed contradictions, were meant to be serious answers to the problems of the age, which were the problems of a late feudal society. There is no indication that any of them was ever seriously considered by the rulers in Mistra. The reason, however, is not

Aristotle portrayed as a late Byzantine, in a fourteenth-century manuscript. *Courtesy of Bodleian Library, University of Oxford. MS. Barocci 87, fol. 33v.*

that they were totally unworkable, but that they would conflict with the interests of the great landowners, both lay and monastic, without whose support the Byzantine Peloponnese would disintegrate. To that extent they were impracticable. The society they envisaged was not a socialist society but a reformed feudalism, which in fact had many of the features of the Byzantine Empire in its earlier and more successful periods.

This was the public aspect of Plethon's thinking. It is noteworthy that it passes over in silence a large part of Byzantine tradition dealing with the legitimation of the empire as an instrument of divine policy. Government was for him a political and economic problem, perhaps a philosophical problem, but certainly not a religious problem. His ideal state, if it ever came about, would not be the New Israel. In his more esoteric writing, addressed to a limited circle of his closest followers, he pursues to its logical conclusion his rejection of the Byzantine synthesis of Hellenism and Christianity. Christianity is to be totally rejected in favor of a new "Hellenic" religion, with a pantheon of gods headed by Zeus. This is no antiquarian restoration of paganism. For Plethon's gods are not personal deities, but names for philosophical categories. His cosmology is Neoplatonist, as are the ethics which follow from it. He sees the universe as a hierarchy of orders of being, beginning with the One which is called Zeus. From Zeus comes Poseidon, the intelligible principle underlying the physical world, and so on. The higher orders create and maintain the lower ones not by emanation, as the sun emits rays, but by a kind of everlasting overflow of their own being. In this respect Plethon differs from most Neoplatonic thinkers, and his philosophy allows a greater worth to the material world, including man himself. It is difficult, however, to pursue this analysis very far, since most of Plethon's great theoretical work, the *Laws*, is lost irretrievably. After 1453 the new patriarch, Gennadios, ordered all copies to be confiscated and burned.

Plethon has been described as an "odd man out." He certainly had little appeal for his fellow Greeks of the Peloponnese, but he was less isolated than might appear, and had an inner circle of disciples who followed him in rejecting Christianity. A letter written by one of his

disciples, Juvenal, in 1438 speaks of a "phratry" or secret society of
Hellenes. Juvenal was expelled from Constantinople by John VIII at
the request of the ecclesiastical authorities and later, in the Peloponnese, had his tongue and his right hand cut off and was thrown from
a cliff into the sea. He bore his barbarous punishment with fortitude,
claiming before he was finally dispatched to be a "martyr of the first
principle of all things." Had the Ottoman conquest and the protection
which it gave to the Orthodox church not "frozen" the situation, it
may be that Plethon's rejection of the Byzantine synthesis of Hellenism and Christianity would have found more adherents in Byzantine
intellectual circles. As it was, it was in Italy that the seed which he
sowed bore fruit, not only in the Platonic Academy of Marsilio Ficino,
but also in the Platonist character of much Renaissance philosophy.
Raphael's great fresco of the School of Athens in the stanze of the
Sistine Chapel owes much to the visit to Florence of George Gemistos
Plethon nearly a century earlier.

The general improverishment of late Byzantine society prevented
monumental building on any scale, but small churches continued to
be built all over the former territory of the empire by local benefactors.
Architects no longer followed Constantinopolitan models. In much
of peninsular Greece a basilical pattern was preferred to the cross-
in-square. Curious compromise patterns were sometimes adopted,
combining features of the basilica and the cross-in-square. Western
features were not infrequently introduced, such as a free-standing or
attached campanile or an arcade. The end of cultural domination by
the capital meant a new freedom of experiment for local architects
and master builders, who readily drew on regional traditions and were
ready to absorb foreign influences. The range of styles in use during
this period can be seen in such cities as Thessalonica, Mistra, or Mesembria, where many churches of the period survive. Noteworthy examples are in Thessalonica—Hagia Aikaterine (thirteenth century),
Holy Apostles (early fourteenth century), Prophet Elias (fourteenth
century), St. Panteleimon (thirteenth century), Taxiarchoi (fourteenth
century), Transfiguration (fourteenth century), St. Nicholas Or-
phanos (fourteenth century), monastery church of Vlattades (four-

teenth century); in Mistra—the Metropolis (1291–92), St. Theodore (1295), which was one of the last examples of the cruciform octagonal pattern common in central Greece in the eleventh and twelfth centuries, the Aphendiko (1310), Hagia Sophia (fourteenth century), the monastery churches of Peribleptos (fourteenth century) and Pantanassa (1428), Evangelistria (fourteenth/fifteenth century), St. George (? fourteenth century); in Mesembria (Nesebŭr, in Bulgaria)—Pantocrator (thirteenth/fourteenth century), St. John Aliturgetos (thirteenth/fourteenth century), St. Theodore (fourteenth century), St. Paraskeve (fourteenth century), and Archangels Gabriel and Michael (fourteenth century). The variety of styles and patterns displayed by these buildings is an eloquent testimony to the flexibility and receptivity of the late Byzantine architectural tradition. There are many monastic and other churches of the period scattered about the northern Balkans, in particular in former Serbian territory. The monastery churches of Gračanica, Studenica, Arelje, Sopočani, Mileševa, the Peribleptos at Ohrid, the small church of Bojana near Sofia, the churches of Žiča and Čučer, exemplify this north Balkan architecture, which must certainly be seen as a manifestation of late Byzantine culture. In the capital itself, the monastery church of Chora (Kariye Camii) and the church of St. Mary Pammakaristos (Fethiye Camii) are the principal monuments of the period.

Several nonreligious buildings of the late Byzantine period survive in Mistra. There is little to compare them with, since lay edifices were more readily demolished than churches. The two-storied Lascaris mansion is an interesting example of an aristocratic private house. The monumental Palace of the Despots embodies constructions of various dates from the late thirteenth to the fifteenth century. Its north façade recalls early Italian Renaissance palaces. Another private mansion, the Palataki, probably dates from the early fourteenth century. All these dwellings were fortified, and therefore follow different patterns from Constantinopolitan houses and palaces.

It is easier to assess late Byzantine painting than late Byzantine architecture, and it is intrinsically more interesting. Many churches of this period still preserve their mosaic or fresco decoration. Far more

The First Steps of the Virgin, a superb mosaic from the church of the Kariye Camii in Constantinople, executed about 1320. *Courtesy of Josephine Powell, Rome.*

portable icons, either painted or in miniature mosaic, survive than from earlier periods, though it is rarely known with certainty where or when they were executed. Very many late Byzantine illuminated manuscripts remain. The surviving paintings are entirely religious in content—secular painting was practiced, but no examples have survived. Most art must have been religiously inspired, since more than in earlier periods the Church, its institutions and its benefactors were the principal source of patronage.

Until recently late Byzantine art was often dismissed as uninteresting or positively decadent. A misleading biological analogy led people to think of societies as passing through periods of youth, maturity, and old age. The late Byzantine period was almost automatically regarded as one of decline. Another factor contributing to the undervaluing of late Byzantine art was the view of Ainalov, one of the founding fathers of Byzantine art history, that the period of Latin occupation had exposed Byzantine artists to powerful influences from western Europe, and that consequently the art of the last two centuries of the empire was in a large measure derivative. Studies by specialists in the last two generations have shown that this theory is not merely oversimplified but positively wrong. They have also revealed a richness, vitality, and variety in late Byzantine art which makes it the very reverse of decadent. There are still many problems of dating and attribution and provenance to be solved, but some guidelines can be discerned.

Among the best-preserved groups of church decoration are those in the monastery of the Chora at Constantinople—the Kariye Camii in Turkish—which was restored and redecorated by Theodore Metochites shortly before his downfall in 1328. The church itself and its inner and outer porticoes are decorated in mosaic, including cycles illustrating the life of the Virgin and of Christ which display not only exquisite delicacy of draftsmanship and classical naturalism of modelling and pose, but also a refined humanity which gives individual importance to all the minor characters in the scenes. Classical architectural and landscape backgrounds are delineated with sureness of touch and unobtrusiveness. Throughout the cycles there is a warm sympathy for the characters which never degenerates into sentimentality. The marvellous, crowded, but orderly picture of the Nativity of the Virgin, and even more that of the First Steps of the Virgin, are striking examples, but it would be invidious to single out any one of these numerous pictures for special admiration. They are all art of the highest quality. Parallel to the main church building is a parecclesion or side chapel, sharing a common entrance portico. It is decorated in fresco; less brilliant and glittering than the mosaics, these paintings are in some ways even more successful. They show the same combination of classical naturalism, superb draftsmanship, and human sympathy for every character. The huge Descent of Christ into Limbo in the apse and the even more impressive Last Judgment in the vault show the artists' sureness of touch in large compositions. The same sureness emerges in details such as the angel holding the scroll of heaven in the corner of the vault. In the outer portico, over the main door, is a mosaic of the donor offering his church to Christ. Metochites, with his neatly trimmed beard, his elegant curving eyebrows, his gorgeously decorated robe of office, and his extraordinary turban-like hat, is depicted with realism. This is no doubt a flattering portrait of the great man—there is not a grey hair in his beard—but it is not an idealizing portrait. This was how the statesman, scholar, and poet appeared to the men of his time.

Of a similar date are the mosaics of the church of St. Mary Pammakaristos or Fethiye Camii, which was endowed by a certain Michael Glavas at the end of the thirteenth century and decorated shortly after 1315. The figure of Christ Pantocrator appears on the dome, surrounded by twelve prophets. The apse is occupied by a Deesis— Christ with the Virgin and St. John the Baptist who intercede with Him. Only portions of the wall mosaics survive, comprising prophets and saints and a scene of the Baptism of Christ. The mosaics are of good quality but rather different in style from those of the Chora church. Their lines are less flowing, and their colors sometimes harshly bright, but they aim at the same kind of classicizing naturalism. Another small church, the Kilisse Camii—probably the church of St. Theodore Tyro—also preserves a little mosaic work of the same period. Coarser in texture, with large cubes, it is inferior in quality to the Chora or Pammakaristos mosaics, but still shows the same naturalistic, humanist tendency. The portraits of the kings of Israel in the outer narthex are highly individualized.

Of comparable date is the mosaic and fresco decoration of the church of the Holy Apostles in Thessalonica. There is perhaps greater realism here than in the Constantinopolitan work, for instance, in the Entry into Jerusalem. But the general style is not markedly different, and the pictures may well have been executed by metropolitan artists. How much of this metropolitan mosaic and painting of the early fourteenth century has been lost is uncertain. But it is known that a painter named Theophanes, who went from Constantinople to work in Russia after the middle of the century, and whose work survives in the church of the Transfiguration at Novgorod and elsewhere, had executed paintings in forty churches in Constantinople and its imme-diate neighborhood before his departure. Not a trace of this work survives.

At the very time when the mosaics and paintings of the Chora and Pammakaristos churches were being executed, Giotto was painting his frescos in the Arena Chapel in Padua. The resemblances are strik-ing—the interest in the individual, the sure and flowing line, the imaginative composition and the sophisticated use of color. The ques-tion has been asked whether these resemblances are coincidental, or whether influences can be traced in either direction. It is not easy to answer. There is no record of movements of artists between Constan-tinople and northeastern Italy, and little is known of individual artists at all in the Byzantine world. That they did readily move from place to place is clear, and Venice, under whose rule Padua passed, had a large Greek colony and was a center of Byzantine cultural influence in Italy. Acquaintance by one artist with the work of another cannot be ruled out. But a common intellectual and aesthetic climate, which has been discussed in connection with Byzantine literature and thought, is the most likely explanation of such parallel tendencies as exist in the visual arts.

In Macedonia also lively artistic activity took place in the late thirteenth and fourteenth centuries, both in the areas under Byzantine rule and in those belonging to the kingdom of Serbia. One of the centers of this activity was Mount Athos, where the wealthy monasteries provided regular patronage. The paintings in the Protaton at Karyes, though their date has been disputed, are now generally believed to belong to the reign of Andronikos II. The rather tense, angular poses and the brilliant colors are very different from anything in the Constantinopolitan paintings discussed above. The same style probably marks the early fourteenth-century decoration of the monastery churches at Chilandari and Vatopedi, though both were heavily overpainted in the early nineteenth century. The same combination of garish color and angular, dramatic poses is to be found in many churches in northern Macedonia, which were probably decorated under Serbian patronage. The frescos at St. Clement in Ohrid (c. 1300) at Staro Nagoričino (1317), at St. Nikitas in Čučer (1307), at Studenica (1314), at Gračanica (1321) and at Dečani (c. 1329) all exemplify this style in some degree. Some of the painters signed their names. There has been much largely inconclusive discussion of the ethnic origin of these painters, and much has been made of the language of the inscriptions upon the paintings—usually Greek, but occasionally Old Slavonic. What does appear significant is that this so-called Macedonian style continues many of the features and tendencies of monastic painting in earlier centuries, including a striving to express intensity of emotion and an angular style of drawing quite different from the flowing naturalism of much metropolitan work. That this provincial style should have been so widely practiced, and should have been chosen by Serbian monarchs in preference to the style of Constantinople for the churches which they endowed, is an indication of the new polycentrism of Byzantine cultural life.

The monumental painting of Mistra not only epitomizes, by the variety of its styles, the lively richness of late Byzantine art, but provides a series of examples from the end of the thirteenth century to the middle of the fifteenth. The frescos of the church of St. Demetrius, founded in 1291, include paintings of reserved and conservative style, recalling metropolitan art of the twelfth century, and others in which

Fresco depicting the Betrayal in the church of St. Clement, Ohrid, c. 1300. The vivid colors and over-full compositions found in late Macedonian wall paintings are in marked contrast to the restrained delicacy of Constantinopolitan art of the same period. *Courtesy of Josephine Powell, Rome.*

the new interest in crowd scenes and elaborate, evocative backgrounds appears. Two different artists or schools of artists seem to have been at work. The two churches in the Brontocheion monastery are slightly later and already display the humanist style of contemporary art in Constantinople. The splendid head of the Prophet Zacharias—which recalls the equally dramatic John the Baptist in the Serbian monastery of Gračanica—and the scene of the Healing of the Blind Man in the Aphentiko church show two different aspects of the new style—the one forceful, the other tender. The small church of the Peribleptos, probably decorated shortly after 1350, is decorated with almost miniature-like intimacy and refinement of detail. The lively Entry into Jerusalem, with its gay crowd in bright costumes, and the almost mystical Nativity, show two directions which the skill of the artists took. It has been suggested that these paintings are influenced by Hesychasm, which was dominant at Mistra at the time. But it is very difficult to detect any signs in Byzantium of a specifically Hesychast art. Perhaps the inward-looking concentration of the mystic was not easily combined with the artist's keen interest in the outward and visible aspect of the world. The last major decorative cycle at Mistra is that of the monastery church of the Pantanassa, founded about 1350 and restored and decorated by John Frangopoulos in 1428. These last major monumental paintings produced in the Byzantine world bear impressive witness to its artistic vitality at a time when its political freedom of action had been reduced to vanishing point. The Entry into Jerusalem is a composition of splendid gaiety. The Annunciation combines naturalistic drawing and spiritual profundity. The superb Raising of Lazarus, with its sophisticated and quite unnaturalistic use of color, foreshadows the work of El Greco. This is the work of an artist or artists of the very highest quality.

The tendencies visible in monumental painting are reflected in the portable icons, mosaic and painted, of which many survive. Unfortunately it is usually impossible to establish their provenance or date with any certainty. Some recall the style of the Chora decoration, such as the Annunciation from Ohrid, now in the Museum at Skopje, and the very fine Annunciation and Death of the Virgin in the Museum of Fine Art in Moscow. They are certainly metropolitan work. Other examples, sometimes displaying different styles, are the mosaic icon of the Annunciation in the Victoria and Albert Museum in London, the Twelve Apostles in the Pushkin Museum in Moscow, the large icon of Christ in the Hermitage, which was presented to the monastery of the Pantocrator on Mount Athos in the 1360s, and the Virgin and Child in the Tretyakov Gallery in Moscow—Our Lady of Pimen—which some scholars believe to have been painted in the Adriatic region. The field is rich and varied, and many of the works are of very high quality indeed.

In book illumination the old tradition of portraits of emperors and other great dignitaries continues, but a new feeling for their individuality comes in along with a more natural and less flat delineation. Examples are the portrait of the Grand Duke Alexios Apokaukos in a manuscript of Hippocrates[19] dating from the early 1340s, with its solid-looking furniture and its characterful features; the double portrait of John Cantacuzenus as emperor and monk[20] of c. 1370; the group of Manuel II, the Empress Helena and their three children in a manuscript of Pseudo-Dionysius the Areopagite (Paris, Musée du Louvre) of the early fifteenth century; another portrait of Manuel II in a copy of his funeral oration on his brother Theodore[21] probably written at Mistra shortly after 1407. A somewhat different, more rigid style is found in the beautiful portraits of an imperial prince and princess of the late fourteenth century in a Typikon, or corpus of rules for a monastery, now in Lincoln College, Oxford. Evangelist portraits, too, often have a new solidity of form and a new individuality of feature, as do portraits of classical writers and others. An example is the portrait of St. John in a bilingual Gospel made by a Greek artist for a Latin patron c. 1250.[22] Another is the portrait of Hippocrates in a manuscript already mentioned above.[23] Western styles and costumes are occasionally found in illustrations to classical authors, such as the later fourteenth-century Oppian[24] with a series of charming hunting scenes. The same tendencies are at work here as in the adaptation of western stories and motifs in the early vernacular literature. Amid much conventional, elegantly drawn work there are a surprising

Fourteenth-century miniature mosaic icon of the Annunciation, one of the most delicate examples of the many portable works of art created in the late phase of Byzantine art, now in the Victoria and Albert Museum, London. *Courtesy of Victoria and Albert Museum, London.*

number of paintings which astonish by their unusual composition, their moving emotionalism, or their original use of color. One of the most striking is the Transfiguration in the manuscript of John Canta-cuzenus mentioned above, with its dominant blues, its sense of lim-itless space and its spiritual depth. Here, perhaps, we see the art of Hesychasm, if such an art exists.

Enough has been said to establish that the political collapse of the Byzantine state was not accompanied by a collapse of Byzantine cul-ture. The unhappy events of the mid-fourteenth century may have undermined the brittle, self-consciously élitist world of classicizing literature, though it certainly did not destroy it. And late Byzantine theology and philosophy may have shown an unhealthy narrowness of interest. But vernacular literature remained lively, and in the years immediately after the capture of the city by the Turks, four historians chronicled the last days of the empire from very different points of view and in different styles. Dukas, writing in easy and unpretentious Greek, expressed the ideas of the not negligible group of Latinizers, who saw the only hope for Byzantine society in absorption by the vigorous Latin west. Sphrantzes wrote movingly and yet without par-tisan prejudice as a former courtier and statesman under the last em-peror, Constantine XI. Kritoboulos represents the pro-Ottoman point of view of those who saw adaptation to the new conditions of Turkish rule as the only real option open to Byzantine society; his history is a panegyric of Ottoman power and grandeur. Finally Chalkokon-dyles—the cousin of that Demetrius Chalkokondyles who taught Greek in Padua and saw the first printed Homer through the press—described and analyzed, with a range of vision recalling Herodotus or Polybius, the expansion of Ottoman power to fill the vacuum left by the disintegration of the Byzantine Empire. The vitality and vari-ety of the visual and literary arts, even under the restricted patronage of an impoverished society, have been illustrated suffficiently. Byzan-tine church music, too, took on a new character in the late thirteenth and fourteenth centuries, when the originally simple melodies were transformed and embellished by elaborate coloraturas, and new melodies in the new, ornamented style were composed by such masters as John Glykys, John Koukouzelis, and John Lampadarios.

If the historian is asked why the Byzantine Empire, after more than a thousand years of vigorous life, collapsed so ignominiously, he will doubtless reply that there was no single reason. Factors of many kinds were at work, from improvements in seagoing ships to climatic changes in central Asia, from the growing independence of landed proprietors to debasement of the coinage in order to increase the money supply. If there was a single fatal blow, it was struck in 1204 when the territory of the empire still stretched from the Adriatic to the gates of Syria, and not in 1453, when Constantinople fell to the rulers of a vast, enveloping empire as an over-ripe fruit falls from a tree. It was the power vacuum created by the Latin invasion which enabled the orthodox Slav states of the Balkans to strike out on a course of their own, freed from the field of force of Byzantium, and in the end condemned them to fall one by one to the Ottoman conqueror. Rivalry and intrigue replaced the firm and traditional political leadership which might have enabled the Balkan world, with its immense manpower and its largely common culture, to offer effective resistance.

Fortunately, Byzantine society and Byzantine culture remained in being until the western world was mature enough to want to learn from them. What they learned was not a dead body of doctrine or an artistic iconography, but rather the living and developing tradition of a society which carried a great cultural heritage without being overburdened or paralyzed by it. The west's process of learning from the Byzantine world was not completed in the Renaissance and the Reformation. Both in the domain of religion and in that of politics, the seventeenth century found the Byzantine world of absorbing interest, as the many publications of Byzantine texts in the period bear witness. The Age of Enlightenment, though it might turn its back upon the Middle Ages, found that Byzantium exercised a disquieting fascination, which emerges strikingly in the pages of Edward Gibbon. To judge by the number of books published, our own age has a new awareness of the Byzantine world. Perhaps we may find illumination of political and cultural problems which in the brash heyday of imperialist self-confidence we thought we could ignore—problems like east-west relations, or the dynamic of traditional societies. At any rate we are still learning from the Byzantines.

NOTES

1. Leo VI, *Tactica* 12.72 (MPG 107.826).
2. P. de Lagarde, *Johannis Euchaitorum metropolitae quae in codice Vaticano gr. 676 supersunt*, Göttingen 1881, No. 43.
3. Cod. Paris gr. 139 fol. 435ᵛ.
4. *Ibid.* fol. 1ᵛ.
5. Cod. Athon. Stavronikita 43 fol. 10.
6. *Ibid.* fol. 5ᵛ.
7. Cod. Paris gr. 139.
8. Cod. Paris gr. 510.
9. Venice, Biblioteca Marciana, cod. gr. Z.17.
10. Cod. Vat. gr. 1613.
11. Cod. Coislin gr. 79.
12. C. Sathas, *Mesaiōnikē Bibliothēkē* 5 (Paris, 1876); 242–43.
13. Niketas Choniates, *History* 7.3, p. 269 (Bonn ed.).
14. Cod. Paris suppl. gr. 1262 fol. 35.
15. Cod. Vat. Urb. gr. 2 fol. 20.
16. BM Add. Ms. 11870 fol. 174ᵛ.
17. *Ibid.* fol. 60.
18. Cod. Oxon. Bodl. Misc. 136 fol. 231ᵛ.
19. Cod. Paris gr. 2144 fol. 11.
20. Cod. Paris gr. 1242 fol. 123ᵛ.
21. Paris suppl. gr. 309 fol. vi.
22. Cod. Paris gr. 54.
23. Cod. Paris gr. 2155 fol. 10.
24. Cod. Paris gr. 2736.

CHRONOLOGICAL TABLE

1022	Annexation of Armenia complete
1055	Seljuq Turks take Baghdad
1071	Seljuq Turks defeat and capture Romanos IV and overrun much of Asia Minor. Bari captured by Normans
1082	Alexios I grants trading privileges to Venice
1097	First Crusade
1133–43	Victorious campaigns of John I in Cilicia and Syria
1147	Second Crusade. Normans capture Corfu, Corinth, and Thebes
1155	Successful Byzantine campaign in Italy
1176	Seljuq victory at Myriokephalon
1182	Massacre of Latins in Constantinople
1185	Normans capture and sack Thessalonica
1204	Capture of Constantinople by Fourth Crusade and establishment of Latin Empire
1259	Nicaean army defeats Latins and Epirotes at Pelagonia
1261	Recapture of Constantinople by Nicaean force and end of Latin Empire
1274	Council of Lyons. Michael VIII accepts Church union
1282	Sicilian Vespers: defeat of Charles of Anjou
1308	Ottoman Turks take Ephesus
1321–28	Civil war between Andronikos II and Andronikos III
1329	Turks take Nicaea
1337	Turks take Nicomedia
1341–47	Civil war between John V and John Cantacuzenus
1347	The Black Death
1354	Turks take Gallipoli
1365	Turks establish their capital at Adrianople
1376–79	Civil war in Byzantium
1387	Thessalonica surrenders to Turks
1393	End of Bulgarian state. Turks occupy Thessaly
1396	Defeat of crusaders at Nicopolis
1397	Manuel Chrysoloras begins teaching Greek in Florence
1397–1402	Siege of Constantinople by Sultan Bajezid
1422	Murad besieges Constantinople
1430	Turks recapture Thessalonica
1439	Council of Florence proclaims Church union
1444	Turks defeat Hungarians and crusaders at Varna
1453	Turks take Constantinople on 29 May. Death of last emperor
1460	Turks take Mistra
1461	Turks take Trebizond

LIST OF EMPERORS

Constantine I   324–37
Constantius II   337–61
Julian   361–63
Jovian   363–64
Valens   364–78
Theodosius I   379–95
Arcadius   395–408
Theodosius II   408–50
Marcian   450–57
Leo I   457–74
Leo II   474
Zeno   474–75
Basiliscus   475–76
Zeno (again)   476–91
Anastasius I   491–518
Justin I   518–27
Justinian I   527–65
Justin II   565–78
Tiberius II Constantine   578–82
Maurice   582–602
Phocas   602–10
Heraclius   610–41
Constantine III and Her-
   aclonas   641
Constans II   641–68
Constantine IV   668–85
Justinian II   685–95
Leontius   695–98
Tiberius III   698–705
Justinian II (again)   705–11
Philippicus Bardanes   711–713
Anastasius II   713–15

Theodosius III   715–17
Leo III   717–41
Constantine V   741–75
Leo IV   775–80
Constantine VI   780–97
Irene   797–802
Nicephorus I   802–11
Staurakios   811
Michael I Rhangabe   811–13
Leo V   813–20
Michael II   820–29
Theophilus   829–42
Michael III   842–67
Basil I   867–86
Leo VI   886–912
Alexander   912–13
Constantine VII   913–59
Romanos I Lakapenos   920–44
Romanos II   959–63
Nicephorus II Phokas   963–69
John I Tzimiskes   969–76
Basil II   976–1025
Constantine VIII   1025–28
Romanos III Argyros   1028–34
Michael IV the Paphlagon-
   ian   1034–41
Michael V Calaphates   1041–42
Zoë and Theodora   1042
Constantine IX Monomachos   1042–
   55
Theodora (again)   1055–56
Michael VI Stratioticus   1056–57

Isaac I Comnenus 1057–59

Constantine X Dukas 1059–67

Eudocia 1067

Romanos IV Diogenes 1068–71

Eudocia (again) 1071

Michael VII Dukas 1071–78

Nicephorus III Botaneiates 1078–81

Alexios I Comnenus 1081–1118

John II Comnenus 1118–43

Manuel I Comnenus 1143–80

Alexios II Comnenus 1180–83

Andronikos I Comnenus 1183–85

Isaac II Angelos 1185–95

Alexios III Angelos 1195–1203

Isaac II (again) and Alexios IV Angeli 1203–4

Alexios V Murtzuphlous 1204

(ruling from Nicaea, 1204–61)

Constantine (XI) Laskaris 1204

Theodore I Laskaris 1204–22

John III Dukas Vatatzes 1222–54

Theodore II Laskaris 1254–58

John IV Laskaris 1258–61

Michael VIII Palaeologus 1259–82

Andronikos II Palaeologus 1282–1328

Michael IX Palaeologus 1294–1320

Andronikos III Palaeologus 1328–41

John V Palaeologus 1341–91

John VI Cantacuzenus 1341–54

Andronikos IV Palaeologus 1376–79

John VII Palaeologus 1390

Manuel II Palaeologus 1391–1425

John VIII Palaeologus 1425–48

Constantine XI (XII) Palaeologus 1449–53

BIBLIOGRAPHY

GENERAL

Ahrweiler, Hélène. *L'idéologie politique de l'empire byzantin*. Paris, 1975.

Baynes, N. H., and H. St. L.B. Moss. *Byzantium: An Introduction to East Roman Civilization*. Oxford, 1948.

Beck, H. G. *Das byzantinische Jahrtausend*. Munich, 1978.

Beckwith, J. *The Art of Constantinople*. London, 1961.

Browning, R. "Byzantine Literature." In *The Penguin Companion to Literature*, edited by D. R. Dudley and D. Lang, vol. 4, pp. 179–216. Harmondsworth, 1969.

Cutler, A., and J. W. Nesbitt. *L'arte bizantina e il suo pubblico*. 2 vols. Turin, 1986.

Demus, O. *Byzantine Art and the West*. New York, 1970.

Ducellier, A. *Byzance et le monde orthodoxe*. Paris, 1986.

———. *Les Byzantins: histoire et culture*. Paris, 1989.

———. *Eglise Byzantine*. Paris, 1990.

Geanakoplos, D. J. *Byzantium: Church, Society and Civilization as seen through contemporary eyes*. Chicago, 1983.

Guillou, A. *La civilisation byzantine*, Paris, 1974.

Hussey, J. M. *The Orthodox Church in the Byzantine Empire*. Oxford, 1988.

Hussey, J. M., et al. eds. *The Cambridge Medieval History*. Vol. IV, 2 parts. Cambridge, 1966–1967.

Kazhdan, A. P., and G. Constable. *People and Power in Byzantium*. Washington, 1982.

Kazhdan, A. P., et al., eds. *The Oxford Dictionary of Byzantium*. 3 vols. New York, 1991.

Lazarev, V. *Storia dells pittura bizantina*. Turin, 1967.

Lemerle, P. *The Agrarian History of Byzantium from the Origins to the Twelfth Century*. Galway, 1979.

Maguire, H. *Art and Eloquence in Byzantium*. Princeton, 1981.

Mango, C. *Byzantine Architecture*. New York, 1970 and 1976.

———. *Byzantium: the Empire of New Rome*. London, 1980.

Meyendorff. J. *Byzantine Theology*. 2d ed. New York, 1987.

Nicol, D. M. *Byzantium and Venice: A Study in Diplomatic and Cultural Relations*. Cambridge, 1988.

Obolensky, D. *The Byzantine Commonwealth: Eastern Europe 500–1453*. London, 1971.

Ostrogorsky, G. *History of the Byzantine State*. Madison, 1958.

Rice, D. Talbot. *Art of the Byzantine Era*. London, 1963.

———. *Byzantine Art*, 2d ed. Harmondsworth, 1968.

Runciman, S. *Byzantine Civilization*. London, 1933.

———. *Byzantine Style and Civilization*. Harmondsworth, 1975.

Schug-Wille, C. *Art of the Byzantine World*. New York, 1969.

Vasiliev, A. A. *History of the Byzantine Empire*. Madison, 1958.

Weitzmann, K. *The Classical Heritage in Byzantine and Near Eastern Art*. London, 1981.

Wellesz, E. *A History of Byzantine Music and Hymnography*. 2d ed. Oxford, 1961.

Whitting, P. *Byzantium: An Introduction*. Oxford, 1971.

CHAPTER I

Barker, J. W. *Justinian and the Later Roman Empire*. Madison-London, 1966.

Beaucamp, J. *Le statut de la femme à Byzance (4e–7e siècle)*. Paris, 1990.

Bowersock, G. W. *Hellenism in Late Antiquity*. Cambridge, 1990.

Brown, P. *The World of Late Antiquity*. London, 1971.

Brown, T. S. *Gentlemen and Officers. Imperial Administration and Aristocratic Power in Byzantine Italy*. Rome, 1984.

Browning, R. *Justinian and Theodora*. London, 1971. Revised ed., London, 1987.

Downey, G. *Constantinople in the Age of Justinian*. Norman, Oklahoma, 1960.

Grabar, A. *Byzantium from the Death of Theodosius to the Rise of Islam*. London, 1966.

Guillou, A., ed. *La civiltà bizantina dal IV al IX secolo*. Bari, 1977.

Haldon, J. F. *Byzantium in the Seventh Century*. Cambridge, 1990.

Jones, A. H. M. *The Later Roman Empire 284–602: A Social, Economic and Administrative Survey*. 4 vols. Oxford, 1964.

Mainstone, R. J. *Hagia Sophia: Architecture, Structure and Liturgy of Justinian's Great Church*. London-New York, 1988.

Patlagean, E. *Pauvreté économique et pauvreté sociale à Byzance, 4e–7e siècle*. Paris, 1977.

Ure, P. N. *Justinian and His Age*. Harmondsworth, 1957.

CHAPTER 2

Bury, J. B. *A History of the Later Roman Empire from Arcadius to Irene*. 2 vols. London, 1889.
————. *A History of the Eastern Roman Empire from the Fall of Irene to the Accession of Basil I (AD 807–67)*. London, 1912.
Head, Constance. *Justinian II of Byzantium*. Madison, 1972.
Lemerle, P. *Byzantine Humanism: the first phase*. Canberra, 1986.
[————. *Le premier humanisme byzantin*. Paris, 1971.]
Martin, E. J. *A History of the Iconoclastic Controversy*. London, 1930.
Stratos, A. N. *Byzantium in the Seventh Century*. 5 vols. Amsterdam, 1968–80.
Treadgold, W. T. *The Byzantine Revival, 780–842*. Stanford, 1988.

CHAPTER 3

Browning, R. *Byzantium and Bulgaria*. London, 1975.
Cheynet, J.-C. *Pouvoir et contestations à Byzance (963–1210)*. Paris, 1990.
Guillou, A., ed. *La civiltà bizantina dal IX al XI secolo*. Bari, 1978.
Harvey, A. *Economic Expansion in the Byzantine Empire, 900–1200*. Cambridge, 1989.
Hussey, J. M. *Church and Learning in the Byzantine Empire 867–1185*. Oxford, 1937.
Jenkins, R. *Byzantium: The Imperial Centuries, AD 600–1071*. London, 1966.
Runciman, S. *The Emperor Romanus Lecapenus and His Reign*. Cambridge, 1929.
————. *The Eastern Schism*. London, 1955.
Starr, J. *The Jews in the Byzantine Empire, 641–1204*. Athens, 1939.
Toynbee, A. J. *Constantine Porphyrogenitus and his World*. London, 1973.

CHAPTER 4

Angold, M. *The Byzantine Empire 1025–1204: A Political History*. London, 1984.
Brand, C. M. *Byzantium Confronts the West, 1180–1204*. Harvard, 1968.
Diehl, Ch. *La Société byzantine à l'époque des Comnènes*. Paris, 1929.
Makk, F. *The Árpáds and the Comneni: Political Relations between Hungary and Byzantium in the Twelfth Century*. Budapest, 1989.
Runciman, S. *A History of the Crusades*. Vols. 1–2. Cambridge, 1951, 1952.

CHAPTER 5

Angold, M. *A Byzantine Government in Exile: Government and Society under the Laskarids of Nicaea (1204–1261)*. London, 1975.

Bowman, S. B. *The Jews of Byzantium 1204–1453*. Alabama, 1985.

Fine, J. V. A. *The Late Medieval Balkans: A Critical Survey from the Late Twelfth Century to the Ottoman Conquest*. Ann Arbor, 1987.

Geanakoplos, D. J. *Byzantine East and Latin West*. Oxford, 1956.

———. *Interaction of the "Sibling" Byzantine and Western Cultures in the Middle Ages and Renaissance*. New Haven-London, 1976.

Guillou, A., ed. *La civiltà bizantina dal XII al XV secolo*. Bari, 1980.

Head, C. *Imperial Twilight: The Palaeologos Dynasty and the Decline of Byzantium*. Chicago, 1977.

Laiou-Thomadakis, A. E. "The Byzantine Economy in the Mediterranean Trade System, XIIIth-XVth Centuries." *Dumbarton Oaks Papers* 34–35 (1982): 177–222.

Meyendorff, J. *Byzantium and the Rise of Russia*. Cambridge, 1980.

Miller, W. *The Latins in the Levant: A History of Frankish Greece, 1204–1566*. London, 1908.

Nicol, D. M. *The Despotate of Epirus*. Oxford, 1957.

———. *The Last Centuries of Byzantium, 1261–1453*. London, 1972.

———. *The End of The Byzantine Empire*. London, 1979.

———. *Church and Society in the Last Centuries of Byzantium*. Cambridge, 1979.

Rice, D. Talbot. *Byzantine Painting: The Last Phase*. New York, 1968.

Runciman, S. *The Sicilian Vespers*. Cambridge, 1958.

———. *The Fall of Constantinople, 1453*. Cambridge, 1965.

———. *The Last Byzantine Renaissance*. Cambridge, 1970.

———. *Mistra*. London, 1980.

Underwood, P. A. *The Kariye Djami*. 4 vols. New York, 1966–75.

Woodhouse, C. M. *George Gemistos Plethon: The Last of the Hellenes*. Oxford, 1986.

INDEX

The Byzantine Empire
was composed in 11.5/14 Granjon
by World Composition Services, Inc.,
Sterling, Virginia; printed and bound by
BookCrafters, Chelsea, Michigan; and
designed and produced by Kachergis
Book Design, Pittsboro,
North Carolina.